THE
Missile
AND
Space Race

THE
MISSILE
AND
SPACE RACE

ALAN J. LEVINE

Westport, Connecticut
London

Library of Congress Cataloging-in-Publication Data

Levine, Alan J.
    The missile and space race / Alan J. Levine.
       p. cm.
    Includes bibliographical references (p.) and index.
    ISBN 0–275–94451–4
    1. Outer space—Exploration—History. 2. Space vehicles—Design
and construction—History. 3. Arms race—History—20th century.
4. Cold war—History. I. Title.
TL788.5.L47 1994
387.8′0973—dc20   93–23673

British Library Cataloguing in Publication Data is available.

Library of Congress Catalog Card Number: 93–23673
ISBN: 0–275–94451–4

First published in 1994

Praeger Publishers, 88 Post Road West, Westport, CT 06881
An imprint of Greenwood Publishing Group, Inc.

Printed in the United States of America

∞™

The paper used in this book complies with the Permanent
Paper Standard issued by the National Information Standards
Organization (Z39.48-1984).

10 9 8 7 6 5 4 3 2 1

Contents

Preface

On May 25, 1961, President Kennedy declared, "I believe that this nation should commit itself to achieving the goal, before this decade is out, of landing a man on the moon and returning him safely to earth."[1]

That goal was achieved; and it is of interest not just as humanity's first venture to another world, but as one of the few national goals the United States accomplished after the 1950s. This book deals with the events that led up to and accompanied the decision to go to the moon; the events that followed; and the interplay between the development of space travel, the Cold War missile race, and the international politics of the quarter of a century following World War II. However deplorable many may find it, the first steps in space travel were a product or byproduct of the Cold War and the arms race. This is not to say that mankind would not have reached space sometime or other, for purely peaceful reasons; but space travel began when it did, and how it did, as part of a great world conflict. Most of the rockets that made it possible were either modified military missiles or used engines that stemmed ultimately from military programs, and particularly from the intercontinental ballistic missiles whose development was a central and critical event of the Cold War. The development of the Intercontinental Ballistic Missile (ICBM), by the Soviets and Americans, and its impact on the Cold War struggle, is a principal theme of this book; it is an exciting story that has been dealt with by a handful of outstanding specialists, such as Edmund Beard and Jacob Neufeld, but whose full interest and impact has not been properly appreciated. With the victory of the Western powers in the Cold War, there may be a tendency to underestimate the dangers it involved; but, as I hope to show, those dangers were considerable, and perhaps much greater than has generally been supposed. I have attempted to present a more detailed and accurate account of the impact of Sputnik, and of the subsequent missile-gap era and its fears, than any available previously.

As far as the development of space travel and the technology behind it is concerned, I have tried to correct fallacies or omissions of earlier accounts. While the development of ballistic missiles was the primary route to space flight, it was not the only one; space flight also came out of aviation via the rocket research plane. I have also tried to correct or at least compensate for the obsession of most writers with the development of vehicles and give due attention to the (in many ways more critical) development of engines and fuels. In this connection I have tried to give overdue attention to the abortive attempts to develop nuclear propulsion. I have also tried to correct some ideas about the relative importance of some of the pioneers of space flight, notably Goddard and his German rivals, about Goddard's concepts, and about the place of the Germans in the postwar American effort.

I would like to thank the following individuals for their help: Roger Launius and Len Saegesser of the NASA History Office, Dr. James Dewar, Professor Paul Gottfried, Israel Levine, and my editor, Dan Eades. All responsibility for any errors is mine.

1

Prelude and Background to the Development of Rocketry and Space Travel

The rocket was an old form of propulsion, periodically used in war (as well as for fireworks) ever since its invention in China during the European Middle Ages. By the late nineteenth century, it was a toy rather than a weapon. Then some began to suspect that new types of rockets could help realize the old dream of visiting other worlds. Unintentionally, they made possible the revival of the rocket as a weapon.

THEORETICIANS AND PIONEERS

The most outstanding of these theoreticians was the Russian Konstantin Tsiolkovskiy. Despite deafness and a limited education, this provincial schoolteacher provided the first mathematically sound study of space flight and invented many of its basic concepts; they were first published in his book, *Exploration of Outer Space with Reactive Devices*. Initially interested in aviation and inspired by Jules Verne, Tsiolkovskiy became fascinated with space travel in the 1890s. He insisted that only rocket engines powered by liquid fuels would make flight beyond the atmosphere possible, and in 1903 he predicted that liquid hydrogen (first produced only in 1898), burned with liquid oxygen, would be the most powerful practical chemical fuel. Realizing that even with that it would be difficult for a single rocket to reach orbit around the earth, much less escape its gravity, he proposed the multistage rocket ("rocket train")—one rocket would boost a smaller one, or a succession of smaller ones, thus discarding the dead weight of empty tanks and plumbing. Eventually, space stations would be built in orbit around the earth as refueling stations and bases for interplanetary flight. Later, solar-powered factories and permanent colonies would be established in space. Much manufacturing could be done better in space with zero gravity and abundant solar power.[1]

Tsiolkovskiy never built any rockets; although honored by the Soviets, he remained almost unknown outside Russia. Robert Goddard, a professor of physics at Clark University, did more. His work has often been belittled, and even misinterpreted, but in many ways he was the towering figure in the development of rockets and space flight. Goddard had become interested in space travel after reading Jules Verne and H. G. Wells. Fearing ridicule, he avoided discussing it at length in his published writings, stressing high-altitude atmospheric research as his immediate aim. Unlike Tsiolkovskiy, who was treated with respect in "backward" Russia, Goddard was widely deemed a crank in the 1920s, although he was treated more respectfully later. Independently of Tsiolkovskiy, he conceived of liquid-fueled and multistage rockets and recognized that hydrogen was the most potent practical chemical fuel, although he was never able to use it.

During World War I, Goddard worked on rockets launched from airplanes and developed a portable rocket launcher, the forerunner of the bazooka. Even before the war, he had conceived of the ion or electrical rocket for space-to-space propulsion. Functioning only in a vacuum, it provided a small, continuous thrust with a stream of charged particles. (Goddard also tried to devise electrical systems that were usable within the atmosphere.) By the 1920s, he privately visualized methods of communicating with other intelligent races, and unmanned probes to other planets to be followed by manned interplanetary travel, using the moon as a refueling station. However, he continued to concentrate on practical problems of rocket development.

In 1926 he fired the first liquid-fuel rocket, using a combination of gasoline and liquid oxygen. It flew just 184 feet. Unfortunately, Goddard was something of a lone wolf. Although one of the founders of the American Rocket Society, he avoided close association with other scientists. Perhaps because of this, he never realized that his engines were inefficient due to a simple failure to use enough oxygen with the gasoline. Fundamentally, however, he was not too interested in the fuel problem. Unable to get liquid hydrogen, which he deemed essential for manned space flight, he stuck to gasoline and concentrated on solving the basic problems of control and engine functioning.

Charles Lindbergh met Goddard in 1929 and took a deep interest in his work. Lindbergh was interested in boosters to assist aircraft takeoffs and provide bursts of speed for conventionally powered warplanes and, ultimately, space travel, with rocket-powered planes as an intermediate step. Although the main line of Goddard's work lay in building ballistic rockets (sometimes launched with catapult assistance), he too had long been interested in rocket planes. It has usually been assumed that his concept of space flight revolved purely around the construction of bigger and bigger multistage, chemically fueled "pure" rockets, fired vertically from the ground. That proved to be the primary, although not the sole, way to space in the next several decades; it was not, however, the only line of development Goddard envisaged or wanted. He devoted much thought to the "rocket turbine," a hybrid engine that could convert from an air-breathing device to a "pure" rocket as it neared the limits of the atmosphere. He hoped that this, or other devices he conceived for getting a spacecraft to the edge of space before switching to rocket power, might eliminate or reduce the use of multistage rockets. There is even a hint, in his papers, that he hoped to supersede rockets by developing a solar-powered spacecraft (probably using propellers in the lower atmosphere and an electrical propulsion system higher up) and that he saw rockets as a way to get the data about the upper atmosphere needed to make such a system work.

Lindbergh helped Goddard secure a Guggenheim grant, which enabled him to move his work to New Mexico and build bigger, more complex rockets. Goddard originated, or at least anticipated, virtually all important developments in liquid-fuel rockets for the next fifty years. Among other things, he developed cooling systems for engines, gyro-stabilization apparatus, and deflector vanes in the exhaust nozzle—as well as fins—to provide control. Later, he mounted engines in gimbals so they could swivel to provide flight control, avoiding the loss of thrust caused by vanes in the exhaust. In 1935 his rockets began passing the speed of sound. As early as 1931, he saw that his rockets would soon be too big to use gas pressure to feed fuel to the engine; but lacking money to develop pumps, he concentrated on the control problem. By the time he started work on pumps, in the late 1930s, he was being overtaken by the Germans, who had greater resources.

By 1941 Goddard had pump-fed engines capable of producing 985 pounds of thrust. He was satisfied that he had solved most of the basic problems of rocket development, although he may have underestimated the difficulty of scaling up engines. With his gimballed engines, he was still ahead of the Germans in controls. His achievements (even though he worked with relatively little money and few assistants) were remarkable. But by then the Germans had an engine with 56,000 pounds of thrust.[2] Wernher von Braun later remarked, however, that "Goddard's experiments in liquid fuel saved us years of work, and enabled us to perfect the V-2 years before it would have been possible."[3]

Herman Oberth, a Transylvanian German, learned much from Goddard and wrote a well-known book, *The Rocket into Interplanetary Space*, that developed far-reaching theories like Tsiolkovskiy's. He convinced many people that space travel was practical. Unlike Goddard, he remained basically a theorist, but he played a major role in the German *Verein für Raumschiffahrt* (VfR, or Society for Space Travel) founded in 1927. Oberth, and most of the VfR, focused on vertically launched ballistic rockets; but an Austrian founder of the VfR, Max Valier, and some others thought that manned spaceships would emerge from the development of rocket planes. (They did not achieve much, but to an extent not often recognized, space flight did come about in this way.) Oberth, the VfR, and space flight enjoyed much publicity in Europe. But the VfR first flew a liquid-fuel rocket only in 1931. It turned to a combination of oxygen and alcohol, the most popular rocket propellants for the next two decades, and devised "regenerative cooling"—fuel was used to cool the engine walls before being fed into it. The VfR collapsed during the Great Depression, but rocket development soon found a wealthy patron.[4]

THE GERMAN WAR ROCKETS

The German Army's use of long-range guns had been severely limited by the Treaty of Versailles, but the treaty had not spoken of rockets, which seemed a substitute. In 1931 the German Army contacted and secretly subsidized the VfR. In 1932 some important members of the VfR, including Wernher von Braun, then just twenty, joined the Army's weapons department. Despite his youth (he obtained a Ph.D. in physics in 1934), von Braun became the most trusted civilian subordinate of Colonel Walter Dornberger, who supervised rocket work. Although the importance of von Braun and the German effort in the development of rockets has often been exaggerated, von Braun and the team of scientists and engineers he formed played an extremely important role in the next forty years. Von Braun, a charming, suave Silesian nobleman, favorably impressed almost everyone. His interest in space flight was the result of reading science fiction— specifically, Kurd Lasswitz's *Auf Zwei Planeten*. The opposite of the Junker stereotype, von Braun ran things in a loose, democratic manner; the astronaut Frank Borman once described him as "as Prussian as James Stewart, and about as likeable."[5]

The Germans developed a series of experimental rockets. In 1936 von Braun and Walter Riedel began designing an operational weapon, the

A-4 (better known as the V-2), a 46-foot missile that could carry a metric ton payload up to 190 miles. It needed an engine capable of generating 25 tons or more of thrust, and it posed unprecedented problems. It required fuel pumps; von Braun found that modified centrifugal pumps of the sort used to fight fires, but powered by the decomposition of hydrogen peroxide, would do the job. The Germans began surpassing Goddard, at least in terms of scale.

The A-4's powerplant ran into most of the problems common in building large rocket engines: pumping fuel, injecting it into the combustion chamber, and cooling that chamber. Large engines were plagued by "combustion instability," analogous to knock in a car engine, but more violent. Even fifty years later, developing big engines was slow, "trial and error" work; they could not be transferred from drawing board or computer screen to test stand in a short and reliable way. The Germans failed to develop a good fuel injection system; Colonel Dornberger grumbled that the resulting engine was hard to produce, and a relatively simple and satisfactory substitute was ready only near the end of World War II. Guiding and stabilizing the missile was also a major problem.

The war was half over when the A-4 flew successfully at Peenemunde on October 3, 1942. Like some of von Braun's later American military superiors, Dornberger had been infected by von Braun's real concerns. At a party celebrating the success, he commented that "today we have invented the spaceship!" Only as an afterthought did he note that the immediate task was to perfect a weapon.[6]

The Nazi leaders had earlier entertained only a modest interest in rockets. But by late 1942, Hitler was desperate for a way to retaliate against Allied bombing, something the Luftwaffe's planes were less and less able to do. He gave the A-4—renamed the V-2 (*Vergeltungswaffe* [vengeance weapon])—a high priority. It became important enough to be a focus of intrigue; the SS tried to seize the project. Von Braun and two of his colleagues were arrested by the Gestapo and held for a time. Although von Braun's real crime was loyalty to the Army and rejection of SS bribes, he had incautiously told an informer that he was more interested in space travel than the war, a view the Nazis regarded as treason. Due to the time spent readying the V-2 for mass production, working the bugs out of the production model (it blew up frequently), and Allied bombing, the V-2 only went into action in September 1944.

Built under gruesome conditions by slave labor at Nordhausen, the V-2 was still not really ready for production. It was unreliable—a fourth of those fired failed—and grossly inaccurate. Only half fell within an 11-mile radius of the aiming point; only a very big city could be hit at all. V-2s killed thousands of people in London and Antwerp, but had little military effect and were very costly. The V-2 used up scarce underground factory space; was competitive with important items in plane, submarine, and electronics production; and used up much liquid oxygen and alcohol. The latter might have extended Germany's fuel resources by 10 or 15 percent. The Germans might have been better advised to devote the effort to the *Wasserfall* antiaircraft missile then under development, although it is doubtful that it could have seriously harmed the vast Allied bomber fleets. Coldly considered, the V-2 was a foolish waste of resources. Von Braun and Dornberger, albeit unintentionally, hurt the Nazis more than many carefully planned Allied blows. But the fact that the V-2 was, at the time, impossible to intercept, and the subsequent development of nuclear weapons, meant that after World War II the long-range rocket would appear in a different light. Nuclear warheads transformed it from an absurdly costly way to harass enemy cities with high explosives to a weapon of annihilation.

In addition to short-range battlefield weapons, von Braun's team worked on improved versions of the V-2 and designed the two-stage A-9/A-10, the America rocket. The lower stage, the A-10, developed 440,000 pounds of thrust. The A-9 upper stage was basically an upgraded, winged V-2. Instead of slamming down through the atmosphere, like the V-2 and other ballistic missiles, it would reenter at a shallow angle and glide to a target. With a range of 3,000 miles, it could hit targets like New York on the east coast of North America. Technically, it was a (barely) intercontinental glide missile, not an ICBM. One model of the A-9 would be a manned bomber. A winged V-2, called the A-4B, was tested in early 1945 with partial success; it became the first winged vehicle to break the sound barrier, reaching a speed of 2,700 miles an hour (although a wing tore off on the way down).

The A-10 never left the drawing board. Two bigger rockets, A-11 and A-12, remained design concepts. In combination, they could put a winged version of A-10, and a payload of 30 tons, into orbit. This scheme was the basis for the system von Braun proposed in the early 1950s to build and supply a space station. It is remarkable that he worked on this during World War II.[7]

ROCKET DEVELOPMENT IN THE UNITED STATES

The other major belligerents concentrated on short-range battlefield missiles, mostly unguided solid-fuel rockets and what was misleadingly called "jet-assisted takeoff" (JATO)—jettisonable rockets to help heavily laden planes take off. These seemingly unspectacular objectives, however, led to considerable work on new propellants and larger engines.

During the 1930s, rocket development in the United States had remained on a small scale, but others had joined Goddard in the field. The American Rocket Society (originally the American Interplanetary Society), founded in 1930, developed small but efficient engines. (Its founders were not only influenced by science fiction, but wrote it.) It had some contact with the VfR before the Nazis took over, and two Soviet enthusiasts became members, albeit of an honorary sort. In 1941 some members founded Reaction Motors, Inc. to build JATO units for the military.

Goddard also turned to war work, developing JATO units for the Navy. He built a throttleable rocket engine capable of producing a maximum 1,000 pounds of thrust; when he died in 1945, he was working on a bigger engine that ultimately powered the X-2 rocket plane.

A more diversified effort grew up at the Guggenheim Aeronautical Laboratory at Caltech (GALCIT), which, directed by the great Theodore von Karman, had already made many advances in aviation. In the late 1930s, von Karman's student Frank Malina (converted to interest in space by reading Jules Verne as a boy) and some others formed the GALCIT Rocket Research Group. It worked on high-altitude research rockets. The far-seeing commander of the Army Air Corps, General Henry H. Arnold, became interested in the research group, and in 1939–1940 it took up military work, developing liquid- and solid-fuel JATO units. Some members set up a private company, Aerojet, to build engines.

Vannevar Bush, the director of U.S. wartime research, had rightly rejected GALCIT proposals to build long-range missiles. It was unlikely that they would be ready during the war, or accurate enough to be useful. The V-2, however, sparked a change in Washington. Although the Air Force was little interested, Army Ordnance backed a modest missile program called "Ordcit." The GALCIT group, renamed the Jet Propulsion Laboratory (JPL) in July 1944, undertook to develop short-range solid-fuel rockets, the "Private" series, and "Corporal," a liquid-fuel missile with a range of 150 miles and a half-ton payload. In November 1944, the Army also contracted with General Electric to study and develop both air-breathing and rocket-powered missiles, but JPL was the main focus of the effort.

Corporal was too big to build in one step, so a smaller rocket, "WAC Corporal," was designed as an interim step and to serve as a high-altitude research rocket—carrying 25 pounds to 100,000 feet. Even it was a big jump; a scale model, "Baby WAC," was tried first. The full-size WAC Corporal appeared in the fall of 1945. Sixteen feet long, it burned aniline and nitric acid for a thrust of 1,500 pounds. It was really the upper stage of a two-stage rocket; a small solid-fuel rocket served as a first stage. On October 11, 1945, a WAC Corporal reached a height of 230,000 feet. JPL, starting late and with less money than the Germans, had largely duplicated their work in a very short time. The United States was not nearly as far behind Germany in rocketry as is usually supposed.

JPL's postwar role was disappointing. Without the drive of war, work on the full-scale Corporal was very slow; it was not ready until well into the 1950s and its range was slashed to 75 miles. JPL lost Malina and two of his most important colleagues, Martin Summerfield and H. S. Tsien. Malina and Summerfield had been Communist sympathizers and were considered security risks; Tsien was apparently not pro-Communist but was so alienated by bungling security measures that he decided to return to China. JPL gradually switched from propulsion work to building instrument packages for space probes.

In controls, the Americans were ahead of the Germans, who had not duplicated Goddard's superior gimballed-engine steering; in propellants they were actually overtaking the Germans. They had duplicated all German developments except for the use of hydrogen peroxide, which proved a dead end as far as large powerplants were concerned. Unlike the Germans, they had begun small-scale work on liquid hydrogen, the most potent chemical fuel and the best fuel—or rather working fluid—for nuclear rockets. Dr. Herrick Johnston of Ohio State University, working for the Manhattan Project, had built a plant to produce liquid hydrogen. In 1944 the Army Air Force became interested in liquid hydrogen as a jet and rocket fuel, and in July 1945 Johnston began work on this, studying its effects on metals. He tested liquid hydrogen rocket engines in 1947. The Navy was also interested and in 1945 gave Aerojet a contract to investigate liquid hydrogen rockets.[8]

SOVIET ROCKETRY

The Soviets preceded even the Germans in starting an official rocket research program; but in scope and results their effort more nearly resembled that of the Americans. There was intense interest in space travel in the 1920s, as well as much work on solid-fuel rockets for military purposes. A laboratory specializing in rocket work, later called the Gas Dynamics Laboratory (GDL), was established as early as 1921 to work on propellants. In 1929 Soviet technologists, led by Valentin Glushko, began work on liquid-fuel rockets with military backing. Glushko may have been the first to propose gimballed engines, although Goddard developed them independently and was the first to build one. While Glushko and the GDL worked in Leningrad (St. Petersburg), another group in Moscow, led by Friedrich Tsander and Sergei Korolev, flew the first Soviet liquid-fuelled rocket in 1933. Korolev would be the galvanizing force in the Soviet missile and space effort after World War II. Originally an aircraft designer, he inclined, for a time, toward the view that the way to space lay in rocket planes. In 1933 the Moscow and Leningrad researchers were fused into the RNII, the Reaction Propulsion Research Institute. They tested various fuels and worked on sounding and antiaircraft rockets and a throttleable engine designed to power a winged "flying bomb," somewhat like the German V-1 cruise missile but far smaller. But few of these projects were finished. The RNII suffered heavily in the Great Purges; it had been closely connected with Marshal Tukhachevsky, the chief target of the Purges. Korolev spent a year in one of the worst labor camps before being transferred to a prison design bureau to work on planes; his health never recovered. As war approached, the disrupted Soviet rocket effort concentrated on small solid-fuel battlefield rockets. It did build some large liquid-fuel engines as boosters for fighter planes, finally producing an engine with nearly 3,000 pounds of thrust. The Soviets even built a rocket-powered interceptor, the BI-1, which flew in 1942. But, unlike the Germans, who wasted much effort on the *Messerschmitt* 163, they saw that the rocket fighter's short endurance made it a poor investment, and thus they did not mass produce it.[9]

By the end of World War II, the basic problems involved in building large liquid-fuel rockets were apparent. So were the limitations of chemical fuels. Tsiolkovskiy's view that liquid hydrogen and oxygen would be the most powerful practical chemical combination was confirmed. (A few marginally more powerful combinations—fluorine-hydrogen and fluorine-beryllium—were very costly, hard to handle, and produced toxic or corrosive exhausts.) Over the next few decades, there were no dramatic discoveries of superfuels. The most powerful propellants were already known. Instead, work revolved around learning to use liquid hydrogen effectively and finding propellants that were more convenient, if less powerful, than hydrogen and other cryogenics that had to be kept at very low temperatures. The search was for storable and hypergolic liquids that would at least approach the power of the familiar cryogenic combinations, could be kept in a rocket for long periods at normal temperatures, and would spontaneously ignite when fed into an engine without a cumbersome, tricky ignition system.[10] Such propellants were obviously desirable for military missiles but also useful for certain space applications.

More powerful solid fuels were also sought, and here there would be some pleasant surprises. Solid fuels that were more powerful than anyone expected would be made; although far less powerful than the best liquids, they eventually edged out liquid fuels for most military rockets. Whether any sort of chemical fuel would really make space travel, at least beyond the near-earth region, economically practical was doubtful. As early as the 1920s, Robert Esnault-Pelterie, a French aviation pioneer who helped organize the VfR and popularized space travel in Europe, had suggested to Goddard that chemical fuels would be inadequate for space flight, which would need atomic energy.[11]

2

The Immediate Postwar Era: Abortive Progress and Hiatus, 1945–1950

Right after World War II, there was intense interest in rockets and space travel. The V-2 deeply impressed everyone; space travel, almost a joke to many people before the war, now seemed a real possibility, even an imminent one. Many imagined that atomic power, the utility of which was exaggerated (at least in the short run), would soon be applied to spaceships. There was a less happy conviction that push-button warfare, with nuclear warheads carried by missiles, was also just around the corner. Even at a sober official level, there were bold proposals for satellites and inter-continental missiles. There was a brief flurry of activity not seen again until the mid-1950s. However, because of budget constraints and short-sighted policies at the highest levels, the results were limited. In practice, American efforts in rocketry consisted of launching captured V-2s and developing new sounding rockets. There was work, although not pushed energetically, on short-range battlefield missiles and bigger rocket engines. Other Western countries did even less.

OPERATION PAPERCLIP

Despite its insignificant impact on the war, the V-2 unnerved the Allies. They were conscious of, and indeed exaggerated, the extent to which the Germans were ahead in rocket and jet development. In December 1944, the U.S. Army decided to secure V-2s to aid General Electric's "Hermes" program. Later, it decided to round up many German scientists, engineers, and technicians involved in work on all sorts of advanced weapons, not just rockets, and perhaps take some to the United States. It was hoped that something of immediate value in the war against Japan, which was expected to last into 1946, might turn up. The U.S. government even hoped to fire captured V-2s, as well as American-built copies of the V-1, against Japan. But by V-E Day, at least some of those involved in what became known as Operation Overcast, and later Operation Paperclip, wished to at least prevent the increasingly hostile Soviets from getting the German researchers.

As the Allies advanced, a special mission entered Germany to secure 100 complete V-2s or their equivalent in parts. Von Braun, and most of his team, had been evacuated to southern Germany to escape the Soviets. His group surrendered to the Americans and guided them to a stash of valuable documents dealing with rocket development. The Germans were interrogated, in a disorganized way, by the Army and General Electric researchers. (General Dornberger fell into British hands; they finally dropped the idea of trying him as a war criminal and released him with other noncriminal German generals in 1947. He later reached the United States and worked for Bell Aircraft.)

The Americans carried off an advanced supersonic wind tunnel. They also had access to the Nordhausen V-2 plant, where 250 V-2s lay in various states of completion. Nordhausen was in what was to be the Soviet occupation zone, but the Americans removed 360 boxcars full of material from the plant before they withdrew in July. This was less of a coup than is sometimes claimed; for there were 1,000 V-2s in field storage in the Western zones (although many lacked control equipment) and even more in the east, although many were developmental models slated for scrapping. Strangely, neither side made use of these missiles before they deteriorated into junk. And the Americans left the production facilities at Nordhausen intact.

Von Braun's team was the real prize. Von Braun and a few others were quickly sent to Aberdeen Proving Ground, where they did important work sorting and cataloging documents dealing with the rocket program. Later they were joined by the other German rocket specialists at Fort Bliss, Texas. Originally it had been planned to bring in a limited number of researchers for just a year. In 1946 a more active recruitment program began; families were brought in, and the chance of citizenship was offered. Finally 127 rocket workers (of 642 Germans and Austrians brought in under Overcast-Paperclip) reached the United States. As their presence gradually became known there was strong opposition by diverse elements ranging from Albert Einstein to J. Edgar Hoover. Later, after Sputnik, they abruptly became American national heroes for a time. But the earlier attitude never evaporated.

The Germans, kept under close surveillance, helped fire V-2s at White Sands Proving Ground as part of the Hermes program. The armed forces and General Electric gained experience in handling big rockets, conducted research on the upper atmosphere (this part of the program was largely directed by the Naval Research Laboratory, NRL), and used V-2s as flying testbeds for new devices.

After an initial failure, the second V-2 fired at White Sands, on May 10, 1946, flew as planned. Despite the haul at Nordhausen, the V-2 program proved more difficult than might be expected. Some parts were abundant, and others were scarce. Only two V-2s could be assembled from purely German parts; the Americans built replacements and new, lighter warheads adapted to carry instruments. In some ways, the V-2 was not well suited to research work. It had, after all, been designed to deliver a set load over a set range and was not very flexible. Unstable after leaving the atmosphere, it often tumbled wildly. Sometimes the Americans would have liked to send a light load of instruments far higher, but the V-2 had to have a high minimum weight in its nose; at White Sands it often carried 500 to 1,000 pounds of lead ballast. The Americans fired seventy V-2s between 1946 and June 1952; in 1951 one reached a height of 132 miles. Eight V-2s were modified to become the first stage of the two-stage "Bumper-WAC" vehicle; WAC Corporals served as the second stage. On February 24, 1949, a Bumper-WAC reached the then fantastic height of 250 miles.

By 1947 the Germans were no longer needed to launch V-2s. Two of von Braun's top men, Walter Riedel and Gerhard Heller, were loaned to North American Aviation's new rocket division to introduce its engineers to the mysteries of large rocket engines. Others designed a 300,000-pound thrust engine that was never built, or played a subordinate role in the erratic Hermes program, whose objectives kept changing. They worked on an antiaircraft missile, on other tactical weapons that were never produced, and on a ramjet-powered intercontinental missile that was canceled as unnecessarily competitive with the Air Force's "Navaho." Hermes C, a study of an intermediate-range glide missile, somewhat like the A-9, eventually evolved into the shorter-range Redstone ballistic missile. While some things were learned during Hermes, the program was not too useful.[1]

After their first role in sorting documents and giving advice, the Germans' part in the American rocket effort was small—not because they were not able, but because they were not used. After incurring the trouble, expense, and unpopularity of importing them, the U.S. government did little with them. Except for a few individuals who left von Braun's group, they took no part in the U.S. satellite and ICBM programs; when the missile effort revived in the 1950s, they were given relatively minor tasks. Again, except for one or two individuals, they took no part in the critical field of propulsion development; von Braun's later work depended on engines developed by others. Only late in the 1950s did the Germans play a major role in the U.S. space program.

Only Britain, of the other Western countries, made a stab at exploiting German developments. The British actually fired a few V-2s before the Americans; but this early effort was not followed up. In one of many blunders that undermined Britain's once great aerospace industry, the government showed little interest in missiles, much less space travel. The British Interplanetary Society advanced an imaginative proposal, "Megaroc," to modify a V-2 into a human-carrying suborbital vehicle, but the government would not listen to it. Megaroc would have been much like the Mercury-Redstones that took the first Americans into space. As David Baker later noted, Britain could have had a man in space by 1950.[2] Megaroc is one of many things showing that the development of rocketry and space flight could have been pushed much faster than it was.

THE U.S. NAVY SATELLITE PROGRAM

Before any contact with the Germans, bold proposals to launch earth satellites circulated in the U.S. Navy's Bureau of Aeronautics. On August 10, 1945, Lt. Robert Haviland proposed that the Navy embark on a space program and eventually build a manned orbital station, which would be useful as a communications relay station and a navigational aid. Lt. Commander Harvey Hall, a physicist, supported him and urged using liquid hydrogen fuel in a one-stage rocket with a very light structure, thus avoiding the complexities of a multistage vehicle. He helped guide Aerojet, which was already investigating propellants, into working on liquid hydrogen.

The Bureau formed the Committee to Evaluate the Feasibility of Space Rocketry in October 1945. It favored an unmanned satellite, but there were doubts about whether Hall's proposed single-stage launcher, cautiously called a "High Altitude Test Vehicle" (HATV), would work, and the Bureau asked the Jet Propulsion Laboratory to examine it. JPL preferred a multistage rocket but conceded that Hall's concept was reasonable. The Navy chose to pursue it and gave study contracts to the Martin Company and North American Aviation. They submitted similar preliminary designs. North American, slightly more conservative in its assumptions, envisaged an 86-foot, 51-ton stainless steel vehicle with nine clustered engines generating 300,000 pounds of thrust; it would put a half a ton into orbit.

The Committee approached the Army Air Force (AAF) to propose a joint project; the AAF representatives favored it but were overruled. Curtis Lemay, the Deputy Chief of Staff for Research and Development, rejected the idea, perhaps out of sheer interservice jealousy. The AAF's new think tank, Project RAND, examined the satellite problem. Its May 1946 report, "Preliminary Design of a World-Circling Spaceship," dismissed a single-stage launcher. Instead it suggested a four-stage rocket using alcohol and liquid oxygen, or a three-stage rocket using hydrogen, to lift a 500-pound payload into orbit. RAND pointed out that a satellite would be a major scientific tool and would have tremendous political repercussions, but it would not be a weapon—although its launcher could serve as an ICBM.

Neither service had the money for a full-scale satellite program (estimated at $150 million for a dozen vehicles over five years), but the Navy tried to pursue it. The Philips company got a contract to develop a solar power device for a satellite, and Aerojet got a contract for a design study of a 300,000-pound thrust engine using liquid hydrogen; Aerojet was actually building a 1,000-pound thrust engine using gaseous hydrogen for test purposes. Aerojet finally fired a tiny liquid hydrogen rocket in January 1949—a year and a half after Ohio State University, working for the Air Force, had accomplished this feat. Aerojet's rocket had considerable difficulties in storing and carrying liquid hydrogen.

In 1948 the Research and Development Board of the new Defense Department reviewed satellite proposals; it concluded shortsightedly that satellites had no military or scientific utility commensurate with their cost. That ended the Navy satellite effort. Small-scale exploration of liquid hydrogen as a fuel went on at Aerojet and Ohio State, but it trailed off during 1950–1951. It was still available only in small quantities; and with no set mission, there seemed no need to solve the problems involved. Interest in liquid hydrogen persisted at the Lewis Flight Propulsion Laboratory of the National Advisory Committee on Aeronautics (NACA, NASA's predecessor), while the H-bomb project promoted the development of ways to make and handle it on a large scale. Interest in satellites did not entirely die. RAND kept them under study for the Air Force; in 1949 it noted that satellites did have a military use—reconnaissance.[3]

Canceling HATV proved shortsighted, even in military terms. Had it been built at an early date, the United States might have had reconnaissance satellites during the Korean War, at a time when the West knew little of what went on behind the Iron Curtain.

LONG-RANGE MISSILES

General H. H. Arnold maintained early on that piloted planes were doomed to obsolescence. In his postwar report in late 1945, he declared that nuclear-armed rockets would replace bombers in the not too distant future. Eventually defenses would probably cope with rockets. In that case, the armed forces had to be ready to launch attacks from "true spaceships, capable of operating outside the earth's atmosphere. The design of such a ship is all but practicable today; research will unquestionably bring it into being within the forseeable future."[4] But the Air Force proved far less interested in space flight and missiles than might be expected; the service that might have been expected to be in the forefront of technological advance in general and the search for ways to deliver nuclear weapons in particular took an unimaginative, erratic approach toward ballistic missiles. Arnold was unusually bold and imaginative; the service he built was dominated by pilots and devoted to winged, manned aircraft. Many who had grown up developing manned bombers proved almost as resistant to missiles as ground generals and battleship admirals had been to air-power, while the Air Force's scientific advisors were unenthusiastic about ballistic missiles and favored an emphasis on air-breathing weapons. Yet the air generals suspected, at some level, that missiles would eventually be important, and they wanted them securely under Air Force control. A running interservice battle over missiles lasted from the latter part of World War II to the late 1950s.

In 1944 Army Ordnance had received jurisdiction over the small effort put into ballistic missile development. The AAF's war experience with rockets was limited to small, unguided solid-fuel weapons. Its guided missiles used almost every sort of engine *except* rockets; its organization for dealing with missiles was odd and inefficient. It tried out conventionally powered robot and drone planes, jet-propelled cruise missiles, glide bombs, and radio-controlled vertically dropped bombs—but it had little luck with any type except the last.

Beginning in 1946, a series of interservice agreements gave the Air Force domination of most missile development, and specifically of all air-launched and strategic weapons. (Operational control continued to be a matter of dispute.) The Army kept only tactical missile development. It may seem surprising that von Braun's team remained with the Army when the Air Force became fully independent; for if they had something special to contribute, it was in the field of large rockets. But neither service really viewed the issue as settled; so the Army wished to hang on to the team, while the Air Force had little interest in acquiring it. Even while part of the Army, the Air Corps/Army Air Force had developed its own approach to research and development. The Army had long maintained a system of arsenals in which government scientists and engineers did much of the Army's research on weapons (and even some production) and closely supervised industry. The Germans fit neatly into this system. The Army air arm had depended on the arsenals for guns, ammunition, and bombs but had depended on NACA and private industry for research and development of aircraft. It lacked an in-house research capability; it felt some unease at this, so it promoted the formation of RAND and other think tanks. But it basically rejected the arsenal system. It integrated a large number of Germans into its School of Aviation Medicine and the Air Research and Development Command, but there was no place for von Braun's team in its scheme of things. In the 1950s this led to a head-on collision of two contrasting approaches to missile development.[5]

The Air Force's research and development effort remained primarily oriented toward bombers; it had some interest in air-launched standoff weapons to help bombers penetrate enemy defenses. What interest there was in long-range missiles was largely in air-breathing cruise missiles. In 1946 the Air Force gave the Northrup Company a contract for 5,000-mile turbojet-powered cruise missiles, the subsonic "Snark," and the supersonic "Boojum." North American Aviation began Navaho, a complicated project with several phases. Navaho I would be a winged rocket with a range of just 500 miles; Navaho II and III would be ramjet-powered Mach 3 cruise missiles launched by rocket boosters, using follow-ons to the engine developed for Navaho I. Only Navaho III would have intercontinental range. (In 1948 the original Navaho I was dropped in favor of an early ramjet test vehicle.) Neither Boojum nor Navaho was ever deployed; Snark appeared belatedly and was of little value despite immense expenditures. But Navaho, for reasons that will be explained later, contributed greatly to rocket development.

There was *some* interest in intercontinental ballistic missiles. In April 1946 the Air Force gave Convair a one-year contract, MX-774, to study three types of missiles to deliver nuclear warheads over a range of 5,000 miles—a subsonic cruise missile, a glide missile like the A-9/A-10, and a purely ballistic missile. Convair's engineers were not too interested in the glide or cruise missiles; realizing the cruise missile duplicated Snark, the Air Force stopped work on it in December 1946. Convair was more interested in the ICBM concept, MX-774B. It was not supervised much by the Air Force, which seemed uninterested in the project although it sweetened the contract with more money in June 1946.

The head of the MX-774 project, Karel Bossart, was a Belgian-born engineer specializing in weight reduction; he had worked on the short-range Navy "Lark" missile. Bossart carefully studied the V-2 and was not particularly impressed. Everything about it was heavy and wasteful. The whole V-2, built of steel (for economic reasons), had been designed to reenter the atmosphere. It used separate fuel tanks, and the control vanes in the exhaust wasted thrust. Bossart decided that only the warhead need reenter; the rest of the vehicle could thus be built far more lightly. Integral fuel tanks could be used, with the body of the rocket serving as the tanks' walls. Bossart went a step farther; instead of using an internal framework, the structure would be supported by nitrogen gas under pressure—which also helped feed the propellants to the engines. The missile would be steered by swiveling the gimballed engines. The pressurized structure concept had been devised by Oberth and Goddard, and gimballed engines by the latter; whether Bossart conceived of them independently is unclear.

To build an ICBM in one jump was too hard—neither big enough engines nor enough money were available. The Air Force approved of building ten small MX-774B test vehicles, also known as RTV-A2s or "Hirocs," to test the design concepts. The 30-foot rockets, resembling baby V-2s, used small alcohol/liquid oxygen engines built by Reaction Motors. Originally developed for JATO work, the engines were to be used in the X-1 and Skyrocket research planes. They were uprated to develop 8,000 pounds of thrust for the MX-774B, which was to send a payload of 100 pounds to 670,000 feet. But the project was hampered by a general slash in research funds in December 1946; another cut in funds ended the ICBM program in May 1947. The Air Force judged that no adequate fuels for ICBMs were available; nor was the problem of warhead reentry solved. Developing an ICBM would take up to ten years. Cruise missiles seemed to offer more payload and range and to be more dependable, although some in the Air Force and its advisory organizations suspected that ICBMs would be less vulnerable than the ramjet missile and could be built just as fast. But the ICBM was only revived during the Korean War.

Convair was allowed to finish and test three MX-774Bs between July and December 1947; all three failed. The engine of the first cut off prematurely, apparently because of an electrical failure; the second blew up when excessive pressure built up in an oxygen tank. The third also suffered premature engine cutoff; apparently an oxygen valve shut due to excessive vibration. Yet the rockets had flown in a stable manner and the crashes were not due to Bossart's innovations, which seemed sound.[6]

Nevertheless, the ICBM was dead. The development of large rocket engines might well have stopped completely, since there was no space or ballistic missile program that needed them. Since engine development is time-consuming and is usually the pacing item in building missiles and space vehicles, a halt in large engine work might have had long-lasting and catastrophic consequences even after ballistic missile development resumed during the Korean War. Oddly, the Navaho cruise missile preserved the possibility of an ICBM and an American space program and, perhaps, prevented the defeat of the West.

In 1949–1950, in the face of budget restrictions, Boojum was canceled, and Snark should have been; it was reduced to a low level of component development for a time. But the Air Force stuck with Navaho despite serious difficulties. Ramjets proved harder to develop than expected, and the program (which was not well managed) fell farther and farther behind. A complicating factor was that Navaho, like all ramjet-powered vehicles, needed an additional propulsion system. Theoretically, ramjets are the most efficient form of jet engine at high speeds, but they have to be moving several hundred miles an hour to work at all. The Air Force chose to supply the needed initial boost with a liquid-fuel rocket. It was perhaps not an inevitable choice. Turbojets, or even a ramp or catapult, might have been simpler and quicker ways to do the job.

Navaho's final version needed really large engines to launch it. Their development was the main job of North American's new Rocketdyne division. Its engineers, after instruction by the Germans, Thiel and Heller, took off on their own. Their reaction to the V-2's engine was much like Bossart's reaction to its structure; as the Germans themselves saw, it was too complicated. They replaced its eighteen separate fuel injectors with a single injector, simplified the turbopump, and designed a combustion chamber that could run under much higher pressure. By March 1950, they were testing a 75,000-pound engine burning alcohol and liquid oxygen. Originally intended for Navaho I, it was available for the Army's Redstone missile, the first operational American ballistic missile. North American's engineers went further. Switching from alcohol to the more powerful kerosene, They developed a new type of engine for Navaho II. Instead of heavy double walls, its twin combustion chambers were formed of bundled thick-walled tubes, through which fuel circulated to provide cooling. A turbopump driven by a gas generator (using the same fuels used for propulsion) fed both chambers, each of which generated 120,000 pounds of thrust. Successive versions of this engine, later uprated to 135,000 pounds of thrust per chamber, powered the Atlas ICBM, the "Thor" and "Jupiter" intermediate-range missiles, and the Saturn I space launcher. The critical nature of the Rocketdyne effort will be understood when it is noted that no other rocket engines under development in the United States in the late 1940s and early 1950s generated more than 20,000 pounds of thrust. In addition, Navaho provided other benefits. It helped develop elements of guidance systems; lessons were learned in the use of titanium; and it helped supply the airframe of the "Hound Dog" standoff missile. The Navaho program dragged on until 1957, long after it should have been canceled, and cost $680 million. But the poky and misguided Navaho contributed far more to American defense than many more sensible and successful projects.[7]

VIKING AND AEROBEE

The supply of V-2s was limited. A replacement was needed if high-altitude research was to go on, and a research vehicle designed as such would be more useful than the V-2. Although the Navy had not gained support for a satellite program, research on the ionosphere, with its immediate importance for radio and radar work, was obviously needed. The Naval Research Laboratory proposed two different vehicles—a small unguided rocket, and a bigger V-2 replacement.

Johns Hopkins University's Applied Physics Laboratory designed an efficient-sounding rocket, the Aerobee, capable of sending 120 pounds to a height of 80 miles. Like WAC Corporal, it had a solid-fuel booster and a main stage using aniline and nitric acid feed under gas pressure. It relied on external fins for stability. First fired in November 1947, it was used into the 1970s. It was also developed into the second stage of the Vanguard satellite launcher and part of the Able and Delta vehicles.

Viking, the larger rocket, was a true advance. In August 1946 NRL selected a design offered by the Martin company; Reaction Motors was to develop a 20,000-pound thrust engine. Viking's other features compensated for the relatively weak engine. The first big rocket built of magnesium and aluminum, it incorporated integral (but not pressurized) tanks, and the engine was gimballed—features apparently developed independent of the MX-774B, although the Viking project engineer, Milton Rosen, never hid his debt to Goddard.

After the usual delay with the engine—it took two years instead of the expected fourteen months and was weaker than expected—the first Viking reached a height of 51 miles on May 3, 1949. It and its successor suffered premature engine cutoff, apparently due to leaks in the turbopump; the third, the first fully instrumented research vehicle, suffered a control failure. Later Vikings, however, were generally successful; more were ordered. Viking 10 provided the most dramatic incident of the high-altitude research of the era. On June 30, 1953, it blew up on takeoff. A fire was quickly put out, and the Viking still stood on its shattered tail. But a vacuum developed in the alcohol tank as fuel leaked out, threatening to collapse the rocket. The Navy project officer shot a hole in the tank with a carbine to let air in. Although the engine and tail section were ruined, most of the rest of the rocket was salvageable. Rebuilt at half the cost of a new rocket, it flew to 136 miles on May 7, 1954. The main Viking program finished in early 1955. The Vanguard satellite launcher's first stage was a much-redesigned version of Viking.

Viking's success rate was fairly high by the standards of the time, and its development was remarkably economical, costing under $6 million and requiring the services of only 100 engineers, technicians, and workers of all sorts. The Vikings made possible the measurement of temperatures, atmospheric density, and wind velocity at high altitudes, and they made it possible to detect ultraviolet, cosmic, and X-rays and to take solar spectrograms without atmospheric interference. Much was learned about the ionosphere and the sun.[8] Along with the V-2s and the Aerobees, the Vikings proved a far better investment than anyone realized in the 1950s. The seemingly hum-drum task of upper-atmosphere research was more than a slight recompense for the failure to pursue more "glamorous" things like satellites. As would become clear in the 1980s with the threats of destruction of the ozone layer and global warming, gathering as much data about all levels of the atmosphere was not merely interesting, but of life-and-death importance.

POSTWAR SOVIET DEVELOPMENTS

The Soviets, too, were intensely interested in the V-2. Their exploitation of German efforts was at first more focused and energetic than that of the West, despite the latter's luck in getting von Braun's team and the Nordhausen V-2s. In some ways, the Soviet rocket effort in general was better planned and more efficient than that of the Americans, and although there was an (almost literally) cut-throat competition between design bureaus, the Soviets avoided interservice rivalry. They simply classed rockets as artillery weapons and put artillery generals in control of their efforts—rather surprisingly, this worked well. Given American laxity, the Soviets were in a good position in the late 1940s to gain an unbeatable lead. However, not for the first or last time, they were foiled by their own hypersuspicion and security mania. After initially using the Germans more effectively than the Americans, they threw them away and disrupted their own efforts.

In the summer of 1945, the Americans had noted the Soviets trying to tempt the von Braun group into the Soviet zone. In general, the Soviets enjoyed little success, but they scooped up many lesser engineers and technicians who had remained east of the Elbe. One senior scientist, Helmut Grottrup, who had worked on guidance and control systems at Peenemunde, disliked the American terms and moved East; he was recruited by the Soviets to lead the Germans under Soviet control. Using the facilities at Nordhausen, the Soviets revived V-2 production. They had Grottrup's team design a successor to the V-2, and they asked for German suggestions to aid a separate, purely Soviet design effort under Korolev. Grottrup's group proved bolder in innovation than von Braun's team, and it suggested the use of separable warheads, pressurized tanks, and fuel pumps driven by bleeding exhaust gases from the engine. But their design was never built. Korolev's design, the R-2 (or V-2A when it was used for high-altitude research), was more conservative; basically it was a V-2 with a more powerful engine, separate warhead, and 400-mile range. In the fall of 1946, the Soviets abruptly transferred all rocket work and personnel from East Germany to the U.S.S.R. Thereafter the Germans continued design work, but none of their missiles were ever put into production. The Germans were used as a check on the Soviets' own work and increasingly kept apart from the main Soviet program. The Soviets thus failed to integrate the Germans into their program, probably due to a mania for security—an unnecessary worry, for there seems to have been no reason to think that the Germans were disloyal to their new masters, and, in Stalin's U.S.S.R. there was not much danger that any spies among them could pass information outside the country.

In October 1947, the Soviets finally fired their first V-2 (R-1). R-1s and R-2s (called SS-1 Scunner and SS-2 Sibling by NATO) were deployed in limited numbers with the first Soviet rocket divisions and were used for research. Unable to carry nuclear warheads, they were not too important militarily, but they provided operational experience with large rockets. A later version of the R-2, the R-11, became famous as the "Scud" missile of the 1990–1991 Gulf War.

Stalin wanted truly long-range weapons. Despite advice that the project was not practical, he was at first more interested in an abortive German project, the Sanger antipodal rocket bomber (see Chapter 9), than in ballistic missiles. Eventually Stalin became more receptive to advice from the rocket experts Grigori Tokaty-Tokaev and M. V. Keldysh. In April 1947 he formed a State Commission on Intercontinental Missiles under the powerful and unpleasant police general, Ivan Serov; ballistic weapons would be pursued. Tokaty-Tokaev actually designed a three-stage ICBM during 1947. He later held that, if this project had been pushed all out, the Soviets could have had ICBMs and Sputniks by 1952. But a new series of purges started. Tokaty-Tokaev's group was broken up; he escaped to the West. Korolev was reimprisoned. After 1950 the Germans ceased to play an important role; later they were sent home. The ICBM received low priority, while work concentrated on standoff missiles for bombers. Like the Americans, the Soviets wasted effort on cruise missiles; work on Navaho-type weapons (begun shortly after Stalin's death), although eventually consigned to aircraft design bureaus, dragged on until 1960 before being canceled. Since the Soviets were already developing large engines for ballistic rockets, this was sheer waste, without the "fallout" that made Navaho worthwhile for the United States.

Work did proceed on the R-5 ballistic missile (NATO designation SS-3 Shyster), which was comparable to the American Redstone but longer ranged. The Soviets also worked on a huge rocket engine designed by Glushko, whose two versions were eventually designated the RD-107 and RD-108. It essentially consisted of four improved V-2 engines that burned kerosene and oxygen with much higher chamber pressures, grouped together and fed by a single turbopump driven by a gas generator that used gasoline and oxygen. It developed 228,000 pounds of thrust, far greater than any engine the Americans contemplated until the mid-1950s. Its development was not a complete secret; beginning in 1951–1952, the Americans received reports that an engine of 265,000 pounds of thrust (or even more) was under development or being tested and that work had started on one twice as powerful. Such reports helped revive the American ICBM program. The Americans mistakenly assumed that the Soviet engine consisted of one big combustion chamber, which they considered conventional. (The Soviets had tried to build a single-chamber engine with the thrust of the RD-107, but failed.) This misunderstanding made the Soviets seem farther along in engine development than they were, and it contributed to the tendency to overestimate their lead after Sputnik. In reality, although some ingenuity was involved in its design, the Soviets had built a big rocket engine in the crudest and most conservative way possible. Their work on fuels, too, remained conservative. They stuck to the combination of kerosene and oxygen. They did develop storable fuels, but they showed little interest in "exotic," high-energy fuels. Unlike the Americans, they did not waste huge sums exploring boron compounds, but they apparently did no work on liquid hydrogen, either. The conservative pattern set in engine and fuel development eventually hampered the Soviet space program.[9]

3

The Race for the ICBM

The Cold War was not a Soviet-American duel in which other countries played a minor role. However, other countries *did* play a minor role in the strategic arms race, and particularly missile development. This element of direct competition gives the race for the ICBM a special interest.

So far, despite the insanities inflicted under Stalin and the awful situation in agriculture, the Soviet form of industrialization had worked well—it was more or less competitive in the old heavy industries, where it copied what the West had. Whether it would compete in an era of automation, computers, and synthetic materials was not clear; but its high production of engineers and scientists, and the apparent early success of some of Khrushchev's reforms, suggested that it might do well. Instead it fell farther behind, and the failure to see much improvement eventually demoralized the Soviet people. The economic system remained inefficient, and in most fields the U.S.S.R. lagged behind the West.

However, the Soviet Union's chances of victory in technological and military competition were not nonexistent. Success, however, depended on unusual adeptness and concentration of resources, and American bungling or neglect. Precisely because of the centralization and inertia of their bureaucracy, the Soviets needed more intelligent direction than the Americans to succeed. Sometimes these conditions existed.

There was nothing "soft," contrary to what is widely believed, about Khrushchev's foreign policy—an idea incompatible even with a careful reading of his memoirs. He was a tough and dedicated enemy of the West.

Khrushchev was a reformer in military as well as domestic affairs.

Although Stalin had invested heavily in nuclear weapons, he had, at least for public consumption, played down their revolutionary nature and denied that surprise attack could be a decisive factor in war. These views were probably shared by many senior officers. Even in the late 1950s, Soviet doctrine assumed that even in an all-out war, land battles—not a nuclear exchange between the Soviet and American homelands—would decide things. After Stalin's death, military thinkers, encouraged by Khrushchev, focused on nuclear weapons and the related issue of surprise. There was a shift to primacy for nuclear forces. Khrushchev at least implied—and at least one authoritative general, Nikolai Talensky, openly argued in 1958—that the ICBM all by itself was a decisive weapon. In practice, however, Khrushchev obtained a second-best position in what Americans regarded as strategic weapons, securing only a few bombers and ICBMs capable of striking the United States. Bombers and missiles capable of hitting Eurasian targets were built in large numbers—larger than the West expected. This seems to have been due to a long-standing strategic conception (related to the ideas of the more conservative marshals) that nearby foes, and American forward bases, must be covered before anything else. It was also due to the inadequacies of Soviet long-range bombers and "first-generation" ICBMs. They were not built in large numbers, because as weapons they were not very good.[1]

The most striking features of the United States in the 1950s were its prosperity, progress, and high morale. Although they were perhaps less optimistic than in the 1940s and feared war and Communism, Americans were confident about the future of their society. Some on the right and left were not, but even the latter (still mired in the attitudes of the 1930s) often found little concrete to complain about. A situation in which most people had attained a comfortable middle-class way of life was so novel that even the most carping critics were stunned into silence. Most Americans had confidence in the country's basic institutions and the probity of their leaders.

After a careful review of all alternatives, the Eisenhower Administration completed a transition, begun under Truman, to a long-haul military policy aimed at maintaining a high degree of readiness over many years rather than meeting a designated year of maximum danger. The Administration thought general war was unlikely; at least the Soviets were unlikely to start one deliberately. The West was too strong, and soon both sides would be in a situation of "atomic plenty" in which all-out war would probably ruin everyone. Nevertheless, the Administration was very careful to ensure that the strategic balance was not upset, and it would convene several high-ranking panels to check just this point.

In formulating its policy, the Administration was strongly influenced by fiscal constraints, as well as a desire to deter aggressions of the Korean type and avoid a costly stalemate if a local war did break out. Eisenhower feared the economic impact of continued military expenditures, deficits, and taxation on the Korean War level and even the development of a garrison state. (He also stressed the danger of spending too little on defense.) He stressed airpower and nuclear weapons. The Air Force and naval airpower dominated the defense budget, which shrank drastically in the mid-1950s; Eisenhower was unique in the post-World War II era in actually reducing federal expenditures.[2] The lowered budgets proved consonant with security and even with remarkable innovations in weapons, although once or twice the Administration would cut costs in ways it would regret.

THE REVIVAL OF THE MISSILE PROGRAM

The Korean War had been a turning point in American missile development, as it was in other elements of the Cold War. In early 1950, Senator Lyndon Johnson (beginning a lasting interest in both military missiles and space travel) and Hanson Baldwin, the *New York Times* military expert, had drawn public attention to the lack of progress in missiles. When the Korean War started, not one missile of any sort was operational.

In July 1950, the Army began developing a mobile missile (later called the Redstone after the new Army missile center at Huntsville, Alabama) to carry a 5,000-pound nuclear warhead 500 miles. At first there was little drive behind the program. In October 1950, under public pressure and urged on by the Undersecretary of the Air Force, John McCone, the Administration named Kaufman T. Keller, the Chairman of the Chrysler Corporation, as a special adviser to coordinate all work on missiles. McCone and some others wanted Keller to head a special missile agency along Manhattan Project lines, but Keller conceived of his task in a far more limited way. Operating with a small staff, his main aim was to eliminate interservice duplication of effort and rush weapons already under development into production. In December 1950 he made Redstone a serious effort. But he was more interested in antiaircraft weapons than offensive ones, and his relations with the Air Force (which accused him of favoring the Army) were bad. By galvanizing the overall missile effort, Keller helped revive the ICBM, although he had little to do with it directly.

The Redstone was scaled down to a 200-mile range. Built of aluminum, with integral tanks and a separable warhead, it was powered by the engine developed for Navaho I. It used alcohol as a fuel and steered with vanes in the exhaust. It had the first inertial guidance system in an American missile, but otherwise it was not a distinguished design, and it entered service only in 1958. It was not an impressive weapon; fighter-bombers carrying nuclear bombs could probably have accomplished its mission more cheaply. It would be surprising if von Braun's team felt much enthusiasm for a clone of the V-2, which if fired in anger would probably hit targets in Germany. But it marked their return to serious development work and gave the Americans valuable experience. Furthermore, Redstone (which was insignificant for military purposes) proved important for space exploration. It provided the launcher for the first American satellite and the first Mercury astronauts.

The Soviets were well ahead of the Redstone. They deployed the R-5 (which had a cluster of combustion chambers using kerosene rather than alcohol and a range of 700 miles) much earlier. This should be recalled when it is suggested that the Soviets were never ahead of the West in rocketry.[3]

REVIVING THE ICBM

The Korean War, the resulting availability of money for military development, Keller's impact, and changes within the Air Force revived the intercontinental ballistic missile—but only on a small scale. Along with the H-bomb, the ICBM was the critical weapons development of the Cold War era. And, as we shall see, the principal launch vehicles of the space program in the 1960s and later (and even today) were products or byproducts of the ICBM effort. For many reasons, therefore, the development of the ICBM is worth close study. There was a long struggle before it got the support needed for success within a reasonable period, and there were conflicts over the size and form the missile should take and how to run the program. Under Truman, the ICBM effort remained limited, although critical decisions were made about the fundamental features of its design.

Well before the Korean War, many officers, and the Air Force's Scientific Advisory Board, had regarded the Air Force's approach to technical matters as inadequate. At their recommendation, during 1950–1951 a separate Air Research and Development Command (ARDC) was split off from the old Air Material Command, which nevertheless feuded with the new agency. General John Sessums, head of the ARDC, was an important force in pushing the ICBM and deciding its design.

In January 1951, Convair, which had continued small-scale work on intercontinental weapons on its own, received a small study contract to work on an intercontinental missile which became known as the Atlas.

It was not certain, for a time, that this would be a ballistic missile. Convair's engineers became convinced that a winged glide missile would weigh less and be cheaper and easier to build. The ARDC doubted this, for the whole vehicle would have to be able to reenter the atmosphere, and it would be slower and easier to intercept. In September 1951, the ARDC made Convair concentrate on an ICBM based on Bossart's concepts. It seemed, however, that it would be massive and unwieldy. Carrying a 7,000-pound warhead to hit within 1,500 feet of its aiming point, the first version of the Atlas needed seven 120,000-pound thrust engines and was 160 feet long. It was expected to take a decade to build. There was little drive behind the project; the Air Force remained oriented primarily toward bombers and secondarily toward air-breathing missiles.

In August 1952, an intelligence review of what was known about the Soviet missile effort concluded that it concentrated on weapons like Snark and Navaho. Reports of large rocket engines, however, worried Sessums and others. With the development of thermonuclear weapons, it became clear that the Atlas's warhead could be lighter. In December 1952, the Scientific Advisory Board's missile committee, headed by the physicist Clark Millikin, urged reducing both payload and accuracy requirements. The Air Force rejected the latter idea but favored the weight reduction. By the spring of 1953, the Atlas was scaled down to a 110-foot, five-engine missile. It was still expected to take up to ten years to develop. Its design had a peculiarity it retained through many changes; it was a one-and-a-half-stage or parallel-stage vehicle. Unlike conventional multistage vehicles, in which whole stages of both tanks and engines fired and were discarded successively, the Atlas took off with all engines firing; at a certain point all but one sustainer engine would be dropped. This avoided any problems involved in starting an upper stage at high altitude.

Little real progress had been made when there was a dramatic turn in the program.[4]

IN THE NICK OF TIME?

The Eisenhower Administration turned a leisurely effort into a crash program. This was the ironic result of what was originally an attempt to cut the defense budget, as well as the work of a few deeply concerned men. The defense budget was not cut, but the West, perhaps, was saved.

Three men played a vital role in this: the great mathematician John von Neumann; the engineer and businessman Trevor Gardner, who was Special Assistant for Research and Development to the Secretary of the Air Force from 1953 to 1956; and Colonel Bernard Schriever.

Gardner was a brilliant and exceptionally able man who had occupied important posts in connection with military research during World War II. He was also unpopular; the U.S. Air Force (USAF) brass, in particular, disliked him. He depended heavily on the backing of Air Force Secretary Harold Talbott.

In June 1953, Secretary of Defense Charles Wilson ordered Talbott to form a committee that would review all missile projects to eliminate waste and duplication. Talbott gave the job to Gardner; his committee changed missile procurement procedures but otherwise had only limited immediate results. But Gardner was worried by intelligence that indicated Soviet progress in missiles. He thought the Air Force approach to ICBM development was wrong. A briefing by Convair engineers impressed him, and he asked Convair for proposals for a crash program and instigated another review of missiles, but this time separate groups dealt with strategic and tactical missiles. He may already have favored setting up a separate development agency, operating outside regular channels, to build an ICBM.

The Strategic Missiles Evaluation Group (SMEG), more often called the Teapot or von Neumann Committee, first met on November 9. Gardner had stacked it with proponents of the ICBM. Its chairman, John von Neumann, was responsible for many achievements in different branches of mathematics (among other things, the theory of games and the theories behind electronic computers). As an adviser to the Air Force, he had already suggested cutting the Atlas's warhead weight further. Other members included scientists with a long record of service in major development projects: Clark Millikan, Charles Lauritzen, George Kistiakowsky, and Jerome Wiesner. The military was represented by Colonel Bernard Schriever, then an assistant to the Deputy Chief of Staff for Development. An exceptionally able officer and engineer with influential connections, he had served in the Pacific, rising from bomber pilot to Chief of Staff of the Fifth Air Force. Since World War II he had specialized in development projects and was a long-standing missile advocate. Unlike the cold, abrupt Gardner, he was a personable man with a gift for leadership. Two members of the SMEG, Simon Ramo and Dean Wooldridge (old acquaintances of Gardner's), had recently left Hughes Aircraft to form the Ramo-Wooldridge Corporation (the nucleus of the great computer firm, TRW). Their company would do administrative work for the committee.

Galvanized by von Neumann and Gardner, the committee did not share the Air Force love of air-breathing missiles. It urged derogating Snark to the role of a decoy for bombers. In its report of February 10, 1954, it warned that the Soviets might be ahead in missiles and recommended accelerating ICBM development to reach an operational capability in six to eight years. This required revising outdated specifications; accuracy demands should be reduced from 1,500 feet to 2 or 3 miles, and warhead weight to 1,500 pounds. These changes made Atlas a "city-buster" suitable for destroying big, "soft" targets, not "hardened" military sites protected against nuclear blasts. While praising Convair, the report warned that a radical reorganization transcending the Convair framework was needed for success in a reasonable span of time. There had to be a separate ICBM development group and overall technical direction by an unusually competent group of scientists and engineers, which the aircraft industry could not supply. And the effort must be free of excessively detailed regulation by existing government agencies.

A parallel study by RAND, submitted February 8, came to similar conclusions. Gardner had already drawn up a plan for a development group to be run by a general who was also a vice commander of the ARDC. He now believed that the Soviets were probably ahead of the United States in missiles. In March he outlined his ideas to Talbott, warning that Convair's program and the current Air Force structure were unsuited to rapid development.

The von Neumann Committee's report proved decisive. The successful test of the first deliverable H-bomb on March 1 showed that warhead weights could indeed be reduced. The Vice Chief of Staff of the Air Force, Thomas White, decided that Atlas was vital; on March 16 he endorsed the Committee's main recommendations. Yet many in the service remained hostile and disliked proposals for organizing the program on unorthodox lines. On March 19, Talbott ordered the Chief of Staff, Nathan Twining, to take all necessary steps to accelerate the Atlas. On March 23, Twining approved of relaxing specifications for the Atlas and assigning it to ARDC with a special organization. The Air Force established a new Assistant Chief of Staff for missiles.

Atlas received the Air Force's highest priority on May 14. On June 1, Schriever, now a general, was assigned to head ICBM development. ARDC would manage it through a special field office, its Western Development Division (WDD), under Schriever's command, with a hand-picked staff. On July 1, this Division was established at Inglewood, California, near Convair. Shortly after a Special Aircraft Projects Office, which would handle procurement, was formed there by the Air Material Command. The Air Force disliked these arrangements, but Talbott implacably backed Gardner and the Teapot Group. And the generals feared that if they resisted too strongly, the effort might be moved largely outside the service to a Manhattan-type project, possibly with a civilian head (perhaps the dreaded Gardner).

Gardner never became a missile czar—a position many believed he coveted—but this outstanding, if unlikeable public servant contributed far more to America's defense than many better-known figures. Edmund Beard estimated that without the advent of Gardner (which was a unique and perhaps chance event), the start of a serious ICBM program might have been delayed a year or two. Thanks to Gardner, von Neumann, and Schriever, the ICBM got going and received the correct organizational framework for success. Thanks to them, no real missile gap developed. Moreover, as we shall see, initiatives strongly promoted by Gardner exposed the gap as a myth at a relatively early date.

The problem of internal organization of the project remained. In April 1954 von Neumann's group had been reorganized as the Atlas Scientific Advisory Committee, with most of its original members. New people joined the group, including Charles Lindbergh and Herbert F. York (who was later the chief scientist of the Defense Department). In July the Committee urged strengthening Schriever's authority and suggested that Ramo-Wooldridge take over not just the task of technical direction but responsibility for systems engineering. It would not supply any hardware to the project to avoid conflicts of interest. These ideas were approved on September 8, despite the opposition of not only Convair but the rest of the aircraft industry, which disliked Ramo-Wooldridge as outsiders. Schriever defended his actions by noting that missile projects like Navaho, run along orthodox lines by aircraft companies, had continually fallen behind schedule. His arrangements and leadership proved a brilliant success and the model for many later efforts.[5]

It was a daunting task: The Atlas program alone included 2,000 companies and 40,000 workers, and the Western Development Division went on to direct two more ICBMs, Titan and Minuteman, and the Thor intermediate-range missile. Herbert York, not an admirer of many professional soldiers, praised Schriever: "He used his special authority brilliantly, and much of what we now take for granted in the methodology of systems development and systems management was pioneered under his direction." He estimated that without either WDD, Schriever, or Ramo-Wooldridge, the Atlas would have taken over a year longer and would have cost far more.[6] It must be noted, however, that even Schriever, while ready to tangle with Air Force brass and plane manufacturers, was unwilling to tackle inter-service rivalry, which was particularly fierce in the 1950s. He did not try to use the Army team headed by von Braun, which was still the most experienced group of rocket engineers in the West. (A few Germans, like

Krafft Ehricke and Adolph Thiel, who had left von Braun's group to join Convair and Ramo-Wooldridge, did play an important role in Atlas.)

In December 1954, Atlas was scaled down to a three-engine vehicle, which was the version finally built. The engines were arranged in a row at its tail; the two outer, booster engines, generating 135,000 pounds of thrust each, would be dropped 145 seconds into flight with the "skirt" structure surrounding the tail; the central sustainer engine, with just 60,000 pounds of thrust, continued to fire for another 125 seconds. The missile could lift a 1-megaton warhead with an accuracy of 5 miles. Guidance would be supplied by a semi-inertial system; its computer would depend on correction by radio signals from ground stations. A pure inertial system would replace it on later ICBMs. As things turned out, both the warhead and guidance system would be improved unexpectedly before Atlas went into operation.

Schriever developed new testing procedures to check out Atlas. The program was shaped by the philosophy of concurrency, which Schriever had envisaged in a paper written in 1950: Development, production, and training were timed to be completed simultaneously to reach operational status as early as possible. The related program package concept ensured that all major parts of the program were treated in terms of their inter-relationships and not in isolation. Lastly, the program used dual source or parallel development; there would be two major suppliers for each major subsystem of the missile to guard against bungling by any one company.

This practice led to the decision to develop a more advanced ICBM to follow Atlas—Titan. It would be built using backup subsystems from the Atlas; the subsystems of either missile (e.g., engines) would remain compatible with the other. Titan would be a more advanced, yet in some ways more conventional, vehicle. It used engines supplied by Aerojet (Atlas used North American's Navaho engines) in two sequential stages, and a standard airframe instead of the pressurized structure Atlas inherited from MX-774B. Titan would use a pure inertial guidance system. (Eventually this system would be adopted for Atlas, too.) More importantly, Titan was designed from the start to be placed in underground silos. Late in 1955, the Martin company won the contract for Titan. It constructed a whole new plant at Denver to build it.[7]

SPEEDUP

By 1955 the ICBM program was well underway, but development was not as rapid as it might have been. However, a shift in perspective of the Eisenhower Administration changed things.

Although he thought that basic factors made world war unlikely, the President had convened a Technological Capabilities Panel on March 27, 1954, under James R. Killian of the Massachusetts Institute of Technology (MIT), to investigate the danger of surprise attack. Its "Surprise Attack Study," usually called the Killian Report, was submitted to the National Security Council in February 1955. The Panel had already had a major impact on the course of the Cold War.

There had been widespread dissatisfaction with American intelligence. Many of the CIA's more able officials, notably Richard Bissell, were disillusioned with trying to get agents into the Soviet bloc; this had been a costly failure. The result was a new stress on technical means to gather intelligence. The influence of Bissell, preliminary appraisals by the Killian group, and the efforts of Trevor Gardner persuaded Eisenhower on November 24, 1954 to approve the development of a reconnaissance plane that would fly over enemy countries at very high altitude. Lockheed Aircraft set up a special, super-secret "Skunk Works" to produce the new plane, the U-2, with remarkable speed. Fragile, big-winged, and almost a powered glider, the U-2 first flew in August 1955. In July 1956 it entered Soviet airspace for the first time. It was used cautiously and sparingly— U-2s only overflew the U.S.S.R. about thirty times before one was shot down in 1960. However, they revealed invaluable information. Later U-2s played a crucial role in the Cuban Missile Crisis. In a less spectacular but probably equally important effort, also sparked by Gardner, a super radar was installed at Samsun in Turkey to watch Soviet missile tests.

The Killian Report warned that unless the United States increased its efforts, the Soviets might gain a decisive missile lead by 1960. It recommended giving the ICBM higher priority, and the development of an intermediate-range (1,500-mile) ballistic missile (IRBM) as an interim and supporting weapon. Based in Europe and Asia, IRBMs might fill in before large numbers of ICBMs were ready. It also urged reducing the vulnerability of the Strategic Air Command's bombers to surprise attack.

The Killian Report envisaged the future unfolding in four phases. In Period I, which lasted until 1956, the United States would have great offensive strength yet would be vulnerable to surprise attack; its early warning and air defense system was inadequate. In Period II, from 1956 to 1958 or 1960, the United States would still have enormous nuclear superiority but would be less vulnerable to surprise. It would certainly win a war, although it would be battered severely. Afterward there would be a transitional phase, Period III, in which things might be fluid. The Soviets would have multimegaton thermonuclear weapons and bombers capable of reaching the United States. The United States would still be stronger, but the Soviets might gain a dangerous superiority if the United States was careless or neglected some programs. In Period IV, whose length would be indefinite, an attack by either side would result in mutual destruction. The Killian Panel regarded this as very dangerous; it lacked confidence in the stability of what was later called mutual assured destruction. The United States should prolong Period II as long as possible, avert Soviet superiority in Period III, and get out of Period IV as fast as possible—if it could, for the Report warned that it was impossible to say whether the expected stalemate would be permanent.[8]

The Report impressed the Administration's upper echelons, and some of the opposition was also concerned. Senators Clinton Anderson and Henry Jackson of the Joint Congressional Committee on Atomic Energy met the President on June 30, 1955 to urge speeding up ICBM work. They noted that although the ICBM nominally had top priority within the Air Force, it did not have overriding priority over other defense programs, and they urged relaxing normal procurement regulations. After a full briefing at a National Security Council meeting on July 28, Eisenhower was won over. On September 8, he gave the ICBM the highest national priority, DX. On September 13, he approved development of an intermediate-range ballistic missile. Hyde Gillette, the deputy for Budget and Program Management under the Assistant Secretary of the Air Force for Financial Management, devised a clever way to eliminate administrative delays, which was approved in November. Normal review procedures, which took two or three months for decision, were eliminated. Western Development Division received authority to issue contracts on its own. The Gillette procedures ensured that planning, budgeting, and reporting would be combined neatly on one yearly document. Only two ballistic missile committees, one chaired by the Secretary of the Air Force and one by the Secretary of Defense, would act as reviewing authorities. (No one seems to have thought it peculiar or pondered the full implications of the fact that when something vital had to be done, ordinary procedures had to be dropped.) The ICBM was now a major national effort. In December 1955, Eisenhower ordered that he receive monthly reports on the strategic missile program.[9]

During 1955 the ICBM effort sparked an interesting sideline. The Air Force and the Atomic Energy Commission began work on a nuclear reactor rocket, at first as a possible powerplant for ICBMs (although many involved must have suspected that this was an unlikely use for nuclear engines). This effort did not come under Schriever and did not have the ICBM's priority. (It will be discussed in Chapter 11.)

It is arguable that the decisions of 1954–1955 were the military turning point of the Cold War. They ensured that the West kept strategic superiority, or at least parity, until the U.S.S.R. collapsed—although that by itself did not necessarily guarantee that there would be no Third World War. As may already have become apparent to the reader, a true missile gap might have developed easily at several points. Without the lucky decisions of the late 1940s to develop the Navaho and launch it with a rocket booster, there would have been no large rocket engines under development when a serious ICBM program finally began, and the ICBM would have been delayed hopelessly. Without Gardner and von Neumann, a major effort might not have started until 1956. Without the special organizational framework and innovation of the WDD and Schriever's outstanding leadership, the project would have been run along orthodox lines by the Air Force and aircraft industry. The examples of Navaho and Snark suggest that, even with all-out priority and appropriations, an operational missile might have been delayed until the mid-1960s. Without any one of these things, a very dangerous situation might have developed by the 1960s; without all three—as might have happened easily—catastrophe probably would have resulted.

It was a strenuous, not always successful fight to keep the necessary priorities and funding. The ICBM's all-out priority was eroded slightly and almost immediately by the decision in December 1955 to have WDD develop the Thor IRBM, and by Secretary of Defense Wilson's order on January 20, 1956 (over Air Force opposition) to give it coequal priority with the ICBMs. Gardner, who wanted more spending on research and development than Wilson, was disgusted by the latter decision. It is uncertain whether he was otherwise dissatisfied with ICBM funding (as he later claimed), but in any case he resigned on February 10. He wrote several articles, before and after Sputnik, indicting Wilson's policies.

Beginning in July 1956, the new Secretary of the Air Force, Donald Quarles, urged "stretching out" aspects of the ICBM program. He seems to have believed dogmatically that it was already impossible for either side to win a war no matter what weapons or stratagems were developed, and so he was relatively indifferent to the precise strategic balance. (President Eisenhower thought that such a situation would probably develop soon, if it did not already exist, but was unwilling to stake everything on such a belief.) Quarles favored postponing attainment of an operational capability from March to December 1961, stopping either Atlas or Titan, and reducing effort on the remaining missile. Schriever fended off concerted efforts to stop Titan, but Atlas development suffered. In March 1957, the planned budget for the 1958 fiscal year was cut 20 percent; Titan development was stretched out and dual development reduced, although a token operational capability for Atlas would be reached earlier. In May the budget was cut further from $1.335 billion to $1.135 billion. At Wilson's insistence, overtime was cut greatly and Titan's priority reduced. Officially these changes were expected to delay Atlas by another four months, and Titan by nine months, but Schriever warned that they might delay missile deployment by three years. In August Wilson imposed limits on Titan and IRBM production while testing proceeded. As it turned out, these decisions had no great impact, if only because they were not in effect for long. But the Administration would have reason to rue them: Along with the mishandling of the satellite program and quarrels over the IRBM, they would do it tremendous political harm.

The principal technical problems in developing the Atlas involved guidance and flight dynamics—providing a smooth and stable powered flight, and ensuring that the warhead would survive reentry into the atmosphere. Reentry was a tricky problem; to solve it the Air Force had Lockheed Aircraft hastily build a small, three-stage, solid-fuel rocket—the X-17—to test "heat-sink" nose cones, which used masses of copper to soak up the heat generated by air friction. But this solution proved inferior to an alternative developed by the Army for the Jupiter IRBM—"ablative" nose cones, in which outer layers burned off during reentry. Powering Atlas was less of a problem; by 1955 Navaho booster development was far enough along to provide the needed engines. Oddly, the only real problem was combustion instability in the small sustainer engine.

The first Atlas A, a test vehicle with a dummy nose cone and two booster engines (the sustainer was not yet fitted), was tested on June 11, 1957. It had to be destroyed when an engine failed. A second Atlas A failed on September 25; that did the Administration little good when Sputnik went up shortly after. The third Atlas A succeeded on December 17, but in total only three of eight Atlas A flights went well. Atlas B, still a test vehicle but with a real nose cone and three engines, flew successfully in August 1958, but it did not go full range until November 28—more than a year after the first full-range Soviet ICBM test. The first Titan was tested in February 1959.[10]

THE IRBM: THOR VERSUS JUPITER

The intermediate-range ballistic missile program authorized in September 1955 proved of little direct military significance, but it provided valuable space launchers; later versions of an IRBM were used three decades later. The program involved several ironies and oddities. The shorter-range missile was developed after the intercontinental one, instead of being a stepping stone to the latter. While WDD worked on the crucial ICBM efficiently, and with less publicity until after Sputnik, the IRBM provoked bitter public controversy, partly because of interservice jealousy and partly because of the glamor of von Braun's team. In a further irony, the IRBM, which itself had little impact on the military balance, led to a project which did—the Polaris submarine-based missile.

The Air Force had long pondered developing an IRBM, but there was much disagreement about whether one was needed and how to build it. The Atlas Advisory Committee recommended developing an IRBM from the second stage of the Titan ICBM. Schriever did not want the IRBM, because he felt that it endangered the ICBM's priority. However, he felt that if one were built, it should be done by WDD and take the form of a scaled-down Atlas. Gardner consistently opposed the IRBM as a diversion of effort. For once, his views were widely shared in the Air Force. Apart from questions of priorities, the Air Force disliked the continued dependence on overseas bases that the IRBM implied, something the service had long wanted to escape.

But the Killian Report gave the IRBM strong impetus. The Army, having finished most of its work on the Redstone, was eager to build an IRBM; so in May 1955 the Air Force began to seek proposals from industry. Gardner wanted to help the British build one, but it became clear that they lacked the resources for a serious effort. Meanwhile Commander Robert Truax, a naval rocket expert attached to WDD, and Adolph Thiel of Ramo-Wooldridge, roughed out the parameters for an Air Force IRBM. By August they decided that it should be transportable by air and should use the Atlas nose cone, a single modified Atlas engine, and an all-inertial guidance system.

Attempts to allot the IRBM to one service or another deadlocked; the Joint Chiefs of staff finally recommended a dual program to Secretary Wilson. The Army, with no role in the ICBM effort, knew its missile team was at stake, and the Air Force would not let it do the job alone. Eisenhower and Wilson made it clear that they wanted the Army team employed, and no one cared to argue that the capabilities of the President's old service should not be used. Eisenhower had great interest in the IRBM, and he thought that it might be almost as effective as the ICBM. (It is worth noting that the impetus for the IRBM came from scientists and political leaders, not the armed forces or the "military-industrial complex.")

IRBM no. 1 would be developed by the Air Force; IRBM no. 2 by the Army and Navy. The latter missile would be designed for firing from either land bases or submarines. But the Navy was not enthusiastic about having liquid-fuel rockets on ships.

Wilson, deeming competition a good thing, approved this scheme on November 8, 1955. It was assumed for the next two years that only one missile would actually be deployed. In December, IRBM no. 1 was officially assigned to WDD; Douglas Aircraft would build it under the name Thor. Work on the Thor, directed by a very small team under Dr. Maxwell Hunter, went very rapidly. Schriever believed that he managed to prevent its interfering much with the ICBM. But the Thor had a checkered test history. The first Thor, launched on January 25, 1957, blew up on liftoff. Only the fourth Thor, fired on September 20, was a success.

JUPITER

In its technical aspects the Army IRBM, the Jupiter, developed more smoothly than Thor, but it ran into political heavy weather. The Army suspected that, despite its nominally equal priority, Jupiter was indeed number two, and it felt uneasy about the Navy—an unreliable ally. The Army also believed that it was up against not just the Air Force but the whole aircraft industry, which wanted to end the Army's arsenal system and keep car manufacturers out of the aerospace field; for the Chrysler Corporation was to produce Jupiter after von Braun's team completed development. Even many neutral observers deemed the arsenal approach at best outdated, and at worst having an inherent tendency to unimaginativeness and sluggishness. (Indeed von Braun's men already had a reputation for technical conservatism.) The Army countered that its arsenals were capable of more objective assessments, were more stable than industrial suppliers, and were a safeguard against private malfeasance. (Development aside, government laboratories were needed for quality control.)

The Army Ballistic Missile Agency (ABMA) at Huntsville, Alabama, showed that with top-flight military leadership and the competence of von Braun's team, arsenals could achieve a great deal. In fact, the Agency's efforts, von Braun's already legendary reputation, and several incidents created a widespread false impression that the Agency was the real center of the American missile and space effort. ABMA's head, John B. Medaris, was an unusual character—as might be expected of a general who wound up as an Episcopalian bishop. Theatrically handsome and perhaps a bit slippery, he was more of a maverick than his Air Force rival Schriever, with whom he was on terms of uneasy geniality. An ardent proponent of the arsenal system, he was a harsh critic of the Air Force, but also of some Army practices. A strong advocate of missiles, he persuaded General James Gavin, then Assistant Chief of Staff for Research and Development, to allot funds for basic engine research and test stands for engines of up to 500,000 pounds of thrust. (That was far bigger than any likely ICBM powerplant and suggests that he envisaged a major Army role in space exploration.) His methods differed from Schriever's. He ran a much tighter organization and supervised things more closely; but his ways might not have worked in the Air Force's bigger operation. Benefitting from the Air Force example, he was delegated unusual authority to make contracts and reported through a simplified review system like that designed by Gillette. He could rely on a stable, established team of technical experts. Von Braun had studied an IRBM ever since Redstone had been well underway.

Army concepts of how to build and deploy an IRBM differed greatly from that of the Air Force. The Air Force planned fixed bases; the Army wanted a mobile system. Its engineers disliked the pressurized structure Thor borrowed from Atlas, and they favored different guidance and reentry systems. Essentially a scaled-up Redstone, Jupiter used much of the same ground equipment and a different version of the same engine that powered Thor. Much time was spent making it suitable for Navy use.

Late in 1956, Jupiter suffered two major blows. On November 26, Secretary Wilson gave operational control of all missiles of over 200 miles range to the Air Force and Navy (i.e., land-based Jupiters would be operated by the Air Force). It did not take a genius to see that the Air Force was likely to prefer its own product. In December the Navy, embarking on its own solid-fuel missile, Polaris, left the Jupiter program. Some top Army officers now favored abandoning long-range missile work. ABMA's desperation led to a strange incident.

THE NICKERSON AFFAIR

Colonel John C. Nickerson, a World War II hero and ardent missile advocate, headed ABMA's field coordination branch; he was a key aide to Medaris. His friend von Braun, and many others, credited his clever politicking with creating ABMA and the Jupiter program.

Angry at Wilson's directive, Nickerson sent a vitriolic memorandum, as well as secret documents pertaining to the Jupiter C rocket, to Erik Bergaust, editor of *Missiles and Rockets* magazine. Bergaust returned the documents; at first he did not realize that the memo, mailed anonymously, was from Nickerson. The memorandum also reached several congressmen, contractors, and the columnist Drew Pearson. It made far-reaching charges against Wilson, the Air Force, the aircraft industry, and the Chairman of the Joint Chiefs of Staff. It charged Wilson with favoritism to the Air Force and Thor in particular; he was allegedly biased by the fact that a division of his old company, GM, produced Thor's guidance system. Nickerson bitterly charged the Air Force and its industry friends with plotting to undermine Huntsville and the arsenal system, and he warned that the plane manufacturers were not fit to handle the missile and space field.

This stick of dynamite soon exploded. Pearson's copy of the memorandum reached Air Force public relations and Wilson. On New Year's Day 1957, the Army's Inspector General showed the memorandum to a professedly shocked Medaris. The memo was soon traced to Nickerson; he was charged with espionage (for giving Bergaust secret papers) and perjury. Nickerson hastily retained prominent civilian lawyers, one famous as the Counsel for the Senate Committee in the Army-McCarthy hearings. They prepared to defend Nickerson by attacking Wilson. Pearson, Bergaust, and others cooperated spontaneously. Nickerson was presented as a new General Billy Mitchell (the crusader for air power between the world wars), martyred by Wilson, the Air Force, and Medaris. Medaris had disassociated himself from Nickerson (claiming that he had nothing to do with the memorandum), had warned his subordinates against any such action, and had thought little of Nickerson. Many officers and scientists had thought that the two men were quite close and believed Medaris had instigated the dispatch of the memorandum or had some sort of hand in the business. The publicity given Nickerson was exaggerated; he was no Mitchell. Missiles already had a high priority; the questions Nickerson raised were about the distribution of missions among the services, the merits of individual missile types, and the efficiency of the programs. These were serious enough. Bad publicity may have led the Army to drop the more extreme charges against Nickerson. In June 1957, he pled guilty to violating security regulations and was fined and suspended from rank for a year.

Along with articles written by Gardner, the affair created an impression that the Administration was neglecting or mishandling missiles, which hurt it after Sputnik. It may have discouraged an early decision for Thor—a decision which then seemed likely but inevitably would have seemed to vindicate Nickerson. Medaris was reduced to hoping that he could convince the Strategic Air Command that Jupiter was so much better than Thor that it was worth an embarrassing intraservice fight. That was not likely, although a case could easily be made that it was better than Thor. After initial failures, the third Jupiter, launched on May 31, was a success; Jupiter piled up a good record while Thor had yet to work. The Army waved this record about and argued that Jupiter was less complex, more rugged, more accurate, and mobile, although neither the Air Force nor the British, who would operate the IRBMs based in their country, cared much about mobility. There was also the embarrassing fact that WDD now conceded that ABMA's reentry mode was better than its "heat-sink." The Administration postponed a decision on Thor versus Jupiter until Sputnik caused both to be produced.[11]

In fact, Jupiter was the logical choice. Inasmuch as the IRBM was but a backup to the ICBM, Thor made no sense. The Army alone should have been given the job to avoid hindering the ICBM, if possible roping in the British to help. Wilson's handling of the IRBM was hardly creditable but was probably due to his faith in competition and the dominance of the Air Force, rather than corruption. And while the open interservice rivalry of the Eisenhower era was wasteful, it was perhaps no more so than the cancerous bureaucracy and compromises that operated to suppress it later.

POLARIS

Even after forty years, the submarine-launched ballistic missile seems the most remarkable military development of the 1950s. It required not just a new missile using new fuels, but a way to launch it under water, a new type of submarine, and a precise navigational system to determine launching positions. All of this was achieved, with amazing efficiency, in just four years. Herbert York later judged that Polaris, the first American "fleet ballistic missile," was the first American missile program to affect the strategic balance seriously. It was partly an offshoot of the land-based IRBM program.

Although Admiral Nimitz had visualized submarine-launched strategic missiles right after World War II, his successors were less imaginative. There was nearly as much opposition to ballistic missiles in the Navy as in the Air Force. Submariners focused on attacking ships, while the Bureau of Ordnance (much like the Air Force) emphasized air-breathing missiles. Having liquid-fuel rockets—especially with "cryogenic" fuels—on ships was not attractive, while solid fuels were not yet powerful or reliable enough. What interest there was in rocket-powered strategic weapons centered in the Bureau of Aeronautics. In 1954 Robert Freitag and Abraham Hyatt of the Bureau impressed the Killian Panel with the potential of submarine-launched missiles. Admiral James Raskell, the head of the Bureau, funded a program to explore the idea, despite the opposition of the then Chief of Naval Operations, Admiral Robert Carney. Carney's replacement, Arleigh Burke, was much friendlier, but the Navy lacked the funds to build a submarine-based missile on its own. It had to join in the Jupiter effort. (It would have preferred a sea-going version of Thor, but the Air Force balked at the complications that would have ensued.) To avoid sparking trouble by assigning Jupiter to either the Bureaus of

Ordnance or Aeronautics, the Navy formed a unique Special Projects Office (SPO) under Vice Admiral William Raborn, a much admired man associated with carrier operations. (This also shut out Hyman Rickover, the brilliant but widely hated officer responsible for the nuclear-powered submarine.) Like WDD and ABMA, the SPO received unique powers. It governed not only development and testing but training, and it had unusual independence in financial matters.

The SPO got along surprisingly well with the Army, but an alternative soon appeared. In 1955 Keith Rumbel and Charles Henderson of the Atlantic Research Corporation made an unexpected breakthrough in the development of solid fuels. By adding powdered aluminum to a mixture of plasticized polyvinyl chloride and aluminum chlorate, they produced a more powerful fuel that could be cast in large grains. Large solid-fuel rockets with dependable and predictable performance were now possible.

Even before this, SPO had envisaged a solid-fuel successor to Jupiter, Jupiter-S. Using clusters of the existing inefficient solid-fuel rockets, it would be big and clumsy; very large submarines could carry just four apiece. It was not expected to become operational before 1965. With the new fuels, a far smaller missile was possible. In March 1956, the Navy started an independent solid-fuel program. In April Lockheed Aircraft received a contract for initial work on a solid-fuel missile; Secretary Wilson let the Navy start systems studies and component development. Naval scientists and Raborn's right arm, Captain Levering Smith, urged dropping Jupiter-S. A conference at Woods Hole, Massachusetts, in the summer of 1956 on problems of submarine warfare, convened by the National Academy of Sciences and the National Research Council, clinched things. Distinguished independent observers became enthusiastic about the ballistic missile submarine. One, Edward Teller, pointed out that the Navy had calculated its needs on the basis of excessive warhead weights. When a solid-fuel missile was ready in the early 1960s, there would be lighter nuclear warheads. The Atomic Energy Commission (AEC), officially confirmed this in September, ensuring that an effective small missile could be built. The Navy pointed out that such a weapon would be far cheaper than Jupiter or Jupiter-S, and Secretary Wilson let the Navy switch to a completely independent effort to build the new missile, Polaris, which was officially initiated on January 12, 1957. By March specifications had been established for the missile, providing the necessary parameters for designing the Polaris submarines—a task completed in another three months. This was an amazingly rapid development effort, and the Air Force was sufficiently impressed to become interested in solid fuels, too.

The Navy used neither a single overall contractor nor a systems contractor like Ramo-Wooldridge. Lockheed developed only the Polaris missile itself; Aerojet built the propulsion system; MIT and General Electric built the guidance system. Systems engineering was done by committees of the major contractors and regular naval laboratories, while SPO held the threads of general technical direction. Despite a drastic change in plans after Sputnik, the Polaris effort proved amazingly successful, coming in under budget.

This was widely attributed to a new managerial system, PERT (Program Evaluation and Review Technique), a computerized method of concerted planning and control. Raborn had sought a radical new management system from the start; he ordered a survey of major corporations, which failed to find what he wanted. In the summer of 1956, Gordon Pehrson, an ex-Navy supply officer who had been a civilian budget official in the Bureau of Ordnance and shared Raborn's interest, joined SPO to run its Plans and Programs Division. He developed the basic concept of PERT by early 1957, elaborating it in concert with Booz Allen, a private consulting firm, and Lockheed officials. The concept provided a planning method that broke down Polaris and its subprograms into specific tasks, as well as a way to calculate the time needed to complete each, all with an unusual flexibility. Later elaborate cost-estimating and quality control systems were added. A special management center, with elaborate graphs of progress and weekly staff meetings, was organized.

PERT was well publicized and widely imitated, but with disappointing results. It was not a magic formula; Polaris was a victory of individuals and special circumstances, not a management system. Most participants, both in SPO and the contractors, thought PERT was of no great use and was costly to operate. Success was due to SPO's independence; the ability of Raborn, his Technical Director Smith, and the men they picked to run SPO; and the high morale not only of SPO but those working for the contractors. Polaris was run on a wartime basis. Raborn did not really decide much in the Management Center; he used the meetings there to boost morale at high levels, keeping in touch with field offices both by routine channels and personal contact (by phone and brief visits). While touring plants, Raborn delivered rousing speeches to workers, who (especially after Sputnik) were easily convinced of the urgency of the job. He carefully cultivated politicians, journalists, contractors, and potential enemies. PERT was useful to him, not because it actually accomplished much but because it seemed a radically new and effective device that encouraged everyone to think that SPO was on the right track. In a sense, it was a confidence trick—one that generated confidence.[12]

R-7: THE SOVIET ICBM

After Stalin's death, Soviet missile development shifted into high gear. In 1953 a new state committee to examine intercontinental missiles, under K. N. Rudnev, placed new stress on the ICBM, although fortunately for the West the Soviets continued wasting effort on Navaho-type weapons. A full-scale green light for the ICBM finally came after the R-5 was tested successfully early in 1954.

The Soviet effort was run like ABMA rather than Western Development Division; an artillery general (later marshal), Mitrofan Nedelin, was in charge, while von Braun's counterpart, Sergei Korolev, designed the ICBM. Indeed the similarity between von Braun and Korolev went further; both men were interested primarily in space flight, not weapons. Korolev's protégé, Mikhail Yangel, designed two intermediate-range weapons, successors to the R-5. The R-12 (NATO designation SS-4 Sandal), which was operational in 1959, could carry a 1-megaton warhead 1,200 miles, using storable liquid propellants (kerosene and nitric acid). It was comparable to Jupiter and Thor, although shorter ranged. The R-14 (NATO designation SS-5 Skean), which was operational in 1961, developed from the R-12, but using two new engines, could fly 2,200 miles, much farther than the Western IRBMs. The R-12 and R-14 brought all Western Europe and East Asia within attack range of the U.S.S.R.; later they played a central role in the Cuban missile crisis.

Korolev's ICBM, the R-7 (wrongly believed for many years to have the designation T-3, and called the SS-6 Sapwood by NATO) was bulky and comparable to the early Atlas designs. Its design was frozen before the Soviets realized how light thermonuclear warheads could be made, and it could lift a very big 3-ton warhead. Its unusual configuration employed parallel staging. Four of Glushko's huge RD-107 engines powered four booster stages around a central sustainer that was powered by the RD-108 variant of the same powerplant. All five stages fired on liftoff, generating over a million pounds of thrust. The four boosters dropped off after two minutes; the sustainer continued to fire for another 150 seconds. Instead of swiveling entire engines, as in American missiles, the Soviets used small "vernier" engines around the five main engines for control. Like the U.S. Army, the Soviets developed "ablative" nose cones; a sheath of laminated plywood burned off as the warhead came down.

The R-7 was a clumsy vehicle; its structure was heavy by Western standards, the result of Soviet backwardness in metallurgy. Huge and heavy (takeoff weight was 325 tons), it had to be based on railroad lines. It could not be dispersed effectively or put into silos. Fueling it was a slow business, and fuel could not be kept in it for more than a day. Its guidance was primitive; the target had to be chosen before the R-7 was oriented on the launch platform, and the R-7 needed radio guidance during part of its flight. Accuracy was not high. With a full load, the range was rather short, and part of North America was out of range from practical bases. Overall it was a poor weapon, but a good space launcher, lifting the first Soviet satellites, space probes, and men (and women) into space. It is still in use. Perhaps that was what Korolev had in mind all along. When the R-7 was first exhibited publicly in 1967, some American engineers thought it a clever piece of design by engineers working within severe limitations. They were impressed by the Soviets' feat in simultaneously igniting thirty-two combustion chambers. However, the R-7 was a blunder. Had the Soviets scaled it down (as the Americans did the Atlas) to a two- or three-engine missile, they might have had a formidable weapon much earlier.

A new missile range was built at Tyuratam in Kazakhstan to test the R-7. It is still uncertain when flight tests of the R-7 began; they may have started as early as 1956. It is certain that tests were underway by the spring of 1957, but five failed in succession. On August 3, 1957, there was a successful limited-range test; on August 21 an R-7 flew to its full range of 5,000 miles into the Pacific. Knowledgeable Westerners were worried; but the public in general paid little attention until October 4, 1957, when a modified R-7 put the first artificial satellite into orbit around the earth.

Before Polaris, at about the same time as intensive work on the R-7 began, the Soviets had begun work on submarine-launched liquid-fuel missiles. They had to be launched from the surface, after lengthy preparations, and submarines could carry only two or three apiece. The problems the Soviets ran into tended to justify the U.S. Navy's wariness of liquid fuels. Only well into the 1960s did the Soviets get missiles that could be launched from a submerged position; they gained solid-fuel weapons comparable to Polaris only in 1968. The first result of this program deployed in 1958, a modified R-11, had a range of just 110 miles; two were carried on some modified diesel-powered submarines. This was probably more of a device to gain experience than a fully operational weapon; the Americans seemed to have been barely aware of its existence. The first effective weapon, the R-13 (NATO SS-N-4 Serb), was deployed on specially designed missile subs starting in 1959. It had a range of about 720 miles—far longer, incidentally, than the Americans estimated. Nuclear-powered missile submarines appeared in 1960. Despite their limitations, these missiles were a significant addition to the rather small Soviet capability against North America.[13]

4

Space Exploration and Satellites in the 1950s

Before World War II, space flight had seemed to most people something for the distant future, at best. The V-2, nuclear power, and other wartime technical advances made it seem far more real. Those spectacular developments probably caused two lesser phenomena that themselves promoted interest in space. One was the rise of science fiction to respectability; for the first time major contemporary science fiction writers were published in book form and attracted friendly interest from established literary circles (which made science fiction's principal theme and motif, space travel, more respectable, too). By 1950 Hollywood was working on the first major space-flight movies, *Destination Moon* and *Rocketship X-M*. A less sane development that both reflected and furthered interest in space was the flying saucer craze, which began in 1947 and first peaked in the early 1950s. (This first wave of interest in UFOs was less irrational than later ones.) It was symptomatic of the postwar climate that for a time even the Air Force was inclined to think that UFOs were spaceships from other planets.[1]

With the increase of interest in space travel, many writers popularized the basic concepts of Tsiolkovskiy, Goddard, and Oberth and elaborated on the current expectations of scientists and engineers. The best of these was Arthur C. Clarke, a British engineer and renowned science fiction writer who had invented the concept of the communications satellite in 1945. Much of his work is still valid. In *The Exploration of Space* (1951) and the more technical *Interplanetary Flight* (1950), he visualized the future of space flight as follows: After unmanned earth satellites and probes into near-earth space, multistage, chemically powered rockets would reach orbit. Lunar and interplanetary trips required refueling in orbit and several different types of space vehicles.

Clarke's Type A would be the top stage of an earth-to-orbit ferry rocket, a reusable winged craft that would glide back to earth after leaving orbit. A Type A, refueled in orbit, might make a circumlunar flight. Type B would be a modified Type A, without airfoils, for landing on the moon and other airless bodies. It would be assembled in orbit around the earth, or more probably would be made by stripping a Type A of wings and other unneeded weight. Type C would be a deep-space vehicle that would never land anywhere; assembled in space, it would go from orbit to orbit. A Type B would make the first landing on the moon. Type Cs, carrying Type As or specially designed landing craft, would reach Mars and Venus.

Eventually, if not before the first lunar trip, permanent manned space stations would be built in orbit around the earth to serve as bases for lunar and interplanetary flights, as well as sites for astronomical, meteorological, and biological work making use of weightlessness and vacuum. They would also serve as radio relays and navigational aids. Within a few years of the first moon trip, permanent moon bases would be established. Clarke thought it would be easy to get water on the moon, either by breaking down lunar soil or from ice in caves, which he considered likely. Water could be electrolyzed to supply hydrogen and oxygen for fuels. Deep-space flights could then refuel on the moon; it would even be economical to refuel in earth orbit with propellants sent from the moon, possibly using an electromagnetic launcher. At some point nuclear rockets would be developed that might render some intermediate steps unnecessary. Although such rockets might be unsuited for taking off from the earth, they should at least power Type C ships. Eventually humans would reach the outer planets, and ultimately even the stars. Clarke envisioned the possibility of "terraforming"—altering otherwise unsuitable planets so that humans could live there without artificial aids.

Wernher von Braun, during the late 1940s and early 1950s, elaborated on his own vision of the exploration of near space, the moon, and Mars in books and articles by himself, Cornelius Ryan, and von Braun's old friend Willy Ley. His ideas were further popularized by TV specials produced by Walt Disney; they were extensions of the work done in Germany. They eschewed radical innovations such as nuclear rockets or even the most powerful chemical fuels. (Von Braun's aim, however, may have been to show that *existing* technologies could do the job.) Von Braun envisaged a reusable, three-stage, earth-to-orbit ferry to build and supply a wheel-shaped space station, as well as elaborate expeditions to the moon and Mars using fleets of ships assembled in orbit—all in great detail.

Von Braun's ideas did not rouse universal enthusiasm; some engineers felt that his was not a true systems-engineering approach. Darrell Romick and others at the Goodyear Corporation developed a rival space station scheme, Meteor. They designed a ferry vehicle, all of whose stages were winged and piloted and had auxiliary jet engines. After reentering the atmosphere, these vehicles would land under their own power. At least some upper stages would be built so that they could be taken apart to supply parts for the space station. Unlike von Braun's, Romick and colleagues' space station was designed so that it could expand indefinitely.[2]

These and other visions for manned space flight in the 1950s had major features in common. All assumed a systematic, if not systems-engineering approach. All envisaged several types of reusable space vehicles for different tasks; all assumed, as a basis, an earth-to-orbit transportation system with winged vehicles capable of a controlled return to earth, and they envisaged building a manned space station at an early stage. They envisaged trips to the moon and the inner planets as large, heavily manned expeditions, usually consisting of several ships that would stay for weeks or months; and at least in the case of the moon, they assumed that the first trip would be followed quickly by a permanent outpost.

All of this was notably more rational than the course actually followed.

VISIONS OF THE INNER PLANETS IN THE 1950s

An important factor in the development of interest in space travel was the belief, which persisted until well into the 1960s, that earth's immediate neighbors were readily accessible to explorers (once they crossed the gulfs between the planets) and that they would prove immensely interesting, not just to scientists. There seemed a good chance that Mars and Venus bore life, perhaps even intelligent life; it even seemed possible, although not very likely, that Venus was a fairly earth-like place that could be colonized readily. It is true that most astronomers were less optimistic about such things than they had been decades earlier; as it turned out, Mars and Venus disappointed even the greatest pessimists.

Observation had long suggested that Mars was a smaller, colder version of earth, had a thinner atmosphere and polar caps of water ice, and exhibited seasonal color changes in dark areas that were generally believed to be covered by plants. The "canali" (channels) reported by the astronomer Giovanni Schiaparelli (and later by Percival Lowell, who believed them to be actual canals built by a Martian civilization) attracted enormous attention to the possibility of intelligent life on Mars in the early twentieth century. Although many keen-eyed observers grumbled that they could not see canals, and experiments in 1913 suggested that they might well be an optical illusion, until after World War I most astronomers may have believed that intelligent life on Mars was at least possible, whether or not there were canals. Between the world wars, however, observation suggested that Mars's air was even thinner than had been thought, and its climate more extreme; moreover, spectroscopic observation found no oxygen. Most estimates were that the atmospheric pressure at the surface of Mars was about 8 percent of that at sea level on earth. (The true figure was 1 percent.) By the 1950s, few astronomers believed in the canals or thought intelligent life likely. But most thought there was life on Mars; vegetation was the simplest explanation of the seasonal color changes on Mars. Experiments showed that some earth plants could live under simulated Martian conditions, or what were thought to be Martian conditions. Mars's surface was believed to be mostly flat and sandy, somewhat like Arizona's Painted Desert, with few or no mountains. At the most optimistic estimates, the atmosphere might be dense enough to let people walk around with just an oxygen mask, but most believed that pressure suits would be necessary. At worst, winged spacecraft could glide to a landing and planes could fly, at least near the ground. Exploring Mars, once you got there, did not seem too hard and held out the promise of finding extraterrestrial life. Unfortunately, most of what astronomers thought they knew was wrong.

Venus provided an even more spectacular example of the fallibility of earth-based observations. It seemed a near twin of earth. But it was wrapped in clouds so its surface could not be seen; not even its rate of rotation was known. Although ingenious attempts were made to infer the length of its day and the temperature under the clouds, few placed much reliance on the wildly differing results. Its distance from the sun suggested that, other things being equal, Venus's mean absolute temperature should be only 20 percent higher than earth's, and perhaps less due to its high albedo. The Swedish chemist Svante Arrhenius suggested in 1918 that Venus might resemble earth during the Carboniferous Age or the Age of Dinosaurs. The higher latitudes, at least, might be settled by humans. The "jungle Venus" became a staple of science fiction thereafter. But spectroscopes could not find oxygen or water vapor; observations in 1932 suggested that Venus's atmosphere was mostly carbon dioxide. Most astronomers concluded that Venus was probably not capable of bearing life—earth-type life at any rate. The predominant belief was that Venus was a vast desert, its temperature was about 200°F, and the clouds were probably dust or some organic compound. Some, however, thought the planet might be covered by one huge ocean. And some astronomers still thought it might be quite earth-like, pointing out that the spectroscopes only saw the upper cloud layers, in which water vapor might be frozen and undetectable. Optimists like V. A. Firsoff suggested that magnetic effects and temperature inversions might keep most of the CO_2 in Venus's air high up and oxygen well below the clouds, and that conditions at the surface might be much like those on earth. Firsoff even thought that Venus might have polar ice caps! In 1956 radio astronomers were startled to detect microwave emissions from Venus, which indicated that its surface temperature must be between 600 and 800°F. But most astronomers, even those who dismissed a habitable Venus, tended to doubt that conditions were that extreme, and they thought that there was some error or that the emissions were produced by some phenomenon in Venus's upper atmosphere and told nothing of surface conditions. In November 1959, spectroscopic observations from a stratosphere balloon seemed to show that there was water vapor in Venus's upper atmosphere after all. It was a last, misleading piece of evidence that Venus might not be too different from earth after all. At the beginning of the 1960s, there actually seems to have been a resurgence of the belief in an earth-like Venus.[3] There was a great deal of excitement as the day approached when it would be possible to send a probe to the enigmatic planet.

SATELLITES AND THE INTERNATIONAL GEOPHYSICAL YEAR

Even as Clarke and others outlined schemes for space exploration, the first steps were taken toward unmanned earth satellites. Such satellites had a dual origin; one was military. The advantage of having an eye in the sky over potential enemies led the USAF to start its own highly secret satellite program in 1955 (which will be discussed later in this chapter). However, for once scientific motives took precedence on the road to space. By the mid-1950s, the Air Force was exploring propulsion systems beyond anything likely to be needed for ICBMs. Apart from the nuclear rocket program, it supported research in conventional rockets (at North American's Rocketdyne Division) that pointed to what became the F-1 engine used in the Saturn V moon rocket, as well as work on winged spacecraft.

In 1950 there were proposals for a Third International Polar Year. The first two Polar Years, in 1882 and 1932, consisted of concentrated assaults by researchers and explorers on the polar regions. The advance of knowledge and the drive to learn more were so great that it was suggested that the interval between Polar Years should be shortened from half a century to twenty-five years, neatly coinciding with an expected peak in sunspot activity. The idea gained wide support and snowballed into a larger concept, an International Geophysical Year (IGY) of concerted work on the whole world and near-earth space. The IGY was to run from July 1957 to December 1958. At an International Astronautical Congress in 1953, the American physicist S. Fred Singer suggested orbiting a satellite during the IGY; the satellite was called MOUSE (Minimum Orbital Unmanned Satellite of Earth) and weighed 100 pound. Singer got much support, although MOUSE was an elephant as far as the rockets likely to be available were concerned. During 1954 the International Committee for the IGY, strongly backed by the National Science Foundation, recommended launching a satellite during the IGY. Although the Eisenhower Administration had earlier axed efforts to continue the Viking program, it was intrigued by both the IGY in general and the satellite proposal. Contrary to what was later widely supposed, Eisenhower was very far from being a fogy and was quite interested in space—not just military missiles—from the mid-1950s on. His later reluctance to go all-out for manned space flight was due to horror at its cost, not disinterest.

In 1954 von Braun proposed launching a satellite that weighed just 5 pounds, using an uprated Redstone with three upper stages of Loki solid-fuel rockets. This scheme was called Project Orbiter. The Naval Research Laboratory proposed a more elaborate scheme for a bigger satellite, with more advanced instrumentation and a complete electronic tracking system, using a launch vehicle developed from the Viking. The Air Force offered to launch research satellites with ICBMs. Although Eisenhower was already interested in an IGY satellite, the Soviets did help clinch the case for an American program. In April 1955, they announced that they would launch a satellite during the IGY and indicated that they planned to explore the moon someday with a remote-controlled tank. Nelson Rockefeller, then a special assistant to the President, presciently warned (as did private observers such as Philip Wylie) that American prestige would be hurt seriously if the Soviets were first with so symbolic a scientific and technological advance. Although Eisenhower (who was always skeptical of prestige arguments) never saw the satellite program as a literal race, it was not likely that the Soviets would be allowed to go it alone. In May the National Security Council endorsed a satellite program; it noted that experience gained in tracking a civilian satellite might aid later military work. On July 29 the White House announced that the United States would launch a satellite during the IGY.

The Defense Department formed an Advisory Group on Special Capabilities, under Homer J. Stewart of the Jet Propulsion Laboratory, to select a satellite project. It was ordered to avoid any interference in military missile work, but otherwise to treat the satellite program as a scientific problem without political significance. The first requirement led it to reject an Air Force proposal to orbit a satellite with an Atlas. That left the Navy and Army proposals. The Army had modified the original Orbiter, replacing the Lokis with more powerful scaled-down "Sergeant" rockets (wittily called "Baby Sergeants" or "Recruits") and providing for electronic tracking of the satellite. It had the advantage of using the proven Redstone, and it could be ready by August 1957—or even in 1956 with a crash program. (It is safe to say that had the Administration seen the trouble that would ensue, it would have endorsed a crash program enthusiastically.) But Milton Rosen of the naval group argued that the Army scheme was inherently less reliable. If just one solid-fuel rocket failed, the whole system failed; many on the Stewart Committee thought the whole lash-up was too heavy and clumsy. The Navy proposal, "Vanguard," involved a comparatively simple three-stage rocket; the first stage was built by the Martin company and was based on the Viking, and the second was built by Aerojet and was based on the Aerobee. Only the third stage (a single large, solid rocket) would be entirely new. Vanguard promised a more efficient design and a more effective guidance system. Its advocates claimed that it had more growth potential, although its first-stage engine was far less powerful than the Redstone's.

More important than the launch vehicle was the Navy's better instrumentation and its Minitrack system for following it. The Naval Research Laboratory promised to deliver it for just $12 million—a wildly over-optimistic assessment. The American Rocket Society and the National IGY Committee were known to favor Vanguard. Despite the instructions of the Defense Department, an element of the political did enter the considerations of the Committee. Some members clearly disliked using a rocket designed by the German team and preferred an American development. More openly, some argued that military and scientific projects should be divorced as far as possible. Vanguard was seen as a civilian research vehicle. The Administration later played this up to justify its choice. In fact, the argument was rather unreal inasmuch as Vanguard was ultimately a Navy project and would be fired from Cape Canaveral, then a military base. Nor was there a real reason to regard military participation in exploration as bad; it certainly had many precedents (e.g., the Lewis and Clark expedition). Dr. Stewart, however, maintained that political arguments were not in fact decisive in the choice of Vanguard over his opposition. The committee's members seem to have been persuaded by the Navy's more advanced instrumentation. They ruled out combining an NRL satellite with an Army launcher as too complicated. On September 9, the Defense Department endorsed Vanguard.[4] It was a choice the U.S. government would have cause to rue.

VANGUARD

Vanguard proved an unlucky project, although it was not quite the utter fiasco often depicted later. The controversy over it and the rejection of the Army proposal was one source of a common false impression that Vanguard and ABMA were the real core of U.S. missile and space development, rather than the Air Force's ICBM work and North American's engine development effort. Indeed the development of Vanguard, with a first-stage engine half as powerful as that of the V-2, smacked of reinventing the wheel.

Vanguard's troubles were perhaps largely beyond the control of its director, John Hagen, and technical director Milton Rosen. Perhaps they did very well with a relatively small work force of just 180 people. They had to build their own facilities at Cape Canaveral (to avoid interfering with military work) as well as an elaborate tracking system. After the unrealistic estimate made at the start, Vanguard suffered from too small and sluggish appropriations; contemporary observers like Willy Ley judged that there was too much contracting to private enterprise of tasks that could have been handled cheaper and faster by government labs. There were enormous cost overruns; ultimately the project cost $110 million. Relations with private contractors were bad. The fine team Martin had formed for the Viking had been broken up; the best people were working on the Titan ICBM. Work on the Titan often conflicted with the satellite project. Vanguard had to be redesigned; the vaunted guidance system was too heavy. There were bitter quarrels over the redesign before the directors got their way. Nevertheless, progress was made. the last two Viking rockets were used successfully to test Vanguard's components. But when the first true Vanguard, TV-2—a live first stage with dummy upper stages—arrived, project personnel were horrified. There had been poor workmanship at both Martin and General Electric; both had failed to supervise workers. Dirt was found in the engine. After cleaning and repairs, TV-2 flew well on October 23—three weeks after Sputnik.[5]

JUPITER C

Despite the rejection of Orbiter, the military continued to ponder involvement in research satellites and space probes. There was some interest in a joint USAF-Army lunar probe, using a Navaho booster as a first stage and a Redstone as a second stage, with two solid-fuel upper stages. In 1957, with the ICBM well along, General Schriever publicly spoke of Air Force interest in space exploration.

Homer Stewart advised von Braun to keep Orbiter alive as an ace in the hole if an early satellite launch was needed. The Jupiter IRBM provided a neat justification for this; the Orbiter vehicle could test Jupiter nose cones. ABMA improved it further into the Jupiter C (Jupiter Composite Test Vehicle). In the first example of a process applied to turn many weapons into better space launchers, ABMA lengthened the Redstone's tanks by 8 feet. Instead of alcohol, Jupiter C burned a mixture of hydrazine and diethylene triamine, which was about 12 percent more powerful than alcohol, raising the engine thrust to 83,000 pounds. An additional hydrogen peroxide tank let the turbopump run longer, while the instrument section was lightened and the front strengthened to support the upper stages. The latter were carried in a "washtub," which spun at 750 rpm to smooth out any differences in thrust between the solid-fuel rockets. As a test vehicle, Jupiter C had a second stage of eleven Baby Sergeants and a third stage of three uprated ones. A live fourth stage of just one Baby Sergeant could put a payload into orbit. This was so well known that the Army, fearing that ABMA might pull a fast one, ordered a dummy fourth stage to be filled with sand before the first Jupiter C launch in September 1956. The Jupiter C was a splendid success and set altitude and distance records. Three flights proved the Army case for an "ablative" nose cone. Medaris foresaw another use for the vehicle. He expected Vanguard to fail and thought ABMA would be called on to launch a satellite. On August 21, 1957, he had the nine remaining Jupiter Cs put in protected storage for that day.[6] On these rockets and on Medaris's foresight rested the hopes for an early American satellite.

PIED PIPER

While Vanguard proceeded under the glare of publicity, a secret military satellite program was underway. RAND had alerted the Air Force to the value of reconnaissance satellites. But such satellites needed powerful boosters; probably only an ICBM, with an additional stage, could do the job. In March 1955, the Air Force issued a requirement for Weapon System 117L. In June 1956, it chose Lockheed to handle project Pied Piper. This project involved developing both a satellite and an upper stage to fit atop the Atlas. The project became an additional responsibility of the Western Development Division, although at first it did not have a very high priority. The upper stage used a 15,000-pound thrust engine developed by Bell Aircraft. (Later called Agena, it played a major role in the space program, sending the first probes to Mars and Venus.) The satellite presented difficult problems. It needed specially developed small cameras and had to be stabilized so that it would align them on a target and ensure that pictures taken in one orbit paralleled those taken in others. Then the pictures had to be transmitted to earth or recovered from orbit. During 1957 the CIA in particular urged higher priority and more funds for the project. In August the Eisenhower Administration decided to accelerate the program; after Sputnik, like many other programs, it was changed again.[7]

Meanwhile the Soviets adapted their ICBM to launch a satellite. They revealed little of their precise plans but repeatedly reminded everyone of their intentions; in June 1957 they announced the wavelengths on which it would broadcast. Thus there was little excuse for claims, still heard today, that Sputnik was a surprise.

5
Sputnik and Its Consequences,
1957–1958

Despite ample warnings, on October 4, 1957 Americans were startled to learn that the Soviets had put Sputnik I, a 2-foot sphere weighing 184 pounds, into orbit. (*Sputnik* means "fellow-traveler." Russian astronomers had long used this term to describe hypothetical small natural satellites of the earth.) Sputnik I had little scientific instrumentation, but it carried two radio transmitters that emitted a beep that Americans found maddening. It was far larger than the Vanguard satellite and had to have been launched by an ICBM. On November 3, the Soviets launched the much bigger and heavily instrumented Sputnik II, which weighed 1,120 pounds and carried a dog. (Wits called it "Muttnik.") Moreover, Sputnik II remained attached to the R-7's empty sustainer; over 8,000 pounds had gone into orbit. Some thought Sputnik II had been launched by a new rocket, perhaps using some sort of superfuel, or even a nuclear rocket.[1]

What was known about Sputnik I seemed bad enough. The fact that the Soviets had an ICBM, and a big one, when the United States had yet to test successfully the far smaller Atlas, finally sank in. (That the Soviet ICBM was *too* big was hardly suspected at the time.) And the Soviets, not the West, had the glory of launching what was immediately called the Space Age. This was a vast gain in prestige for the Communist powers and a terrific morale blow to the West. Furthermore, it seemed to imply two related but different dangers that were often confused in the 1950s.

First, if the Soviet ICBM was reliable and effective and put into mass production, and if the Americans failed to catch up or take vital counter-actions, the Soviets might gain a first-strike capability within a few years.

If they turned their undoubted lead in development into a massive superior ICBM force, the West's development lag would turn into what became known as a "missile gap." And this might become an actual "deterrent gap," a situation in which the Soviets could attack without fear of effective retaliation. The distinction between a missile gap and a deterrent gap must be stressed, for the Eisenhower Administration had expected a missile gap for a while but was fairly sure that it could prevent a deterrent gap. (It must also be stressed that the missile gap was a forecast or prediction, *not* a statement about the current balance of power.) The Administration expected to prevent the expected Soviet superiority in numbers from becoming an effective first-strike capability.

The second problem might be called a space or payload gap. The R-7 (not to mention anything bigger that the Soviets might build) ensured that, at least for some years, the Soviets could send bigger loads into space than the Americans, score any number of firsts, and exploit any military advantage that might be found in space. As it turned out, the R-7's defects, among other things, prevented a missile gap. But the space gap was real. The United States matched the Soviet ability to lift heavy loads into space only in 1963. But its superiority in electronic miniaturization and the large number of satellites it launched meant that, in practice, it achieved more than the Soviets in terms of scientific results and utilization of outer space.

Sputnik triggered a political and even social explosion in the West. Even when it was understood, as it was in the United States (but *not* in Europe), that there was no immediate military danger and that the West would retain military superiority at least for the near future, there was a great disillusionment. Many had been sure that the West, and especially the United States, would always have technological superiority and that this would compensate for the (rather exaggerated) numerical superiority of the Communist powers and the political initiative the latter held in the Cold War. Apart from what now seems a touching faith that the United States would always lead the world technologically, most Westerners had assumed that the West must be ahead simply because it was a free society. That state of mind had already survived much contrary evidence—notably the excellence of most Soviet equipment and the actual superiority of their tanks during World War II; their unexpectedly early achievement of nuclear weapons; and the trouble the Mig-15 had given Western pilots in Korea. But the fact that a totalitarian state had led the way into space could not be effaced; and even after it was clear that the West was ahead in military missiles, the Soviets would score spectacular firsts. There were fears that the Soviets might spring almost any kind of surprise; not just bigger and better missiles and satellites, but rocket bombers and nuclear-powered rockets and planes.

There was no counterpart to this general anxiety before or after. The Air Force and some congressional critics had feared a "bomber gap" in 1955–1956, wrongly thinking that the Soviets were building more heavy bombers than the United States. However, that short-lived worry had only a mild effect on defense policy, and there is little evidence that the public was much perturbed. Later anxieties, during the 1970s and 1980s, focused on comparatively narrow issues of Soviet superiority in this or that particular item, possibly gained only by violating arms-control agreements— not a general fear that the Soviets were indeed the wave of the future and about to overtake the West on a broad front. The fears of the late 1950s were thus unique.

For a time, those fears were real and powerful. The *London Times* spoke of a world transformed, in political and psychological terms, by Sputnik.[2] The general belief, rarely questioned at the time, that the West faced a technologically superior enemy that might soon enjoy outright superiority makes that era one of the most interesting (and perhaps most misunderstood) periods of the Cold War. (Contrary to what is often claimed, such overestimation of the other side was not common during the Cold War.) And the fears of Americans in the late 1950s in some way prefigured later fears—or realities—of national decline.

It has been well said that the Eisenhower Administration was under siege at home and abroad from late 1957 until it left office. The attacks on it (for neglecting defense) were mostly wrong, always exaggerated, and sometimes vicious, and eventually this would come to light. Even when they contained a core of truth, such attacks were wrapped in a shell that rendered them misleading. And it is hard not to suspect the sincerity of many critics, some of whom had shown little concern about the Soviets earlier and later manifested total indifference to the Soviet military buildup from the late 1960s onward. In fact, the Eisenhower Administration had already averted a missile gap of the sort feared in the late 1950s. By the time of Sputnik, that was no longer possible. As we shall see, recognition that the anxiety had been overblown, in addition to the efforts of some of the Administration's defenders (and others with murkier motives), later obscured the fact that the Administration shared some of its critics' fears and that it reacted strongly to Sputnik, in a creative and creditable way.

That did not save it, however, or the post-New Deal, middle-of-the-road American society it epitomized. Sputnik put the liberal opposition in a position which, abstractly considered, was rather fantastic. The opposition was able to discredit a conservative, strongly anti-Communist Republican administration, led by the most popular hero of World War II, for not doing enough to defend the country. In addition, fiscal conservatism (or even fiscal responsibility) and the cautious approach to social reform were discredited. The shock of Sputnik was not the sole factor—but a very important factor—in enabling liberals to carry out their programs in the 1960s. For a time there was a convergence of liberal demands for reform and demands for greater military strength that would later seem very odd.

THE POST-SPUTNIK FUROR

Late 1957 might not have been a particularly pleasant time in any case. The United States was in its worst recession since the 1930s, and the President had suffered his second serious illness; this worried even (or perhaps especially) those who did not admire him. Since the Suez crisis and the Hungarian Revolution, international tension had been growing.

After Sputnik, bad luck and blunders by the Administration's officials and defenders made its position worse. The post-Sputnik controversy is arguably a study in how not to handle an issue. Critics pointed to ill-considered official reactions, some by individuals with no responsibility for defense matters, and played up contradictions and misstatements, while the Administration was forced, over the course of a month, to concede that things were worse than it had first admitted.

On October 8, the President declared that there was no space race and that Sputnik had not raised his apprehensions one iota, although he sportingly conceded that it was a great achievement. Yet his first television address in response to Sputnik contained seeming evasions and one or two poorly worded passages that wrongly suggested that he was ill-informed about missiles. Secretary Wilson denied, on October 9, that he had ordered any sort of speedup of the missile program, although he was doing just that, and he insisted that the satellite had no military impact and that the Soviets currently had no operational ICBMs. While those points were perfectly correct, Wilson's offhand manner made a bad impression. Critics quickly unearthed his November 1954 remark that he did not care if the Soviets got a satellite first. Others offered more recent unfortunate remarks. Eisenhower's chief of staff, Sherman Adams, declared that the Administration was not interested in an "outer space basketball game"; he later conceded that to be an "overemphasis on the deemphasis." Clarence Randall, an Eisenhower assistant on economic matters, described Sputnik as a "silly bauble." Admiral Rawson Bennett, head of naval research, derided Sputnik as a "hunk of iron almost anybody could launch." Although that remark was designed to boost the morale of the Vanguard team, it contributed to the impression that the Administration was asleep.[3] Administration spokespeople blunderingly tried to counter critics by inflating expenditures on research and development, reclassifying expenses more properly charged to procurement and production and even housekeeping at research facilities. Some fanatic partisans even suggested that Sputnik was somehow a fake. Many whined that Sputnik was due to the fact that the Soviets had grabbed the Germans responsible for developing the V-2. Even the usually careful Secretary of State, John Foster Dulles, at first gave credence to that absurdity, which was quickly exposed and rebounded against the Administration. Vigorous efforts by Eisenhower, Dulles, and the Vice President never effaced the impression that the Administration was unaware of what was at stake. Dulles, taking a line that he stuck to later, suggested that Sputnik might be a good thing, preventing complacency in the West. A real military danger, he noted, was five or ten years off.

The Administration's critics neatly made their case, which was crystallized by the remark of the most respected American labor leader, Walter Reuther, that Sputnik was a "bloodless Pearl Harbor." However exaggerated that seemed later, the spirit of the Americans of the 1950s was summarized by Reuther's promise that workers would make any sacrifice needed to catch up.

Those with specialized knowledge of missile matters, who had argued for speeding up the ICBM effort before Sputnik, were vocal. Senator Stuart Symington declared, "If this now known Soviet superiority develops into supremacy, the position of the Free World will be critical." Henry Jackson bluntly declared that "we are losing" the race for the ICBM. *Aviation Week* and *Missiles and Rockets*, long critical of the Administration, saw their version of events become gospel. Former Administration officials were powerful witnesses for the prosecution. Gardner's attacks on Secretary Wilson (but not the credit he gave the Administration for reviving the ICBM) were widely cited. Clifford Furnas, former Assistant Secretary of Defense for Research and Development, eloquently blamed Wilson for rejecting repeated requests for more money for research. Wilson, not much liked in or outside the Administration, was a particularly good target; he seemed the very caricature of a Republican big businessman. General Maxwell Taylor, recently retired as Army Chief of Staff, blamed interservice rivalry for the missile lag. The *New York Times* warned in November 1957 that the United States was in a race for survival. It reported von Braun's estimate that the United States was five years behind the Soviets. Even Republican politicians and institutions turned against the Administration; the Luce publications printed indictment after indictment of its real and alleged mistakes, culminating in an incredible article in the November 18 *Life*, accurately titled "Arguing the Case for Being Panicky."

The attack crystallized along the following lines:

1. The Administration had mishandled the IGY satellite program by choosing and mismanaging Vanguard.
2. The Administration had recklessly relaxed the ICBM effort by Wilson's cutbacks during 1957.
3. Champions of the Army team argued that it had been neglected. They pointed to the blundering over the IRBM and raked up the Nickerson court-martial.

These points, the most specific elements of the attack on the Administration, contained a hard core of truth, albeit often eclipsed by exaggeration. Only factors then unknown rendered these faults rather minor, along with the truth (artfully obscured by most commentators) that it was the Eisenhower Administration that had gotten the ICBM and satellite programs rolling in the first place. Eisenhower's defenders reiterated that point; but strangely it failed to sink in.

Ideas of how to fix things were more confused. Many, like Senators Mansfield and Javits, called for a Manhattan Project approach to missiles and space. Such talk faded when Gardner and von Braun testified that the various programs were *too* advanced for that; it would just disrupt existing facilities and teams. There were calls for a missile czar to run everything, and there was a general demand for a speedup of missile development and more money for research and defense in general.

These narrow-gauged, not entirely mistaken criticisms snowballed into a wider attack on the Administration and ultimately American society. Sputnik and the related threat were also blamed on the following:

1. The Administration had tolerated unchecked rivalry between the armed services and allowed some (usually undefined) bad organization in missile development.
2. The Administration had not sufficiently funded scientific research in general; Edward Teller and Vannevar Bush proved the most impressive exponents of this point of view.
3. Some, notably ex-President Truman and Walter Lippman, blamed the Soviet triumph on McCarthyism. They claimed that official persecution had discouraged the best scientists from joining the missile and satellite programs—a view for which there was no evidence.

4. Many blamed Sputnik on the failure of the educational system. There was a spate of publicity for critics, ranging from Rudolf Flesch to Admiral Rickover, who had railed for years (and with good reason) about the state of American education. They variously attacked the sight method of teaching reading, progressive education in general, insufficient emphasis on mathematics and science, and an overemphasis on helping less intelligent children instead of the gifted. Although the faults of the educational system, however real, had nothing to do with Sputnik and the missile situation, the attacks impressed many people. Even Eisenhower endorsed them implicitly in one of his speeches. Sputnik caused Isaac Asimov to switch from writing science fiction to the popularization of science, a task to which he devoted most of the rest of his life. (He sardonically noted that the only difference thirty years later was that the educational situation was still bad, but Americans no longer seemed to care.)

5. There was a vast outpouring of attacks on the alleged social evils of the era. These were not, as might be expected, poverty, ignorance, crime, or racial discrimination, but "conformity," "status-seeking," "consumerism" (which then meant obsessive grasping after material goods), "materialism," and the inadequacies of the "organization man" (or "mass man") to meet the Soviet and other challenges. Already clichés among intellectuals by the mid-1950s, these themes were further embroidered on and publicized by the mass media, although the latter were the greatest of all strongholds of consumerism and the "organization man." Many were widely accepted long after, although it would be difficult to show, for example, that Americans were more conformist in the 1950s than usual. An odd phenomenon of the time was a seeming temporary convergence of two very different criticisms of trends in contemporary society. Many conservatives, too, were unhappy with conformity, for they feared the loss of traditional individualism and creativity. For many on the left, the attack on conformity (when it meant anything concrete) was an opening wedge for a general assault on tradition and the "conservatism of habit," which, ironically, opened the way for new and tighter sorts of conformity than anyone imagined in the 1950s.

This sort of vague moralizing tended to metamorphose into or fuse with more serious, or at least specific, criticisms of American society, which focused on the ills of the "Affluent Society" (a neglect of social capital and what was later called infrastructure in favor of private consumption). This view was popularized by John Kenneth Galbraith and, more cautiously, other influential liberals. Those unimpressed with this view did tend to point increasingly to the persistence of poverty, discrimination, corruption in unions and government, and the maldistribution of wealth. Although (contrary to what is sometimes said) few people had been unaware of these evils earlier, there was a growing tendency to see them not as unfortunate conditions that could be cured by economic growth, education, piecemeal reforms, or some combination thereof, but as part and parcel of the existing order of things—a current that led to the rise of the New Left and a partial radicalization of American liberalism. A subtle but critical transformation took place; the era of the 1940s and 1950s henceforth was pictured statically as a sort of frozen status quo, instead of being seen as an era of rapid progress in dealing with many of these problems—as it really was. Still, in the late 1950s the element of old-fashioned moralizing remained strong, resulting in much pompous talk of the need for sacrifice, national purposes or goals, and the need to restore a drive for excellence. This became an important element in the rhetoric, if not the reality, of the Kennedy Administration.

The generally conservative ethos of the Eisenhower Administration (indeed of the entire period since 1945), which was oriented toward business and private initiative, was discredited. There was a renewal of faith in an enlarged government role in economics and society, in planning, and in what was optimistically called social engineering (social alchemy would have been a more accurate term). Sputnik and the apparent general advance of the U.S.S.R. seemed to validate, if not socialism or nationalization, a more positive role for government. After all, the Soviets seemed to be succeeding and even surpassing the capitalist world. Such ideas influenced many with no sympathy at all for Communism or even democratic socialism. They fused with, and furthered, the pretensions of the social scientists of the era.[4] It would be foolish to attribute the growth of liberal or leftist ideas solely to the shock of Sputnik; however, Sputnik played a serious role in discrediting the existing order, which seemed to have failed in its own terms.

EUROPEAN ATTITUDES

Europeans reacted far more strongly than people in North America to Sputnik. Whatever its other misfortunes, the Eisenhower Administration quickly reassured Americans that the United States was still stronger than the Soviets and that any real danger was still some way off. In Europe, things were different. A week after Sputnik I, a Dutch delegate to the Western European Union attacked the United States for having "helped our enemy" by not getting an ICBM first. The European NATO members became extremely skittish about allowing IRBM bases in their countries. There was a general belief (except in Italy), which persisted until 1961, that the Soviets had already overtaken the Americans technologically and in military strength. There was a corresponding tendency of Europeans to distance themselves from the United States. However, this was not the case among the British, who reacted to the perceived threat by becoming more pro-American.[5] Still, while continental Europeans' attitudes changed, they did not bolt the alliance. NATO was not quite as weak as alarmists periodically suggested; although there was a good deal of trouble, resistance to the Soviets did not crumble.

CHANGES IN POLICY AND THE GAITHER REPORT

The Administration was far from being unruffled. Eisenhower was far more upset by Sputnik than he let on in public. On October 15, 1957, the Science Advisory Committee of the Office of Defense Mobilization, at a meeting scheduled prior to Sputnik, impressed the President with the dangers of the situation. The physicist I. I. Rabi warned that unless vigorous action was taken, the Soviets might indeed overtake the United States. He proposed making James Killian a Presidential Science Advisor and forming a Presidential Science Advisory Committee, ideas the President accepted readily.

Intelligence took a gloomier view of Soviet missile development. The last National Intelligence Estimate (NIE) on the subject, in March 1957, had predicted that the Soviets would have an operational ICBM capability in 1960–1961; the NIE of November 4, 1957 moved the date up to 1959.

An earlier precautionary move now caught up with Eisenhower. In the spring of 1957, the Administration had launched one of its periodic reviews of defense policy. Under the aegis of the Office of Defense Mobilization Science Advisory Committee, a group had undertaken a review of civil defense that soon broadened into a general inquiry on defense policy. Called the Security Resource Panel, it was nominally run by H. Rowan Gaither, a prominent lawyer, former head of the Ford Foundation, and member of the board of RAND. But Gaither was sick during most of the deliberations and had little to do with the resulting Gaither Report. The Panel's members included scientists and defense experts with impressive credentials (and Democratic connections). In early November, the Panel submitted a grim assessment of American defense policy and near future problems. It urged increased spending on basic research, preparations for limited and antisubmarine warfare, reorganization of the Defense Department, and a limited fallout shelter effort. It took an alarming view of Soviet missile development and the possible results given current U.S. deployments and preparations. The United States lacked an adequate early warning system, and the Strategic Air Command (SAC) was too concentrated on just twenty-nine bases, without blast shelters for its planes. Furthermore, its reaction time was too slow even if warning were available. Without a change, the United States might be very vulnerable to surprise attack from 1959 or early 1960 until 1961–1962. The Gaither Panel briefed Eisenhower and the National Security Council in early November. Because the Panel had been denied direct access to U-2 intelligence and some other military data, and perhaps for other reasons, Eisenhower ruled that it was not sufficiently well informed for its suggestions to be taken as a blueprint. But he was impressed with its analysis of SAC's vulnerability, and he accepted the need for more defense expenditures and other changes in policy. He, and other Administration spokespeople, were publicly conceding more cause for worry. On November 4, Dulles had admitted that the Soviets probably led the United States in certain areas. Eisenhower followed suit and finally allowed that Sputnik had some, albeit indirect, military significance. He announced that SAC's dispersal would be accelerated, and its warning and reaction time improved. He made some concessions to the broader themes of many critics; science education would have to be improved. He even indirectly praised Soviet education. He announced the appointment of Killian and the formation of the Presidential Science Advisory Committee.[6] However, parts of the Gaither Report leaked, feeding demands for still stronger action (as did the Johnson Committee hearings).

Lyndon Johnson, Chairman of the Preparedness Investigating Subcommittee of the Senate Armed Services Committee, characteristically saw Sputnik both as a real challenge and a fine chance to make a name for himself. After some preliminary jabs right after Sputnik, he launched a full-scale inquiry on satellite and missile programs, which took place from November 25, 1957 to January 23, 1958. Although the Administration used them to counter some of the wilder charges against its policies, the hearings hurt it. The Army witnesses, led by the retiring James Gavin, proved particularly embarrassing. Eisenhower refused to release the Gaither Report to the public, as the Subcommittee demanded.

The inquiry produced an impressive list of recommendations: reorganizing the Defense Department, forming a national space agency, allowing more money for SAC and research, and developing a million-pound-thrust rocket engine. In fact, the Administration was already working on most of those ideas; Johnson's staff lifted them from classified reports and made it look as though the Administration was acting only under pressure.

The hearings disclosed a split between the armed forces that influenced assessments of the missile balance over the next few years, as well as the military policy of the Kennedy Administration. Unlike the Air Force, the Army and Navy thought nuclear war unlikely and tended to favor nuclear policies of finite or minimum deterrence. It was only necessary to have a modest retaliatory force immune to attack and capable of smashing Soviet cities to deter nuclear war. The Polaris submarine seemed ideal for this. Surprisingly, even General Medaris shared this perspective. The Army and Navy did not yet rule out a missile gap or even a Soviet attack, but tended to think that any gap would be smaller and less important than the Air Force thought. They also believed that any period of danger would be a brief prelude to an era of strategic stability in which war must be suicidal, and hence unlikely. Conversely, however, those services rated the chance of limited war as high, and they stressed preparing for such wars. In the late 1950s, these views were already associated loosely with liberals and the Left.

The Air Force, little interested in the limited war problem, favored seeking or keeping absolute nuclear superiority over the Soviets and was interested in "counterforce" rather than "countercity" strategies. Still believing that, at least in some circumstances, a nuclear war could be won, it wanted the ability to blast enemy missile and bomber bases rather than cities. It tended to view the nuclear balance as more delicate than did the other services, and (projecting its own outlook onto the enemy) it assumed that the Soviets would go all out to get a first-strike capability against the United States if there was any chance to do so.[7]

At this point, the paradoxes in what was later called Mutual Assured Destruction began to become obvious and acute (although some had envisaged them as early as 1945–1946). While often deploring the Air Force view of the world (perhaps correctly) as bloody-minded or just plain obsolete, it was precisely those who favored the smallest, cheapest nuclear deterrent who favored the bloodiest strategy in the event of nuclear war, and who later tended to oppose most vehemently the search for ways to intercept ICBMs. They tended to project their own ideas of strategy onto Soviet minds; and in some respects they manifested a remarkable complacency—on the one hand in the rationality of the enemy, on the other in the ability to maintain an invulnerable deterrent indefinitely. Bent on deterring war, they ensured that it would take the worst possible form if it broke out.

"FLOPNIK"

Despite the Administration's increasingly vigorous actions, the nation and the West were demoralized further on December 6, 1957 by the failure of the first Vanguard satellite.

Shortly after Sputnik, Dr. Hagen personally briefed the President about the next Vanguard firing. Vanguard TV-3 would carry a "minimal satellite" weighing just 4 pounds, but it was primarily the first test of the whole launch vehicle. Hagen warned that success was not guaranteed; in fact a successful satellite would be a bonus. He would have preferred that the launch get no publicity beforehand. But on October 9, the President's press secretary issued a statement which, while technically accurate, lent itself to the interpretation that a successful satellite was expected.

On December 6, TV-3 rose a few feet; then its engine cut off, and it fell back and collapsed in a spectacular burst of flame. If only because of the atmosphere surrounding the episode, it was a sight that none who saw was likely to forget. The exact cause was never resolved precisely, although there was a bitter feud between the contractors. The engine was slightly modified and never failed in the same way again.

But that was small consolation to the public, which was influenced by a press that reacted to the exaggerated expectations it had fostered. TV-3 became not an ordinary failure of an experimental rocket, but a symbol and a national humiliation. Dubbed "Flopnik" or "Kaputnik," it was played up throughout the world. The Americans, it seemed, could not even orbit a mere grapefruit. Those working on Vanguard were treated like lepers; even the successful Atlas test on December 17, militarily far more important than Vanguard, failed to cut through the gloom.[8]

EXPLORER

A real defeatist neurosis was developing. It could have gotten out of hand easily, for the next Vanguard firing, in February, would also fail. Fortunately for the West, the Eisenhower Administration finally used the Army's satellite capability.

The incoming Secretary of Defense, Neil McElroy, happened to be at Huntsville when Sputnik I went up. Von Braun and Medaris promised to orbit a satellite in ninety days if allowed to do so. On October 8, in one of his first policy shifts after Sputnik, Eisenhower ordered the outgoing Wilson to let the Army prepare as a backup. Medaris, on his own, had von Braun de-mothball a Jupiter C and start work. On November 8, it was officially announced that the Army would launch a satellite as part of the

IGY, but the directive that reached Medaris told him only to prepare to do so. Angry, Medaris threatened to resign before receiving an unambiguous authorization.

The Jet Propulsion Laboratory repackaged instruments from Vanguard. Equipment designed for the spherical Vanguard satellite had to be altered to fit into the long, thin Explorer, which used conventional batteries instead of the solar cells used by Vanguard. Explorer I carried two radios to report the temperature of its outer surface and interior, micrometeorite impacts, and the detection of cosmic rays. The cosmic-ray experiment had been designed by James Van Allen of the University of Iowa.

By late January 1958, the Jupiter C was ready. (Officially, it was the Juno I when carrying a live fourth stage and satellite, but in practice that name was hardly used.) Explorer I was launched on January 31; jetstream winds kicked it into a slightly higher orbit than planned. The satellite and the attached fourth stage together weighed just 30 pounds; but there was great jubilation and relief. Within a short time, Explorer I made the first great scientific discovery of the Space Age: the Van Allen radiation belts.[9]

Explorer was a landmark in the space program. It was not just its first great success, but the first time that von Braun's group, which had been in the United States for over a decade, was used properly. The group had been underused or shunted to secondary tasks; only now did it move to the center of American rocket development—and for space exploration rather than military missiles.

SPEEDUP AND REORGANIZATION

Explorer and ABMA involvement in space were only the first, most visible examples of a general post-Sputnik shift in Administration policy during 1957–1958, which affected both military and space efforts. Contrary to what is sometimes claimed, Sputnik had a considerable impact on the conduct of American defense.[10] Defense expenditures were increased. In January 1958, the Administration requested an additional $1.37 billion for defense, and in April it returned to Congress for another $1.45 billion. The late Eisenhower era military buildup did not equal that of the Truman, Kennedy, and Reagan Administrations, but it was nevertheless considerable. Its main peculiarity was that it was limited to strategic weapons; their share of the military budget peaked in 1959, reaching a proportion never equaled before or after.

Even while downplaying Sputnik, Secretary Wilson had begun changing his position on plans for the ICBM program. Schriever's Ballistic Missile Division (as the Western Development Division was now called) had anticipated this and had new plans ready on October 8. On November 22, the restrictions on overtime work on ICBMs were ended. Plans for an ICBM force before Sputnik had been tentative, limited to eight squadrons of eighty Atlases and Titans through 1961; in the first of many changes in plans, the Administration decided in December to form no less than nine squadrons of Atlas alone. (Plans for Titan were not yet resolved.) In late 1957, the Air Force decided that a solid-fuel missile, which could be kept in underground silos for years and fired at a moment's notice, was a practical proposition. In February 1958, the Air Force was allowed to proceed with developing Minuteman. Late in 1957, the Administration decided to accelerate the reconnaissance satellite program, now named Sentry. Instead of waiting for Atlas-Agena to become available, an experimental version of the satellite, called Discoverer, would be launched using the Thor. On November 25, Secretary of Defense Neil McElroy decided to produce both Thor and Jupiter and to accelerate both programs, so a limited Thor capability might be operational as early as mid-1958. This was perhaps the most politically influenced decision of the whole period, in several ways. General Medaris, who favored it, suspected that it was aimed to spare the Administration embarrassment at the Johnson hearings, while the whole IRBM concept was more popular with Eisenhower and Dulles than with the Pentagon. In January 1958, ABMA was authorized to proceed with development of the Pershing (a solid-fuel replacement for the Redstone) and the Nike-Zeus, the first of several never-deployed systems designed to intercept ICBMs.

To protect the existing deterrent, the Air Force hastened the dispersal of SAC and work on the Ballistic Missile Early Warning System (BMEWS). Its three radars—in Alaska, Greenland, and England—ensured at least fifteen minutes' warning of an ICBM attack.

The most dramatic speedup of an offensive program was that of Polaris. On December 9, the Secretary of Defense advanced the date on which it would become operational by three years, to 1960.[11]

The post-Sputnik shift saw a major change in the government organizations dealing with defense, space, and scientific research. The creation of the presidential advisory apparatus in late 1957 was a first step; it was followed by the creation, in February 1958, of the Advanced Research Projects Agency (ARPA) in the Defense Department. ARPA was designed to be a small agency to evaluate and coordinate (not manage directly) the research efforts of the services and ensure that novel and valuable proposals that were of no particular interest to any one service were investigated. Unofficially, it was expected eventually to take over direction of military space programs. ARPA's creation was followed by a major reorganization of the whole Defense Department.

At the recommendations of the Johnson Committee and the Presidential Science Advisory Committee (PSAC), the Administration decided to form a civilian space agency out of the old National Advisory Committee on Aeronautics, although this was not finished until 1960, when von Braun's team was finally transferred to it. Meanwhile the Army and Air Force initiated a spate of research satellites and moon probes with existing boosters. During 1958 they started three programs critical to later space efforts. The Air Force contracted for a huge conventional engine, the F-1 (which had been under study since 1955), and an upper stage, Centaur, which had a liquid hydrogen engine and was designed to be launched by ICBMs and to propel space probes. ABMA, using Redstone and Jupiter components, started to build a major space booster, first called Juno V and later Saturn.[12] (These developments will be discussed in more detail in chapter seven.)

Some (perhaps most) of the aforementioned changes and programs might have taken place sooner or later; but the impact of Sputnik cannot be doubted. A major change in national civilian policy stemmed directly from it. Federal aid to education had been debated since the 1940s, but feuds over aid to parochial schools and segregation in the South had blocked action. Sputnik broke the logjam, producing the National Defense Education Act of September 1958, which provided student loans and fellowships. Aimed at promoting science and language education, it opened the way for a much broader program of aid to education.[13] At least for a time, it improved science education; but the long-run effect (or lack of it) would have shocked everyone: Incredible sums would be expended while education actually declined.

THE LONG-RUN IMPACT OF SPUTNIK

The commotion after Sputnik showed the Americans of the 1950s at their best, but also at their worst. On the one hand, there was an outpouring of real concern and energy and a determination to overtake the Soviets and cure the country's ills, much in contrast to the bickering and languid response to decline characteristic from the late 1960s onward. On the other hand, there was a good deal of foolishness and profiteering, and a misuse of patriotism by people with axes to grind, as well as ostrich-headed reactions by those who pretended that the Soviet rockets did not exist or that it was all because "we captured the wrong Germans." Some of the attacks on the Eisenhower Administration were sheer lies.

John Foster Dulles had speculated, as early as October 16, 1957, that Sputnik would prove a good thing, a salutary shock jolting Americans out of their complacency and reenergizing American society. (This was a curious revelation in that even at the top of the Administration some shared the prevailing ideas of social criticism, at least in their conservative form.) Elaborating on this three months later, Dulles suggested that Sputnik might mark a decisive turn in the Cold War precisely because it would boomerang by causing Americans to react.[14]

Five or ten years later, in the high noon of the Kennedy-Johnson Administration, even many who disliked Dulles would have conceded that he had proven farsighted. For all the worry and trouble that had ensued in the three or four years after Sputnik, it had galvanized the United States into taking a new look at its educational system and pour more resources into science and technology as well as its missile and space efforts. Militarily, the United States had maintained—even increased—its lead over the U.S.S.R. Furthermore, the partisans would argue, by embarrassing the staid incumbent it had helped make possible the New Frontier and the Great Society. The late 1950s, it seemed, had been the start of a new burst of energy, activism, and readiness to make things over, all of which promised a better society.

Decades later, the impact of Sputnik seems very different. The criticism of American society, which was fashionable in the late 1950s and afterward, contributed nothing to a better world, or less than nothing. The ranting against conformity and materialism of the 1950s seems ludicrous. Except for racial discrimination (in decline since at least the 1920s), none of the real social evils that such criticism had sometimes indicted were overcome; most became far worse, or indeed were exacerbated by new evils unthinkable in 1957. Appearances had not been entirely deceiving in the late 1950s; there was a burst of energy and creativity. But most of it was misdirected; and what resulted was not the regeneration but the derailment of a society, which despite its faults had been progressing rapidly.

No more damning judgment can be imagined.

6

The "Missile Gap" and After

Sputnik I was followed by some of the tensest years of the Cold War. Some of the crises of the era were triggered by local issues and forces, but others were related directly to the missile race, and all were influenced by it. The period of 1957–1961 was overshadowed by a looming Soviet superiority, crystallized in the term "missile gap." Beliefs about the strength of the two sides, almost more than the reality, powerfully affected world opinion. The reality presented a seeming paradox. Contrary to near-universal expectations, the Soviets failed to turn their lead in development into a massive ICBM force. The long-dreaded gap opened in reverse, even while Khrushchev tried to bluff the West into retreating. By 1961 the United States had shot ahead and maintained its strategic superiority, and Khrushchev's bluff was exposed. Meanwhile the Soviets had carried out a far less publicized, massive buildup of shorter-range missiles covering Western Europe and U.S. overseas bases. In relation to those targets, Khrushchev acquired what was later called overkill (a point that has often eluded Americans). Then, having seemingly forfeited the ICBM race and with their weakness in intercontinental weapons exposed, the Soviets used some of their intermediate- and medium-range missiles to close—perhaps more than close—the gap between the superpowers' ability to strike each other's homelands. This led to the Cuban Missile Crisis. Khrushchev was eager for great gains. At first his policies had clearly ruled out taking any real chance of war. Perhaps the very frustration of his hope to intimidate the West peacefully into a general retreat led him to take fantastic risks—perhaps even more fantastic than has been generally realized.

THE MISSILE BLUFF

The seeming anomaly of small-scale deployment of ICBMs against the United States, together with a massive one against Western Europe, resembled the earlier Soviet deployment of bombers. In both cases, contrary to what is often said, the Soviets' production effort was great. The cause of the disproportion was that while the medium-range Tupolev-16 bombers, and the R-12 and R-14 missiles, were satisfactory weapons and could be built in numbers more than sufficient to cover the enemy near at hand, the Tupolev-95 and Myasishchev-4 heavy bombers, and the R-7 ICBM, were far less successful. The speed, altitude, and range of the bombers, as well as the range limitations and handling characteristics of the R-7, left the intercontinental weapons so inadequate that the Soviets decided to manufacture them only in token numbers and delay building a major intercontinental striking force for a time. It was not the lack of desire for intercontinental forces, but Soviet technical limitations, a tendency to spread limited resources over too many intercontinental projects (e.g., the Sorokovka and Burya Navaho-type missiles), and the blunders of the design bureaus (as well as the political favoritism that gave the incompetent Myasishchev a critical role) that delayed the development of a Soviet ability to attack the United States far beyond even the most optimistic American assessment in the 1950s. In the 1960s, when the Soviets finally got their act together and acquired soundly designed ICBMs, they quickly deployed them in large numbers—larger, in fact, than the Americans expected. There are widespread beliefs that in the 1950s the Soviet ruling group deliberately rejected starting nuclear war and consciously chose a policy of finite deterrence, but both of these beliefs are doubtful. The latter, particularly, seems incompatible with the known Soviet military doctrine of the period, the massive nature of the missile deployment against Western Europe, and the 1962 decision to send missiles to Cuba—much less compatible with the military buildup of the 1960s and 1970s.

The R-7's bulk, the need to base it on railroad lines, and the time it took to ready it for flight rendered the R-7 of little value. The Soviets tried to protect R-7 sites with blast walls, but it could not be based underground. It was of little use as a retaliatory weapon unless it could be completely hidden, which was unlikely with U-2s (and later satellites) roaming overhead. Paradoxically, it was so clearly nothing but a first-strike weapon that it was not even suitable for that. To build a force of several hundred

R-7s might have led to a grave danger of the Americans launching a preemptive attack if they feared that the R-7s were about to be fired; a bomber attack might easily catch them on the ground.

Marshal Nedelin thus concluded in 1958 that the R-7 would not be a suitable ICBM; while Khrushchev's son Sergo, who worked in a design bureau of one of Korolev's rivals, made sure that his father knew of the R-7's limitations and drew his attention to American plans to base the Titan underground. Korolev designed another ICBM, the R-9 (NATO SS-8 Sasin), which, though dependent on cryogenic fuels, could be fueled quickly. It was not too successful; Korolev's protégé/rival Yangel developed the superior R-16 (NATO SS-7 Saddler) using hypergolic fuels, but it was not ready for deployment until 1961. A few R-7s were deployed at a base at Plesetsk starting in 1959.[1]

Soon after Sputnik, at the latest, Khrushchev realized that he could draw profit from ICBMs even without having any in force. By playing on the real achievements embodied vividly in Sputnik, he could create the impression that he had (or, more exactly, was about to get) an ICBM capability—and thus convey the message that the west should prudently get out of his way on issues like Berlin while it could do so gracefully. He knew, of course, that as a last resort in any crisis he must back down, but he hoped that the West would give in first. That hope proved in vain; the West would not cave in on anything vital, although it came close once or twice. Nonetheless, the Soviets' non-Communist allies would be impressed.

The Soviets were helped by the fact that, at least between 1959 and 1961, an American traitor, Colonel William Whalen, fed them the U.S. intelligence estimates of Soviet strength. Soviet claims about their ICBMs were carefully measured to sound plausible while avoiding saying anything too specific that might be checked and refuted. And they were interspersed with more specific, threatening, and well-founded claims of what their missiles could do to the Europeans. Khrushchev repeatedly and bluntly threatened nations harboring U.S. bases, frequently reminding them that a few bombs could destroy them.

The Soviet claims started slowly; at first the Soviets did not specifically claim to have an operational force or that military superiority over the West was imminent. At the November 1957 conference of the world's Communist parties (the last meeting of a more or less united Communist movement), they claimed that there had been a general shift of the correlation of forces in their favor. That broad formulation included all elements of the world struggle, not just the military balance. The Soviets asserted that they had eliminated American military superiority and had neutralized U.S. overseas bases. In November 1958, as the Berlin crisis started, they announced that ICBMs were in mass production. From then on—coinciding with the peak of the American debate over the "missile gap"—the Soviets did everything possible to make the West believe in it, and they intimated that they already had an operational force. They now claimed approximate military equality with the United States. With the brief relaxation of tension during 1959, they played down the issue while reiterating their ability to wipe out European NATO countries. In November 1959, Khrushchev claimed to have a substantial operational ICBM force. His claims reached a peak in January 1960; he flatly claimed that he could destroy the United States and hinted that he had a fantastic new weapon aside from the ICBM. After the U-2 incident in May, Khrushchev retreated from his more exaggerated claims, perhaps fearing that he might provoke Eisenhower into publicly flourishing the evidence that had begun convincing most in the U.S. government that things were not as bad as had been feared. But Khrushchev revived claims of Soviet superiority beginning in July, perhaps assuming that the Americans, no longer able to use the U-2, would be unable to check them. As the Americans began to see through him, he retreated to claims that there was now strategic parity. In late 1961, after the Kennedy Administration belatedly ended the missile-gap myth, the Soviets retreated to denying American strategic superiority, although even in 1962 they sometimes claimed to be the stronger side. Khrushchev, who had earlier belittled the importance of bombers, now admitted their importance (since it was now apparent that the Soviets still depended on them). The Soviets harped on the power of the huge thermonuclear weapons tested in 1961 and their undoubted ability to smash the Western European countries.[2]

ESTIMATING THE THREAT

The United States, of course, never accepted the Soviet claims at face value. Sputnik was the start of a struggle, which lasted several years, to learn what was really going on. Only very late in this effort did the Americans receive the help of a valuable spy, Oleg Penkovskiy. The Americans' chief weapons were the U-2 and the Turkish radar; but neither provided absolutely conclusive evidence. The radar could track Soviet missile launches through most of their trajectory, but it was not always certain if a test had succeeded. Moreover, the U-2 was a wasting asset, as had been fully expected when it was developed. It had never been able to overfly all of the U.S.S.R., and relatively fewer flights were made after early 1958. Grounded for part of that year after a series of crashes, when it did fly it had to be used more cautiously. The latest Soviet ground-to-air missiles could reach its altitude with some control, and defended areas had to be avoided. And the U-2's evidence was of a negative sort. It might show that the Soviets had not yet deployed ICBMs, but not whether they were just about to do so. Some feared, too, that it could be beaten by camouflage.

At the end of 1957, Eisenhower's new Science Advisor concluded that the American missile programs were progressing reasonably well. James Killian believed that the Americans were probably behind the Soviets, but only because they had started later and not because of inferior technology. American test failures, so far, were not inordinate.

In a report on February 4, 1958, the Presidential Science Advisory Committee (PSAC) endorsed George Kistiakowsky's estimate that the Soviets were a year ahead of the United States in propulsion, a year behind in warhead development, and a bit behind in guidance systems. Still, with the very large warheads the missiles could carry, the warhead and guidance lag might matter little. The Soviets might finish the twenty to thirty test firings needed for operational deployment in just six months. Later, in May 1958, the Defense Department's Director of Research and Engineering estimated that the Americans lagged eighteen months behind the Soviets.

What that could mean in terms of a concrete threat was spelled out in a Special National Intelligence Estimate in January 1958. The Soviets might have a small operational force (an initial operational capability in the jargon of the time) as early as mid-1958, and 100 ICBMs by mid-1959. That would make possible an effective strike on SAC before early warning was available. Much, therefore, depended on whether the Soviets could quickly finish testing their ICBM and mass produce it. For the Americans, finishing the Ballistic Missile Early Warning System, dispersing SAC, and quickly deploying an attack-proof retaliatory force—the Polaris submarines—were all urgent. There were two possible subthreats within the "missile gap"—one, a quick Soviet achievement of a modest force able to achieve complete surprise, sometime in 1959–1961; second, and later, the creation of a massive force vastly outnumbering its U.S. counterpart. The latter might not give the Soviets a decisive advantage, since the Americans by then would have early warning, hardened bases, and Polaris. But it was not a pleasant prospect.[3]

Contemporary public estimates of the Soviet missile and space program were gloomy, overestimating Soviet engine development and their ability to build light structures. The Soviets' ICBM was believed to have single-chambered engines of up to 264,000 pounds of thrust each. The Soviets were believed to be developing more advanced missiles, perhaps using "exotic" fuel additives, and were widely thought to be far advanced in work on the "T-4A," the long-rumored Sanger manned "antipodal" rocket

bomber. The Soviets were widely reported to be working on far advanced
nuclear rockets. There were reports that they were testing a 50,000-pound
thrust nuclear rocket engine and working on one with 2.2 million pounds
of thrust. The truth was so prosaic that few at the time would have believed
it; the Soviets were developing better missiles and a winged spacecraft
(the Lapotok reconnaissance spaceplane), but apparently they only studied
more advanced weapons and powerplants. Oddly, their work on submarine
missiles went almost unnoticed during the missile-gap furor.[4]

The ICBM threat seemed bad enough. The term "missile gap" apparently
originated in the Pentagon, where it was simply called the gap, and it was
publicized by the columnist Stewart Alsop in December 1957. The term
appeared occasionally during 1958 but seems to have become common
only in early 1959. (President Eisenhower used it at least once during the
1958 election campaign, but to refer to the developmental lag, not a
threatened Soviet superiority of numbers. Blaming the lag on Truman, he
assured everyone that it was being fixed speedily.) Then internal debates
within the government about the extent of the gap began leaking out; the
Administration, not without a struggle, had settled on a less threatening
estimate of Soviet capabilities.

A National Intelligence Estimate of June 1958 confirmed that the
Soviets could have 100 ICBMs by mid-1959; they might have 500 in 1960
and 1,000 by 1969 (when the United States expected to have no more than
130 ICBMs). But the CIA believed that any failures in the Soviet test series
must push back the emergence of a major threat by six to twelve months.
Since it was already known that the Soviets had had such failures, the
President coolly discounted the estimate. Further, the Soviets had not
tested ICBMs since April; indeed after Sputnik III was launched in May,
no R-7s flew at all for the rest of 1958. ICBM tests resumed only in April
1959, although there were space launches early in that year. There were
two possible interpretations of the halt. The Air Force argued that the
Soviets had finished the requisite tests and were content with the result
(despite the occurrence of some failures). The CIA and the other military
intelligence agencies rightly believed that the Soviets had hit real troubles.
They did not conclude that the R-7 would not be deployed, but they
deemed the threat less acute than had been feared, and they convinced
Eisenhower of this. The NIE of December 1958 predicted a Soviet force
of 100 ICBMs by mid-1960, 300 by 1961, 500 in 1962, and 1,000 to 1,500
in 1963. This estimate essentially shoved the threat a year further into the
future. During late 1958, there was some optimism in the press as well;
von Braun's testimony that the Soviet lead was small and not militarily
significant was widely cited.[5] The new mood soon dissipated, however.

1958: YEAR OF CRISES

The new estimate was one of the few pieces of good news during one of the grimmest years of the Cold War. Other years saw bloodier fighting or more intense crises, but none saw such continuous, complex trouble in far-flung parts of the globe. The U.S. government lurched from one outbreak to another. Eisenhower and Dulles handled these difficulties with skill and aplomb, disguised by their stolidity and preference for maintaining an air of calm and determination instead of posturing for the galleries. The first confrontation was with the Soviets' radical Arab nationalist allies. In July U.S. and British forces landed in Lebanon and Jordan, the former to settle the long-sputtering Lebanese civil war (which had become more menacing in the context of the revolution in Iraq that month) and show the world that the widely feared Soviet superiority had not paralyzed the West. Soon after, the Chinese Communists began the second Taiwan Straits crisis.

In November the Soviets started a crisis that they wanted, demanding an agreement that would end the Western occupation of Berlin within six months. The resulting crisis dragged on in one form or another until 1962.

The belief in the "missile gap" nearly had decisive and disastrous effects. At first, despite differences, the West held together. It ignored the deadline on Berlin and rejected the Soviet proposals. It offered to negotiate if the ultimatum was lifted; Khrushchev tacitly did this in March 1959. At the meeting that followed in Geneva, the West at first seemed firm. But the resignation of Secretary Dulles, months of harping on the "missile gap," and attacks on the rigidity of the Western governments by their internal opponents led the nervous Western leaders to offer an interim solution involving concessions that might well have led to a complete collapse of the Western position on Berlin. However, the Soviets, over-reaching themselves, rejected it.[6]

THE IRBMs

Meanwhile, the Americans frantically tried to overtake the supposed Soviet missile lead. One sort of strategic missile, albeit not too satisfactory, the IRBM, was already becoming available. Work on Thor and Jupiter was rushed to provide a stopgap until ICBMs and Polaris were ready. The first operational Jupiters were built at Huntsville (instead of turning all production over to Chrysler) to get some as soon as possible. Medaris's sensible proposal to reverse the decision on operational control and let Army personnel with Redstone experience handle the similar Jupiter was rejected. It is a comment on the maniacal nature of interservice rivalry in that era that the Air Force, the service most insistent on the danger of the missile gap, still wanted to sink the whole Jupiter program. To be fair, the Air Force had lost enthusiasm even for Thor. The difficulty of finding bases for IRBMs was becoming clear. By January 1959, SAC actually recommended canceling the IRBM effort; much reduced, it went on more as a symbol of American resolve than anything else.

In March 1957, the British and Americans had agreed to equip the Royal Air Force (RAF) with four Thor squadrons. (The warheads would stay in American custody; launching required both American and British consent.) But there was much grumbling even in Britain about the agreement. Apart from the fear of attracting Soviet bombs, some critics warned correctly that the Thors, based above ground at soft fixed sites, were slow firing and vulnerable. Despite the priority given the task and an elaborate airlift that rushed supplies and equipment to Britain starting in August 1958, getting the Thors ready took longer than expected. There were delays in base construction and in training personnel to handle the rockets. The first RAF unit became truly operational in June 1960.

After Sputnik, with the Soviets threatening those who accepted U.S. bases, it was hard to get other countries to take IRBMs. During 1959, unable to get bases in France, Spain, or Greece, the Americans settled for basing two Jupiter squadrons in Italy and one in Turkey. The Italians and Turks would provide launch crews, while both missiles and warheads stayed in U.S. custody. Delays in training local crews forced the Americans to man the missiles themselves for a time. The first Jupiters became operational in Italy in July 1960, but the missiles and their ground equipment suffered severe corrosion problems. The Turkish missiles became operational between November 1969 and March 1962; the turnover to Turkish crews coincided with the Cuban Missile Crisis. The IRBMs had little value. Closely grouped at soft bases, they would have been smashed in any Soviet attack. (It would have been different if the Jupiters' mobility had been used, however.) Their sole value was in complicating Soviet targeting and, perhaps, in indicating that the Americans might strike first themselves in the event of a Soviet conventional invasion in Europe. The Kennedy Administration, however, disapproved of such a first-strike echelon as provocative. It considered canceling the Turkish deployment but did not do so, fearful of offending the Turks. Polaris submarines were a more than superior substitute for the land-based IRBMs; during 1962 the British announced that they would phase out the Thors, and the Americans belatedly moved toward junking the Jupiters. During the Cuban crisis, the fifteen Jupiters in Turkey became an acute embarrassment to the U.S. government—or, at least, that was how it chose to regard them.[7]

THE AMERICAN ICBMs

Atlas and Titan were too far along by the time of Sputnik for there to be much room for speeding up their development, once the cuts and restrictions imposed in 1957 were undone. Plans for deploying the first-generation ICBMs, however, fluctuated wildly for the next three years. This was not due primarily to changing estimates of the Soviet threat; but that was an additional spur to get as many early-model missiles as possible, even if they were not too satisfactory. There were big difficulties in deciding how many ICBMs to procure and how they should be based. The proper configuration of missile sites and control complexes, and how much they should be hardened, were complex issues; data from nuclear tests in 1958 caused major changes in plans. It was unclear what the mix of missiles should be.

Various models of the Atlas differed greatly in hardness, while all were inferior in this and other ways to the Titan I. The promise of later-model missiles, Titan II and Minuteman, complicated the issue, as did Polaris. Both the Navy and the Army favored substituting Polaris submarines for some land-based rockets. Titan II, proposed by Martin engineers in early 1958, was basically a new missile. Using storable fuels and more powerful than Titan I, it carried an 18-megaton warhead and could be fired right out of a silo (Titan I had to be raised to ground level on an elevator). Minuteman was further off, but it could be fired from a silo almost instantly and promised to be very cheap. The PSAC, in February 1958, urged procuring just eighty operational Atlases and then switching over to Titan. Eisenhower liked the idea of giving priority to Titan and the solid-fuel missiles. In December 1958, he approved a plan for nine Atlas and eleven Titan squadrons (nine missiles each) by June 1963. The Air Force, however, agitated for seventeen Atlas and twelve Titan squadrons, including eight Titan II squadrons.

There was much argument over Titan. Some in the Defense Department and Congress favored canceling Titan, or at least Titan II, as wasteful duplications of Atlas. But the dominant pressure of public and congressional opinion was for more of everything, and the Secretary of Defense and the Ballistic Missile Division preferred Titan to Atlas; with the PSAC, they strongly backed Titan. The project survived. In January 1960, Eisenhower approved plans for a liquid-fuel ICBM force of thirteen Atlas and fourteen Titan squadrons by February 1964; this was close to the final mix of thirteen Atlas and twelve Titan squadrons that was eventually deployed. The impact of the "missile gap" fears, therefore, was to cause the Administration to order more of the already obsolescent or at least short-lived Atlases than it would have liked.

Atlas A tests had ended in June 1958. The sustainer engine, first flown on Atlas B, proved unreliable; like the similar Thor engine, it suffered severe problems with its turbopump. Series B tests ended in early 1959. Atlas C, testing new nose cones and various improvements, flew from December 1958 to August 1959; only three of six succeeded. Atlas D, tested from April to December 1959, was the first operational missile. The Atlas had plenty of trouble on the ground as well. Developing a system to fuel the missile quickly and safely proved difficult. Building bases and training personnel proved costly, and some of the early training proved unrealistic. Atlas D was declared operational on September 7, 1959, but that was really for political purposes. Three were mounted in the open on the gantries used for experimental launches at Vandenberg Air Force Base; they could have been fired only with several hours warning. More Atlas Ds became operational in August 1960; they were almost as vulnerable as those at Vandenberg because they were stored above ground with no blast protection. Many authorities considered Atlas E, which was operational in September 1961, the first truly useful model of the Atlas. It had a far better all-inertial guidance system and was kept in semihardened positions—above-ground coffins covered with earth. To be launched, the Atlas E had to be raised and then fueled. Atlas F, the last model, was truly hardened. Stored in a silo, it could be partially fueled while under ground, but it had to be brought up on an elevator to be topped off and fired. It was available in the latter part of 1962. In total, 126 Atlases were deployed. They were never very reliable and at first were downright undependable; Herbert York estimated that in 1960 only a fifth would have reached their targets in a real war situation. Moreover, Atlas never met the desired fifteen-minute reaction time; it could not be fueled fast enough with any safety. It was phased out in 1964–1965.

Titan I was tested—first stage only—in February 1959. After the usual initial failures, its test record proved less checkered than that of the Atlas. It was finally deployed in April 1962; by September of that year fifty-four were ready. Beginning in 1963, the Titan I was joined by, and then replaced with, the Titan II. Titan I was probably the first ICBM to make an important contribution to Western defense.[8]

MINUTEMAN

The weapon that ultimately became the backbone of the ICBM force resulted from the unexpectedly rapid development of a breakthrough that no one had expected. The solid fuels that made Polaris possible had interested the Air Force. The head of the Thor test effort, Colonel Edward Hall (an able scientist who had long been an advocate of solid fuels), was put in charge of work on them. He convinced Schriever of the possibility of a three-stage solid-fuel ICBM, at first called "Weapon System Q." Schriever got the originally separate solid-fuel effort assigned to his Ballistic Missile Division, and he sold Secretary McElroy on the idea despite widespread skepticism in the Air Force. The Air Force's Scientific Advisory Board thought that the advocates of the system banked on improbably low warhead weights. In February 1958, a research and development program was approved for what was now called Minuteman. The Air Force envisaged a flight test by the end of 1960 and an operational force by July 1963. The service envisaged a force of 500 or more missiles, some based on trains, but McElroy limited Minuteman to research and development. Elements hostile to Minuteman were led by William Holaday, the Director of Guided Missiles in McElroy's office, but there were disagreements among the Joint Chiefs of Staff. But the program survived, and in October 1958 the Boeing company became the assembly and test contractor; the three stages of the missile, all of which used different fuels, were built by three separate contractors.

In September 1959, Minuteman got a DX priority, but it never became a crash program during the Eisenhower Administration. There were formidable difficulties in fabricating its propellant charges and controls; the first stage, developing 200,000 pounds of thrust, was the biggest solid-fuel rocket yet built. The third stage introduced both a superior new propellant and fiberglass construction. Nevertheless, progress was remarkably rapid. General Samuel Phillips, the director of the program (who later played a central role in the Apollo project) boldly decided on "all-up" testing—trying all three live stages in the first flight. Tried in February 1961, this was a complete success, although the next two tests failed. Minuteman I's range was not quite adequate, so in 1960 the Air Force decided to base the first missiles at Malmstrom Air Force Base in Montana, which was not only well north but on a high plateau, thus giving the missile an extra advantage. The Kennedy Administration junked the mobile Minuteman, but in March 1961 it made the silo-based weapon a crash program. The first twenty Minutemen became operational in December

1962; ultimately 1,000 were deployed. Unlike the missiles discussed earlier, Minuteman played no direct role in space exploration. It was purely a device of destruction.[9]

POLARIS

Polaris, which had inspired Minuteman, was the sole missile project to add substantially to western power in the "missile gap" era. Unlike the first-generation ICBMs, it was drastically speeded up after Sputnik. In December 1957, a radical change in plans—the possibility of which had been studied before Sputnik—was set in motion. Fortunately, the vital new "jetavator" device, which was to steer the missile, had just been proven in tests with the Air Force's X-17 rocket.

Instead of seeking an operational capability by 1963, the first Polaris submarines were to be ready in 1960. This involved a certain cost: the use of a less effective missile and the adaptation of submarines already under construction instead of building boats designed as missile launchers. The interim Polaris missile, the A-1, would have a range of only 1,200 miles instead of 1,500; it used a less effective propellant and a more primitive fire-control system. (The original Polaris design became the Polaris A-2; a further model, A-3, was developed later.) An originally planned series of test vehicles was canceled. Over Admiral Rickover's opposition, an attack submarine was turned over to the Polaris program and was renamed *George Washington*. It was cut in two, and a 130-foot center section was added to house sixteen missiles, each carrying a 500-kiloton warhead. The five-boat *George Washington* class would be succeeded by five of the *Ethan Allen* class and thirty-one *Lafayette*-class submarines, carrying 656 missiles in all. In an innovation devised in 1959, over much opposition, each submarine would be manned by two alternating crews so they could stay at sea more of the time.

While the Electric Boat Company worked on the submarines (three shifts and overtime), the development of the missiles, launching methods, and a precise navigational system for the submarines took place. No less than eleven different ways to launch the missile were explored before the project settled on blowing the missile out of the tube with compressed air (the rocket ignition took place in the water). Admiral Raborn orchestrated the complex project masterfully, making full use of his independent authority and priorities, playing up his "magic" management technique, and making sure that both officers and civilians in the Special Projects

Office were amply rewarded with promotions. The project was run on a wartime basis, with officers always in uniform. Raborn bought off potential rivals and opponents by suggesting that Polaris missiles could be put on some surface ships. (Plans to do this were eventually canceled.) Raborn made clear to everyone that Polaris was not just another job and that the stakes were enormous. Lecturing not just SPO employees but their families, he told his audiences to grasp the backs of their necks—"those are the necks that will be saved when Polaris is developed!" He toured factories, offices, and laboratories that were working on Polaris in the same spirit. Plants working on Polaris flew special Polaris flags like the E (Excellence) flags flown over outstanding factories during World War II. The key to Polaris's success was that it was not just a program, it was a crusade. Unfortunately, for just that reason, its success could not be duplicated readily. It was one government program that came in on time and on budget.

Without that spirit, or with a lesser leader than Raborn, the project might have slipped badly. Polaris did not succeed without setbacks. There was a serious explosion in a plant that made the propellants, and the missile's test history might have daunted a lesser person. Test vehicles were fired successfully from under-water tubes as early as March 1958, but the missile itself failed spectacularly. In September 1958, AX-1, the first full-scale Polaris, flew up at 40,000 feet when a part in its autopilot failed. When AX-2 was launched in October, the first stage sat on the launch pad, smoking; then the second stage took off by itself. An explosive bolt had failed. AX-3 went out of control when the rocket's exhaust melted its tail. Raborn gambled and kept up the test schedule, trying to fix things between flights. He must have wondered if he had made the right choice, for the same cause destroyed AX-4 and AX-5. AX-6, however, flew successfully on April 20, 1959. After that, development went smoothly. *George Washington* fired a Polaris while submerged on July 20, 1960 and became operational in November 1960. By the time of the Cuban Missile Crisis, nine Polaris submarines were operational. Polaris components were used in NASA's Scout satellite launcher.[10]

Unfortunately, the government never made proper use of Raborn's talents after he left the Special Projects Office. Instead of putting him in the space program, President Johnson made him head of the CIA, where he was a fish out of water. Had the missile gap been real, and the United States survived it, William Raborn would have been recognized properly as a great national hero. He should be remembered as one in any case.

THE CLIMAX OF THE "MISSILE GAP" CONTROVERSY

In 1959 few doubted that the "missile gap" existed; however, there was intense argument over its extent and meaning. Not all agreed with the more optimistic estimate of late 1958. Senator Symington had thought even the June 1958 estimate overoptimistic; he and his sources of information in the Air Force violently opposed the December NIE. Apart from differing evaluations of the Soviet test halt, there were serious differences in opinion at several levels. The PSAC, in January 1959, believed that the Soviets already had an initial operational capability (IOC), which the CIA denied. The President, in close touch with the evaluation process, thought the PSAC might be right, but also correctly held that the real problems involved determining when a big Soviet force would be available and just how accurate the Soviet missiles were. The date of the Soviet attainment of an IOC was a minor item in a puzzle whose solution depended on several factors: how many missiles were being built, their accuracy and reliability, and whether they would be available before the United States had an early warning system and improved, survivable retaliatory forces. It was not clear whether the Soviets would need as few as two or as many as six ICBMs to be sure of smashing an unhardened SAC base; and it was uncertain how hard the planned Titan bases would be.

In January Secretary McElroy tried to reassure Congress in secret testimony, but it and the leaks that reached the public made the "missile gap" a bigger controversy than before. Presenting the new, more optimistic view, McElroy still admitted that the Soviets would probably have more ICBMs than the United States sometime in the early 1960s. But he insisted that the United States need not match the enemy missile for missile and could deter an attack even at the peak disparity of numbers. Symington was openly skeptical.

As the new estimates leaked out of the hearings, articles by a retired Army general, Thomas R. Phillips (based on information leaked by the Air Force), appeared in the liberal magazines *The New Republic* and *The Reporter* and frightened the public. Phillips warned that the Administration grotesquely underestimated the danger. Disclosing the figures from the June 1958 NIE, he claimed that complete ICBM bases already existed in the U.S.S.R. (The Soviets, behind schedule in hacking Plesetsk out of a swamp, would have been delighted had this been true.) Phillips's assessment was based not only on his acceptance of the higher figures for projected Soviet strengths but on a low opinion of Minuteman and Polaris. Others argued, with reason, that the planning and construction of the U.S. ICBM bases left something to be desired. They argued that even Atlas could be better protected if sited in deep canyons or pits. Coincidentally, on a more exalted theoretical level, *Foreign Affairs* published an influential article, "The Delicate Balance of Terror," by the well-known and able strategic analyst Albert Wohlstetter. As its title implied, the article suggested that the strategic balance was less stable than was generally thought; and specifically it stressed the vulnerability of U.S. bomber and IRBM bases.

Symington and others urged quick adoption of a costly airborne alert, as well as buying more first-generation ICBMs. The Air Force used this pressure in its effort to sell the Administration on its program for twenty-nine Atlas and Titan squadrons. Although Eisenhower, in his State of the Union address, had implicitly criticized the idea, General Schriever suggested in April that there would be a period of maximum danger in 1962–1963. Gloom spread with the early failures of Polaris and Atlas; McElroy had to admit that the IOC for Atlas must be put back sixty days.[11]

Shortly afterward, however, the picture brightened. In April the Soviets resumed ICBM tests. It became clear that the optimists had been right about the test halt; and the Soviets were suffering failures in the new tests, too. Even the Air Force decided that it was unlikely that the Soviets would reach an operational capability in 1959. McElroy declared that a Soviet IOC would be about even with the American one (which was artificially advanced for political reasons). General Schriever announced that the Americans and the Soviets were now in about the same stage. Polaris began to fly. Fear receded, for a time.

In December 1959, a new NIE concluded that the Soviets had chosen an orderly rather than a crash program and had no current operational capability. It estimated that the Soviets would have thirty-five ICBMs in mid-1960, 140 to 200 in mid-1961, and 350 to 450 by mid-1963. They would not enjoy more than a moderate numerical superiority. But there still seemed some danger of attack in 1961 before the early warning system was ready, and there was some argument over the basic validity of the estimate. The Army and Navy held even more optimistic views than the CIA, which dominated the NIE, while the Air Force presented far higher estimates. Eisenhower accepted the NIE.

At the urging of Republican leaders and worried about the 1960 election, Eisenhower had the new Secretary of Defense, Thomas Gates, and General Nathan Twining, the Chairman of the Joint Chiefs of Staff, testify about the "missile gap" before Congress. There was intense skepticism about the good news. The President himself tried to reassure the public in his State of the Union Address and at a press conference on January 13; he was a bit shocked to encounter attacks on his personal honesty. (That would not be unusual today, but in the 1950s virtually no one had questioned his integrity.) The hearings backfired. Gates disclosed the new estimates, but his blundering attempt to explain changes in the method of estimating the Soviets' strength was misunderstood; due to a failure in coordination, Twining presented figures slightly different from Gates. That fed suspicions (which were strongly pushed by Senator Symington) that the Administration was "playing politics" with intelligence. And General Thomas Power, the commander of SAC, made a speech suggesting that an attack by 150 ICBMs and 150 IRBMs could destroy SAC before BMEWS was working. The Chief of Naval Operations scoffed openly at this claim, arguing that the Soviets could not launch a closely timed salvo of missiles that would hit all the targets simultaneously and had not practiced the mass firings needed. Twining took the same line in public, albeit less vehemently. Power and Twining, like Gates, stressed that the size and diversity of U.S. forces would make any Soviet superiority less than decisive.

Unfortunately, the Administration's attempts to straighten things out and take precautions against the danger outlined by Power confused things further. In further muddled testimony, Twining and Allen Dulles of the CIA presented different figures of estimated Soviet missiles, and an Air Force general disclosed the fact that the USAF's estimate was far higher than the NIE's.

Meanwhile, in February, the CIA had revised its estimate downward—cutting the projection for mid-1961 to just thirty-five ICBMs. If correct, that made an attack without warning impossible; but some in the Administration still thought an outside chance of that existed. Herbert York told his superiors that, if the Soviets had the maximum capability in mid-1961 listed in the NIE (he probably meant the one of December 1959), there might be "a critical period when they may be able to destroy virtually all our retaliatory forces by a perfectly coordinated surprise attack." He recommended accelerating construction of the Alaska BMEWS station and several Polaris submarines to avert this. Gates favored this; in April the Administration sought funds for six more Polaris submarines and eighteen more Atlas missiles.[12] Unfortunately for the Administration, this completed a picture of apparent confusion (if not dishonesty) and bending under outside pressures finally to do the right thing. But only the element of confusion had any reality.

U-2 AND DISCOVERER

Soon afterward, the U.S. government lost its best intelligence weapon. On May 1, 1960, a U-2 was shot down over the U.S.S.R., shortly before a summit conference was to meet in Paris. This was a major diplomatic embarrassment; and the United States lost the source of 90 percent of its intelligence.

Reconnaissance satellites came to the rescue. On August 11, after a dozen failures, Discoverer 13 was recovered in the Pacific; Discoverer 14 followed a few days later. The CIA's latest estimates, and a parallel assessment by the Defense Department's Weapons Systems Evaluation Group, indicated that there would be no "missile gap" at all. These estimates were known to Democratic leaders; nevertheless, John F. Kennedy made much use of the gap in his Presidential campaign. The role of the "missile gap" in the Democratic victory is imponderable, for many issues have been picked out as decisive in that close election.

In his last State of the Union address, on January 12, 1961, Eisenhower remarked that "the bomber gap of several years ago was always a fiction and the missile gap shows every sign of being the same." General Schriever, in an interview published January 23, endorsed this view.[13] It would be nearly a year before the new Administration admitted that they had been right.

When John F. Kennedy took office, public belief in the "missile gap" was still strong. Robert McNamara, the new Secretary of Defense, convinced by the same evidence that had reassured the previous Administration, soon decided it did not exist. Recklessly, he revealed this to reporters in an off-the-record session on February 6; the story became public the next day. The Administration hastily denied that the briefing had ever taken place. Later it claimed that McNamara had misunderstood the facts.

Officially, there was still a gap; on March 28, in a speech on the military budget, President Kennedy led the public to believe in it. In June 1961, McNamara reverted to a formula the Eisenhower Administration had used in 1959: There was a "missile gap," but no deterrent gap. In fact, the evidence against a gap piled up steadily from reconnaissance satellites and Oleg Penkovskiy, who disclosed that the U.S.S.R. had only a nominal ICBM capability. In May he reported that the Soviets had decided to scrap the R-7, which was already ten months behind schedule, as a weapon. The Americans knew that its successor ICBM had encountered difficulties.

The Administration seemed to have been embarrassed by the prominence of the "missile gap" in the election and unwilling to admit that it had been wrong and worse, that the President had known the truth all along. The

only excuse for its behavior was that Air Force intelligence, alone of
the agencies concerned, still insisted that the Soviets were deploying large
numbers of R-7s under camouflage. (The issue had now become estimating
current strength, and not just projecting the future.) In the summer of 1961,
the CIA concluded that the Soviets had at most thirty-five ICBMs. The
Air Force insisted it was right, but it produced no evidence and was
ignored.[14] In truth, Administration policies had not been based on the
assumption of a "missile gap"; indeed its decision on force levels—how
many missiles to deploy—had hardly been determined by any specific
view of enemy strength.

FORCE LEVELS

In its last days, the Eisenhower Administration had envisaged an
ultimate missile force of about 1,100 ICBMs and Polarises. The program
did not reflect the views of any particular service; the Navy wanted more
Polaris submarines (up to fifty) and the Air Force wanted more ICBMs.
Some Air Force elements wanted as many as 10,000 Minutemen, but the
Ballistic Missile Division thought 1,200 ICBMs of all sorts was sufficient.
The Chief of Staff finally put forward a figure of 1,850 Minutemen and
512 Polarises.

Kennedy and his advisers liked Polaris, the weapons system most
popular with Congress and informed opinion. In March 1961, the Administration decided to accelerate Polaris and Minuteman; SAC would be on
a higher state of ground alert. In total, 160 more Polarises and sixty
Minutemen would be purchased. But two of the eight planned Titan II
squadrons were canceled, along with plans to arm a cruiser with Polaris.
Minuteman's mobile version was deferred (and ultimately canceled). The
Administration decided to phase out some obsolete equipment sooner than
expected. Even then, the Administration did not base its policies on the
"missile gap" or an unlimited buildup of every sort of strategic weapon.
The final program, to be finished in 1967–1968, was set after many months
of bargaining and the public disclosure that the gap did not exist. Despite
many contradictory and even dishonest statements by McNamara about
the reasons for his decisions, the size of the U.S. force was not determined
by estimates of the expected Soviet force, or any particular nuclear
strategy, but by the desire to enforce a figure on the various services that
would please Congress. The Kennedy Administration ultimately settled
on a force of 1,000 Minutemen (although Kennedy's advisers thought 400
to 600 were enough), fifty-four Titan IIs, and 656 Polarises.[15] Thus, after

the gap dissipated, it programmed 75 percent more missiles than the previous Administration!

THE BERLIN CRISIS AND THE END OF THE "MISSILE GAP"

In 1961 Khrushchev resumed the Berlin crisis. He continued to exploit what was left of the "missile gap." The mishandling of the Bay of Pigs, the poor impression Kennedy made at the Vienna summit meeting, and other incidents made it seem that Khrushchev would encounter no great resistance. The 1961 phase of the Berlin crisis may have been more dangerous than was realized; for in the peculiar situation of the divided city, deep inside East Germany, much depended on the Soviets' appraisal of Western willpower. Unfortunately, they were optimistic about this point at least during the early stages of the crisis, even though the nuclear balance hardly favored them. They knew that the U.S. government no longer took the "missile gap" seriously, but Kennedy's reticence on this point let Khrushchev flourish his bogus superiority for a time. Moreover, Khrushchev had something that might partly replace the ICBM for purposes of intimidation— super-powerful thermonuclear bombs of up to 100 megatons. Politically, there were apparent points of vulnerability in the West's position, and the Soviet Ambassador to the United States (who was more extreme than Khrushchev) was known to have advised Moscow that in the last resort the United States would not fight over Berlin. Reportedly virtually all Soviet leaders doubted that the United States would use nuclear weapons over Berlin; and they thought that even if the Americans were so inclined, the Western Europeans would not be. Several unpleasant months followed.

The "missile gap," which had degenerated from a mistaken but genuine fear to a shabby political hoax, was a millstone around the neck of Western diplomacy until late in the crisis. But by September, the facts were leaking out. The respected correspondent Hanson Baldwin, who had long been skeptical of the gap and was not friendly to the Administration, disclosed the true state of affairs in the *New York Times* on September 19, 1961. The Administration itself apparently leaked information to a friendly columnist, Joe Alsop (long an alarmist about the gap) late in September. Deputy Secretary of Defense Roswell Gilpatric made a formal public revelation in October. He warned that a Soviet attack would be suicidal. U.S. forces were so strong and alert that they could deliver a retaliatory strike at least as big as anything the Soviets could deliver by striking first. He derided the Soviet superbombs as mere terror weapons. In fact, the Soviets did regard their superbombs as weapons whose probable aim was to jam radio and radar rather than destroy targets. Their Proton space booster may have been designed originally as a super-ICBM to carry such bombs.[16]

Ironically, Gilpatric's speech was the point at which the Americans swung back from overestimating the Soviets to underestimating them. In an odd fashion, many analysts felt guilty about the overestimation of the opposition manifested in the "missile gap" and the earlier, less influential bomber gap and were determined not to repeat it. (Strangely, few had felt guilt about the underrating of the Soviets, which was common until the last half of the 1950s.) Many who were engaged in defense matters leaped to the conclusion that the Soviets had not built a big ICBM force between 1957 and 1961 because they did not want a first-strike capability, or even a strong nuclear force. In a further illogical deduction, these individuals decided that since the Soviets had not wanted one in the late 1950s, they would never want it in the future. Many blamed Kennedy for provoking the Soviets to an enormous buildup later in the 1960s. The American program indeed ran beyond anything needed to counter the Soviets in the near term; but, judging by their later behavior, it merely set the jumping post higher for their later efforts to overtake the United States. As later analysts glumly concluded, "We build, they build. We stop, they build."[17]

In truth, the failure of the "missile gap" to develop was a near thing. It was due to the exceptional performance of men like von Neumann, Gardner, Schriever, and Raborn, and the Eisenhower Administration as a whole, and to fatal flaws in the Soviet ICBM program. Had the Soviets scaled down the R-7 to a two- or three-engine rocket (as the Americans did the Atlas) and/or devoted the effort to it that they wasted on cruise weapons, they might have had an effective ICBM far earlier. They might have had a force of 150 or more missiles before the Americans had an adequate warning system, Polaris submarines, or hardened bases. If it were not for that blunder, the nightmare of an attack without warning, which haunted the Eisenhower Administration until 1960, might have come to pass.

At any rate, the missile-gap episode was over. Some things written about it later exceeded in silliness anything that had been said in the late 1950s.[18]

THE CUBAN MISSILE CRISIS

The end of the "missile gap" and the unsatisfactory result of the Berlin crisis left Khrushchev desperate for success abroad, but stymied by the unsatisfactory power balance. A strong faction around his rival Frol Kozlov wanted stronger action against the West, while Khrushchev himself was not as peaceably inclined as is sometimes stated. Indeed Penkovskiy maintained that while Khrushchev might not want war just then, he looked forward to one eventually. Some elements in U.S. intelligence thought there were indications that the Soviets were preparing for war, or some action involving grave risks of war.[19] Yet, in view of the basic military balance, this seemed insane.

There was, however, a way to alter that balance radically. Medium- or intermediate-range missiles based in Cuba would pose a deadly threat, for they would outflank the American early warning system and could catch most of the American deterrent force—which still consisted overwhelmingly of bombers and soft missiles—on the ground.

We still know little about Khrushchev's decision to move strategic missiles to Cuba. Apparently he considered the idea in April 1962; he may have been prompted by his old associate Minister of Defense Rodion Malinovskiy. Khrushchev reportedly told the few in the Presidium who were informed of the plan that he would reveal the missiles himself after the U.S. elections. He claimed that if the missiles were discovered, Kennedy would not react sharply; at worst he would negotiate about the matter secretly and would swallow the missiles. He said that he had no plan to go to war. Although Foreign Minister Andrei Gromyko and Anastas Mikoyan warned that the Americans would find the missiles soon and react badly, both went along with Khrushchev. The precise aim of this dangerous move was apparently not made clear even to them, and it has never been explained satisfactorily. The official line after the crisis was that it was to deter an American invasion of Cuba, which the U.S. government did not plan and which Khrushchev probably knew it did not plan. Khrushchev in his memoirs, and other Communist leaders in private, declared that the missiles in Cuba had the additional purpose of making up the difference between Soviet and American strength in strategic weapons. But the move was more likely to provoke an invasion than prevent one, as Gromyko and Mikoyan knew; and there was a vast contradiction involved in the alleged assumption that the Americans were hell-bent on invading Cuba, on the one hand, and that they would accept Soviet missile bases there, on the other. It is hard to believe that, whatever his contempt for Kennedy, Khrushchev did not know that any American leader would have to get rid of those bases when they were revealed; and Kennedy had made clear to Khrushchev's son-in-law Alexei Adzhubei that any further increase of Soviet influence in Cuba would be intolerable. Strangely, Khrushchev made no apparent preparations for the crisis he was making inevitable; everything he did after the missiles were found in October was apparently an improvisation.

During May 1962, the plan was fleshed out. The Soviets reportedly planned to send twenty-four R-12 medium-range missile launchers, with forty-eight R-12s. Each launcher could fire one R-12 and then reload to fire a second in several hours. (According to some accounts, the second missile was just a spare and they never planned to send warheads for every rocket.) Sixteen R-14 IRBM launchers, with thirty-two R-14s, were to be sent; but the crisis broke before any arrived. (Some Cuban accounts, however, have recently reported that the Soviets planned to send over 100 missiles.) Between the R-12s and R-14s, they could hit almost every SAC base in the United States. The missiles were to be ready by a specific date in November or December, which has never been revealed.

Fidel Castro assented readily to the plan; there was a vast movement of soldiers and equipment by sea with remarkably effective secrecy. They landed at the port of Mariel, whose dock area was cleared of Cubans, and moved at night to sites in western Cuba. Work on the missile bases was fast and efficient—but the Soviets made fatal blunders. They did not camouflage their installations; apparently they were in too much of a rush to do so. There may have been a misunderstanding somewhere along the line, for Khrushchev and the commander of the Strategic Rocket Forces apparently expected the missiles to be camouflaged and were shocked to find in October that this had not been done. Moreover, the Soviets started the offensive missile sites before the surface-to-air missiles to defend them were ready. The latter may have been delayed by the discovery that the sites originally chosen were on swampy terrain. The Soviets may have relied too much initially on the existing Cuban radar system, which could not detect U-2s. They acted as though rigidly bound to finish both the R-12 and R-14 sites at the same early date. If it were not for these mistakes, the bases might have been finished undetected.[20]

There was a struggle on the American side over whether to look for the bases. To nearly everyone in the U.S. government, the idea of the U.S.S.R. putting strategic missiles in Cuba seemed unreal. One exception was the head of the CIA, John McCone. He and a few others pushed the Administration into a proper reconnaissance effort. On October 14, a U-2 flew over western Cuba; the next day photo interpreters found that an R-12 base was being built. The greatest crisis of the Cold War was underway.[21]

Although the reverse that the Soviets suffered during the Cuban Crisis has sometimes been exaggerated, it enforced more caution on Khrushchev and his successors. Europe became very quiet. Contrary to what is sometimes said, the Crisis did not cause the Soviet military buildup. That had been decided on before the Crisis.[22] The overall strategic balance, during the rest of the period discussed in this book, was quite stable. War was truly unthinkable, at least for a time. Surprise was no longer possible; indeed it hardly mattered. The growing U.S. missile force, in silos and submarines, could not have been destroyed even if the Soviets had suddenly gained numerical superiority. Missile accuracies were such that it would have taken two or more Soviet missiles to smash each Minuteman.

The situation was changed gradually by a major Soviet buildup, which began to appear in 1966, and new warheads and guidance systems. In 1969 the Soviets overtook the United States in numbers of ICBMs (some far bigger than anything the United States had) and began multiplying their originally small missile submarine force. In the qualitative race, in which the Americans remained ahead, missiles increased greatly in accuracy, and multiple independently targeted warheads were introduced. In theory it became possible for a single attacking missile to blast several missile silos. The rockets themselves, however, underwent relatively little change; Titan II would be replaced by the MX Peacekeeper, and Polaris by Poseidon (really an upgraded Polaris) and then by Trident (a new missile carried by a new class of submarine), but newer models of Minuteman remained the bulk of the U.S. force. The delivery vehicles in the U.S. arsenal by the end of the Cold War did not look too different from those of 1963. Electronics, and new ways to package warheads, became the driving force of the arms race.

There was a general reluctance or inability to predict these developments. In an instance, perhaps, of the "cry wolf" syndrome, the tendency of the late 1950s to overestimate Soviet capabilities was replaced by a long-term swing toward underestimating them, which lasted at least until the mid-1970s. Secretary McNamara, with his usual dogmatism, set the tone for the period when he claimed that the Soviets had just given up on the "quantitative arms race" and that there was "no indication that they were seeking to develop a strategic nuclear force as large as ours."[23] Each year, the projections of U.S. intelligence fell behind reality.

7

The Space Race, 1958–1960

The late 1950s saw the start of a race to be first in this or that aspect of space endeavor, first with unmanned and later with manned craft. Although the stakes in the space race lay in the realms of prestige and general technological and scientific advances, this was not apparent immediately; it seemed possible that space ventures might have direct military applications aside from reconnaissance. In this era, the general opinion was that the Americans were not doing too well in the space race; the far bigger loads the Soviets sent into space, and some of their dramatic firsts, outweighed the more numerous (although too often unsuccessful) American launches, even though the latter had more scientific significance. The U.S. and Soviet efforts jelled into true programs, with the unfortunate accompaniment of bureaucratization. Many vehicles still in use decades later appeared (these were adapted from weapons), and both sides developed large vehicles for "pure" space efforts.

EXPLORER AND VANGUARD

The already existing U.S. satellite efforts—for which the supply of launchers was limited—remained only erratically successful. Explorer I had puzzling results. On its way up, as expected, it had reported an increase of radiation; then its radiation counter had suddenly cut off. It was some time before it was possible to check on what had happened. Vanguard TV-3BU (the backup for the rocket that had failed so miserably in December 1957), launched less than a week after Explorer I, went out of control and broke up in mid-air. The Navy's only comfort was that Explorer II, launched on March 5, 1958, also failed—the Jupiter C's fourth stage did not fire. TV-4 finally put up Vanguard I, the second American satellite, on March 17. Weighing just 3.5 pounds, it carried only a radio transmitter and heat-measuring devices and could not check the radiation problem. But, unlike Explorer, it had solar batteries and reported for seven years from a much higher orbit. Tracking it disclosed the earth's true shape (slightly pear-shaped) and that the earth's mantle was less plastic than had been thought. (This was the beginning of the vindication of the long-ridiculed Wegener theory of continental drift.) It also showed the influence of magnetic drag and that the density of the fringe of the atmosphere was greater than had been thought. Vanguard scored only one more real success. After several failed launches, the project put up a full-scale satellite, Vanguard II, in February 1959, only to have the satellite itself malfunction. (Unlike the Army, the Vanguard program prudently did not number satellites that failed to reach orbit.) Two more launches failed. Left with no more mission launchers, the project salvaged TV-4BU, a leftover backup vehicle from the first phase of the program, and fitted it with a more powerful third stage. On September 18, 1959, it put up an efficiently instrumented 52-pound satellite that explored the earth's magnetic field and detected solar X-rays. The scientific value of the Vanguard program proved out of proportion to its success at orbiting satellites; the unreliability of the vehicle had almost defeated the perfection of instrumentation. Still, as we shall see, the effort put into building the rocket would be recompensed.

The cruder Explorers had a higher success rate. Explorer III, almost identical to Explorer I, flew on March 26, 1958. Like the first, its radiation counter seemed to "die" past a certain height. Aided by clues from earlier sounding rockets, James Van Allen, who had helped plan the radiation experiment in the Explorers, theorized that the counters had been over-loaded by extremely powerful radiation—belts of protons and electrons trapped in earth's magnetic field. Interaction between the belts and the upper air might be responsible for the aurora. Improved instruments were devised for Explorer IV to check the idea. The question of whether the Van Allen belts existed, and the discussion of their nature, suddenly touched on matters of high policy.

Some months earlier, Nicholas Christofilos, a physicist at the AEC's Livermore Laboratory, had observed that artificially injecting radiation into the earth's magnetic field (by exploding nuclear bombs) might produce artificial auroras and could wreck radio communications over a vast area for some time. Van Allen's work, indicating the existence of naturally trapped radiation, focused attention on the possibility that an enemy, by detonating a few bombs at high altitude or in near-earth space, could prevent detection of an attack. It was vital to explore the problem as soon as possible and beat the deadline imposed by the forthcoming nuclear test ban, since the Soviets might know more than the Americans. Sputnik III, orbited in May and the Soviets' sole space launch in 1958, was a 2,925-pound well-equipped geophysical laboratory that made the Explorers and Vanguards look feeble.

A series of tests, Project Argus, was devised hastily. On July 26, Explorer IV went up. Its improved detectors proved the existence of the Van Allen belts. On July 31 and August 10, Redstones fired from Johnston Island in the Pacific lifted H-bombs to heights of 48 and 28 miles respectively, in tests planned in 1957. They produced artificial auroras and blacked out communications in the central Pacific for hours. In Argus proper, three solid-fuel rockets launched from ships in the South Atlantic, in late August and early September, carried small A-bombs to 300 miles. The blasts produced artificial auroras and increased the strength of the radiation belts.

In 1962, after the end of the test moratorium, a later test over the Pacific, Starfish, proved even more spectacular. It increased enormously the strength of the Van Allen belts; its effects, which were unexpectedly severe, damaged several satellites. Although much was learned, the so-called rainbow bomb proved unimportant militarily. Its effects were not entirely predictable, there were limits to how intense it could be made, and the jamming effects could not be produced in the polar regions (which the Van Allens did not cover), which were the most critical points in nuclear warfare.[1]

A FAMILY OF SPACE LAUNCHERS

After Explorer IV, the last two Jupiter C's were expended in failed attempts to put up Explorer V and a small balloon. Jupiter-C and Vanguard would be replaced by a whole family of launchers, later models of which would form the backbone of the U.S. satellite-launching capability into the 1990s. Their development followed the example set by Jupiter C; they were modified military missiles—Jupiter, Thor, and Atlas—combined with various upper stages—Able, Able-Star, Delta, and Agena. Later they would be joined by adaptations of the Titan II and the Centaur and Burner upper stages. The missiles' fuel tanks would be enlarged, their main engines improved and supplemented by strap-on solid-fuel rockets, and the upper stages would be upgraded; but after many changes they would still be recognizable as the weapons that were designed in the 1950s, transformed for civilian purposes. This suggests how well the missiles and upper stages had been designed in the first place. But it may also be a commentary on the relative lack of spectacular progress in space travel after the 1950s.

The Juno II was the first but least useful of the new vehicles. ABMA engineers modified the Jupiter IRBM in the same way used to turn the Redstone into the Jupiter C/Juno I, lengthening its tanks and modifying it to carry the same sort of upper stages, albeit with slightly more powerful solid fuels. First tested in December 1958, it was used to launch more Explorer satellites and Pioneer moon probes. But the upper stages were still underpowered, and some critics thought ABMA was too interested in bigger projects, especially Saturn, to make Juno II work properly. Only ten were launched; Juno II put just three satellites in orbit and was retired after May 1960. But the lengthened Jupiter proved useful in the Saturn project.

Thor proved far more useful; far more Thors would be built for civilian purposes than for war. It was first used in space operations with the Able upper-stage combination (which was simply the second and third stages of the Vanguard vehicle, modified slightly). The Air Force had seen Able's potential in late 1957, as a way to provide high speeds for ICBM nose cone tests and fill in the gap before the specially developed Agena upper stage was ready. (It also considered using Thor-Able as a jury-rig ICBM— Thoric—but that proved unnecessary.) After the usual initial failure, Thor-Able proved effective. With an additional small solid-fuel stage, it was used—unsuccessfully—to launch the first Pioneers. Thor Able-Star used the lower half of the Able combination to reach low earth orbits.

In 1959 the Air Force shifted over to the Thor-Agena combination to launch its Discoverer reconnaissance satellites. NASA used Able only five times and then switched to the new Thor-Delta. Delta was developed from Able; it used a modified version of Vanguard's second stage (with a new guidance system and thrust chamber) and the third stage introduced in the last Vanguard vehicle. Thor-Delta—eventually called simply Delta by NASA—was primarily a civilian launcher; used until the 1990s, it went through thirteen major changes. Thor-Agena and Thor-Delta developed more or less in parallel; the Air Force introduced successive improvements to the Thor booster that were eventually taken over by NASA. First launched unsuccessfully in May 1960, the first version of Delta launched the Echo, Syncom, and Telstar communications satellites, the Tiros weather satellite, and additional Explorers and Pioneers.

In 1962 Delta A introduced an improved first-stage engine. Delta B had a second stage with bigger fuel tanks, enabling NASA to reach a 24-hour, geosynchronous orbit 22,300 miles up, in which a satellite would stay permanently over one point on earth. In 1962 the Air Force had ordered TAT (Thrust-Augmented Thor) with three 53,000-pound-thrust Castor strap-on solid-fuel rockets to increase takeoff thrust, as part of its Thor-Agena B combination. It first flew in March 1963. NASA introduced TAT as the lower part of Delta D in August 1964. Delta E had improved upper stages; the Air Force went on to introduce the Long Tank Thor, or Thorad. Douglas engineers lengthened Thor by nearly 20 percent; this became standard thereafter and was introduced in NASA's Delta L in 1968. Later versions of Delta increased the strap-ons to nine, and introduced redesigned upper stages and a new main engine. Retired in the 1980s, Delta was brought back after the *Challenger* disaster.

Part of the story of Thor-Agena has already been alluded to. Agena was originally reserved for vital military jobs, but in January 1959 NASA decided to use it in combination with Thor and Atlas for its own work. Thor-Agena was used to launch some research and weather satellites. The Agena upper stage went through several models; Agena B was introduced by the Air Force in October 1960 and NASA in September 1962. Agena D, restartable in space, was introduced in 1962 and could move satellites from orbit to orbit. In 1965–1966, the Air Force introduced Thor-Altair, which combined Thor with a solid-fuel upper stage borrowed from NASA's small Scout satellite launcher (developed from Polaris) and yet another solid-fuel upper stage, Burner II. A two-stage version, Burner II-A, was introduced in 1974.

Not all combinations proved successful. The marriage of Able and the Atlas ICBM was a notable failure. All three Atlas-Ables, used to launch moon probes in 1959–1960, failed spectacularly; along with Vanguard, Juno II, and the first Mercury-Redstone, Atlas-Able was a chief cause of the missile-gap era impression that U.S. rockets never worked.

Atlas alone became the first large American satellite; in December 1958, the complete sustainer-core stage of Atlas 10-B was put into orbit; although its useful payload was small, it carried a recorder to transmit the President's Christmas message. Atlas-Agena A, first introduced in February 1960, worked well after an initial failure. Atlas-Agenas launched the Air Force's heavier reconnaissance and experimental early warning satellites, while Thor-Agenas lifted the lighter reconnaissance satellites that depended on radio transmission of photographs rather than recovery of film packs. NASA used Atlas-Agena B to send Ranger probes to the moon and the first Mariner probes to Venus. Atlas-Agena D sent Mariner IV to Mars, provided targets for experimental rendezvous for Gemini manned space flights, and put Lunar Orbiter satellites into orbit around the moon. In 1964 the Atlas itself was stretched to provide a first stage with more fuel. Finally Atlas was coupled with the hydrogen-powered Centaur upper stage; although badly delayed, Atlas-Centaur carried Surveyor probes that could brake to a landing on the moon and large satellites into "geosynchronous" orbit.

Titan II was also adapted for space purposes; it was used to launch Gemini craft. Titan III-A, introduced in December 1964, added a restartable 16,000-pound-thrust third stage, dubbed a "transtage," using the same hypergolic fuels as the lower stages. Titan III-B, introduced in July 1966, had more powerful first-stage engines. With Agena D, it put medium-sized satellites in polar or "geosynchronous" orbits; Titan III-C, already introduced in June 1965, added two huge solid strap-ons (generating 1.2 million pounds of thrust each), which carried the whole vehicle for two minutes after liftoff until the main engines of the Titan proper fired. With a "transtage," it could put 3,000 pounds into "geosynchronous" orbit. Titan III-C, and a later version, Titan III-D, had the heaviest payload of any standard launchers and were used for military work. Titan III-E/ Centaur substituted a Centaur for the "transtage" and in the 1970s launched NASA's Viking probes to Mars, Voyager to the outer planets, and the Helios probe to the sun.[2] The workhorses of the American unmanned space effort, and much of the manned effort, were thus of military origin. The boosters and upper stages generally originated independently, and often preceded the creation of the U.S. civilian space agency.

THE NATIONAL AERONAUTICS AND
SPACE ADMINISTRATION

After Sputnik there was strong pressure to bring the space effort, or as much of it as possible, under one agency. Several elements within the government were potential nuclei for a space effort. The Federation of American Scientists and the powerful New Mexico Senator, Clinton Anderson, favored giving the job to an enlarged Atomic Energy Commission. Although its head, Lewis Strauss, was widely disliked, the Commission had a great deal of prestige among scientists and the public. Although much of its work was military oriented, it was a civilian organization that was already working on nuclear rockets, and that would appeal to President Eisenhower and others who disliked military domination of the space effort. There was, however, support for assigning space efforts to the military. The Air Force, backed by Dr. Edward Teller (then at the height of his prestige as the "father of the H-bomb"), sought control of the space program. In many ways it was a logical candidate; it was already working, successfully, on the biggest rockets the United States had and its own satellite program. It had great experience in managing large development programs. The Army was another candidate. It had been forced into an odd position; it was working on relatively short-range missiles and preliminary designs of very large space boosters. Unless it got the space mission or a big slice of it, it would have little excuse to keep von Braun's team. General Medaris, of course, was proud of ABMA's achievements and was sure that it was more efficient than the Air Force way of doing things. He feared that if the Air Force won, von Braun's team would be discarded and its talents lost. While the Army developed its own program for space exploration (parallel in many ways to that envisaged by the USAF), it did not really expect to vault over the Air Force and get the whole space job. Instead it joined other elements in urging that the space effort be assigned to an enlarged version of the Advanced Research Projects Agency. Medaris, unlike the Air Force, was on good terms with ARPA's imaginative head, Roy Johnson, whom the Air Force's chief scientist, Herbert York, viewed as insane.

Had the AEC gained control of the space effort, it is likely that it would have taken a drastically different course with more emphasis on nuclear propulsion. That might also have been true had a military agency gotten the job. Both the AEC and the military were more inclined to take risks than the National Advisory Committee for Aeronautics, which won the struggle.

Right after Sputnik, NACA's director, Hugh Dryden, started a campaign for the space job. NACA was not an inevitable choice. A small applied-research agency oriented mainly to work on aircraft, it had no experience in developing hardware or managing big programs. Although it had accomplished much, it was not esteemed among scientists, and its chief customers, the armed forces, still blamed it for America's lag in developing jet engines in the 1930s and 1940s. But it was already on at least the fringes of space with the X-15 research craft, and its Pilotless Aircraft Division and the Lewis Flight Laboratory were doing significant research on space (the latter campaigned actively for space activities).

Dryden chose Abraham Silverstein of Lewis to formulate a civilian space program. The inclinations of the top political leaders and their advisers aided Dryden. The Johnson Committee recommended a separate civilian space-only agency that shut out the AEC and the military. Killian and the PSAC, seconded by the Bureau of the Budget, concluded that NACA was the best nucleus for such an agency but must be altered to give it a single executive head and a development capability. On March 5, 1958, Eisenhower approved the choice; Congress quickly followed suit. The

National Aeronautics and Space Administration was formed in October, under T. Keith Glennan as Chief Administrator. It was a complex, perhaps overcomplex, assortment of semiautonomous field centers and programs. In August it was assigned all but overtly military manned space flight. It took control of the Vanguard program and the Jet Propulsion Laboratory in December, although for a long time JPL remained autonomous with an uneasy relationship with NASA headquarters.

Logically NASA should have absorbed von Braun's team, but the Secretary of the Army, loath to see his empire diminish, blocked an early transfer. The Administration, however, specified that von Braun's primary mission would be to support NASA. Finally, in late 1959, the Administration decided to break up ABMA. Von Braun and most of the agency joined NASA in July 1960, forming its George C. Marshall Space Flight Center. In September 1959, the Defense Department gave the Air Force all military space work. In practice, that amounted to controlling reconnaissance satellites; but for nearly a decade the service hoped for its own manned program.[3]

The Army and Air Force had outlined long-term programs, both emphasizing manned flight. The Army plan, elaborated by von Braun in late 1957, envisaged putting a payload of a ton in orbit, soft-landing a probe on the moon as early as 1960, and establishing a four-person space station in 1962 and a manned moon landing by mid-1966, to be followed by a permanent space station and lunar outpost by 1973 and manned trips to the planets. A later version, presented in July 1958, envisaged a fifty-person space station for 1967 and a flight to Mars or Venus in 1977. Von Braun expected the development of winged reusable vehicles and nuclear rockets by the 1970s. Estimates of costs, as well as timetables, were highly optimistic; the Army estimated that it could have a small moon base by November 1966 for just $6 billion. In April 1958, the Air Force presented an elaborate but shorter-ranged five-year plan to culminate in a permanent moon base. Some in the Army and Air Force thought that the base would have a direct military role. In their view, space, and particularly the moon, was "the high ground" which would control the earth. General Homer Boushey argued that at least part of the U.S. nuclear deterrent should be based on the moon. Small moon-based missiles could be controlled en route to targets under permanent observation. That would prevent a Soviet surprise attack, for in order to block American retaliation the Soviets would have to hit bases on the moon two days before any attack on earth.

This was only one of the early schemes for space-based weapons which proliferated in the late 1950s. ARPA especially pondered antisatellite weapons to deal with Soviet orbital bombs, and space-based interceptors to stop incoming ICBMs. In practice, however, offensive tasks could be done better and more cheaply on earth. Space-based defense against ICBMs might hold eventual promise but ran ahead of the available technology. General Schriever, the chief planner of the Air Force program, did not base his arguments for aiming at a moon base on such plans; instead he argued that a moon base would advance technology and aid things that did have military applications. Many officers, notably Medaris, were interested in space exploration for its own sake. Von Braun's military master had become his disciple, just like Dornberger.[4]

ADVANCED ENGINES AND BOOSTERS

The Eisenhower Administration would not buy long-range programs of the sort outlined by von Braun. Nevertheless, in 1958 it authorized development of three items of long-range interest: the Saturn superbooster, the giant F-1 engine, and the Centaur upper stage. NASA inherited these projects from the military, and they proved critical to its success. Without them, the Apollo program, at least in the form it took, would have been inconceivable.

In December 1957, Krafft Ehricke of von Braun's old team, now at Convair/General Dynamics, proposed an upper stage using liquid hydrogen to be mounted atop the Atlas and carry payloads into space. He specifically envisaged it as carrying a Mars probe. When ready, it would match or surpass the Soviet ICBM in lifting capacity. ARPA gave the 30,000-pound-thrust Centaur the nod in August 1958; it was transferred from the USAF to NASA in July 1959. Its development was long, costly, and troubled, but it was the entering wedge for the actual use of liquid hydrogen as a fuel.

Well before Sputnik, both the Air Force and ABMA had contemplated boosters far bigger than ICBMs, but they took different routes to this goal. The Air Force, as before, led in promoting the development of huge new engines by North American's Rocketdyne Division (no precise vehicle was yet envisaged), while ABMA, dependent on the Air Force-Rocketdyne nexus for engines, envisaged grouping existing or soon-to-be-available engines in a specific vehicle. As early as 1955, the Air Force had pressed studies of a 400,000-pound-thrust engine. Rocketdyne argued that it could build one delivering a million pounds of thrust; the service's Scientific Advisory Board suggested that an engine with 5 million pounds of thrust was a desirable target, but the Air Force balked at that. It decided to go for the million-pound goal in two stages. E-1, with 360,000 to 380,000 pounds of thrust, would come first. But North American was already working on models of various components, and a full-scale thrust chamber, for the bigger F-1 by 1958. NASA took over the project; it sought a larger version of the F-1 that would generate 50 percent more thrust and signed a contract for this in January 1959. At about that time, Rocketdyne's first tests reached the million-pound thrust mark, and NASA pondered a vehicle, tentatively called Nova, to use the F-1. The E-1 was dropped.

In April 1957, ABMA had begun design studies for a space booster, at first tentatively called Super-Jupiter, with a first stage developing 1,500,000 pounds of thrust. Later renamed Juno V, it was expected to use four E-1 engines. After Sputnik there was a market for big boosters. ARPA initially inclined toward a smaller design, Juno IV, but Roy Johnson gradually warmed to Juno V. At the suggestion of ARPA engineers, he urged clustering available engines instead of waiting for E-1s, and von Braun decided to substitute eight H-1s, uprated Jupiter engines. It was later estimated that this decision saved $60 million and two years of work. In August 1958, the Defense Department approved the ABMA booster program; von Braun secured its redesignation as Saturn in February 1959. Eventually it would be called Saturn C-1, then Saturn I and IB, as Saturn became the name for a family of vehicles (some of the later ones adopted the F-1 engine). The difficulty of making fuel tanks for a captive test led ABMA engineers to see that Saturn I's first stage could be formed by clustering eight Redstone tanks around a core tank taken from a Juno II— avoiding the slow, costly job of retooling for bigger tanks. What form Saturn's upper stages would take was uncertain; ABMA inclined for a time toward using a Titan ICBM as a second stage and a Centaur, or perhaps a nuclear rocket, as a third stage.

But Saturn hovered on the edge of cancellation. Herbert York, now Director of Defense Department Research and Engineering, argued that it had no military purpose. Any military work could be done by existing ICBMs, although York hedged by arguing that an Air Force proposal, Titan C or Super-Titan, using four clustered Titan engines, could replace Saturn. Medaris denied York's premise and belittled Titan C as just an engineering study, while Saturn was well underway. Bitter politicking resulted. There was much opposition to York in the Defense Department as well as NASA; in September 1959, an interagency review decided to keep it going. Titan C was dropped. Nevertheless, most agreed with York that Saturn was not really a military task. In October 1959, Eisenhower ruled that it should go with von Braun to NASA.

Von Braun and other factions were bitterly at odds over Saturn's upper stages. Von Braun, with bad memories of experiments with liquid hydrogen in the 1930s, favored using conventional fuels. Others thought that using conventional fuels, or simply using Titan and Centaur, was too limited. NASA headquarters inclined toward hydrogen-fueled upper stages, and bigger ones than Centaur, to provide much greater payloads for deep-space missions. A Saturn Vehicle Evaluation Team was established under Abraham Silverstein, a domineering personality and a long-standing proponent of hydrogen. Finally von Braun himself was convinced, and in December 1959 Silverstein's committee unanimously recommended developing hydrogen-fueled upper stages. Saturn I's S-IV second stage would use clustered Centaur engines; the S-IVB, used in Saturn IB, would use a single big engine, eventually designated J-2. (In the end it would be decided not to have a third stage.) Along with the decision to build the F-1, this was an early vital landmark on the road to the moon. In January 1960, Saturn got the highest national priority.

NASA had visualized even bigger rockets, generically called Nova, using the F-1—itself often called the Nova engine. NASA's report on booster development in January 1959 had envisaged a four-stage Nova using four F-1s in the first stage, and one in the second stage, with two liquid hydrogen upper stages. By the end of 1959, Silverstein's committee outlined further versions of the Saturn family, some using F-1s and intermediate in size between Saturn I and Nova. Nova itself grew bigger. By June 1960, as a vehicle for a manned trip direct from earth to the moon, it was expected to use no less than eight F-1s in its first stage. As the Apollo project took form in 1961, both later additions to the Saturn family and Nova grew bigger. Saturn C-8 (never built) had a first stage with eight F-1s, while the last versions of Nova (which was never built either) had ten to twelve F-1s. The Saturn V, which took people to the moon, had a first stage with five F-1s and was actually bigger than the first version of Nova.

NASA had its hands full with Saturn I. Despite the minimization of development of new components, merely scaling up in size caused all sorts of problems. Propellants sloshing around in the tanks proved a problem; the effects of the engine exhausts threatened to melt or otherwise render the rocket's base unstable. Even uprating the well-tried Jupiter engines went slowly.[5]

THE FIRST RACE TO THE MOON

Meanwhile, the Americans tried to use existing equipment to beat the Soviets to the next objective in space—sending a probe to the moon. Many engineers involved, and Roy Johnson himself, were skeptical of success, but in March 1958 ARPA authorized Project Mona. The Air Force would use Thor-Able and the Army Juno II to launch probes under the name Pioneer. The Air Force's Pioneers, packaged by Space Technology Laboratories, were to fly past the moon and, if a retro-rocket worked, go into orbit around it. The much smaller Army probes, developed by JPL, were to near-miss the moon. On August 17, the first Thor-Able blew up shortly after liftoff. On October 11, another Thor-Able got Pioneer I into space, but the upper stages provided less power than planned. The probe reached 71,700 miles from earth and then fell back. But it showed the extent of the Van Allen belts. Pioneer II was launched on November 8, but one stage did not ignite. A Juno II launched Pioneer III on December 6. Like Pioneer I, it did not reach escape velocity and fell back from 66,580 miles out. But its instruments worked better and showed that there were two distinct Van Allen belts. A second Juno II, launched on March 3, 1959, attained escape velocity, but one upper stage burned longer than planned; Pioneer IV went far off course, missed the moon widely, and went into orbit around the sun. In July a third Juno II went off course and had to be destroyed after liftoff. A switch to Atlas-Able proved disastrous. Between November 1959 and December 1960, all three failed.[6]

The Soviets had done little in space since Sputnik III; but they had committed to a full-scale program of probes in late 1957, as well as manned flights. They quickly developed an 11,000-pound-thrust liquid-fuel upper stage for the R-7, and they planned to launch moon shots in 1959, Mars probes in 1960, and Venus probes in 1961. Their first moon probe, Luna 1, launched on January 2, 1959, was intended to hit the moon but missed by a few thousand miles. It was the first human vehicle to exceed escape velocity. Luna 2, launched on September 12, 1959, hit the moon two days later. Its instruments showed that the moon had no magnetic field or radiation belts. This was a tremendous gain for Soviet prestige. The next month, the Soviets scored an even greater success. The 955-pound Luna 3, the first Soviet craft to use solar cells, looped around the moon and photographed its never before seen far side. The automatically developed pictures, transmitted by television, were crude but showed large features like the Sea of Moscow. They disclosed the surprising fact that the far side differed from that facing earth. It consisted mostly of heavily cratered highlands and had few of the dark "maria" common on the near side.[7] Luna 3 was a great achievement, but Americans in 1959 appreciated it through gritted teeth. The Soviets had won the first race to the moon.

PROJECT MERCURY

NACA and the U.S. Air Force had been working on winged maneuverable vehicles to explore at least the fringes of space before Sputnik; but, in addition to other problems, the thrust needed to put them in orbit was years away. Atlas, the biggest available American booster, could put only 3,000 pounds into a low earth orbit.

Even before Sputnik, the Air Force had pondered a simpler craft that would enter like the nose cone of a ballistic missile and could be developed quickly. After Sputnik there was a rash of proposals for capsules of this sort from the armed forces and manufacturers. Early in 1958, the Air Force proposed an essentially automatic capsule, which would carry a passenger rather than a pilot, as part of its overall program pointing toward a moon landing. NACA was interested but withdrew from direct cooperation as part of its campaign to capture space for itself. Although the Air Force's overall program was rejected, ARPA approved the Air Force capsule scheme, called Man in Space Soonest. It was to use a Thor plus an upper stage; later an Atlas was substituted. Army proposals for a suborbital flight using a Redstone were rejected by ARPA and NASA, which inherited the Air Force project when all manned flight was assigned to the new agency. Engineers at its Langley, Virginia center, headed by Max Faget (later the designer of the Space Shuttle), were already designing a capsule. In November 1958, they became part of the Space Task Group and manned satellite program under Robert Gilruth. The Space Task Group later became the nucleus of the Manned Spacecraft Center, which moved to Houston in 1961. NASA and ARPA had already agreed on plans for manned capsule flights in October; the program now included preliminary suborbital flights like those envisaged earlier by the Army, using Redstones and perhaps Jupiters. Specifications were sent out to contractors; in November the project was dubbed Mercury at the suggestion of Abraham Silverstein. In January 1959, McDonnell Aircraft, which had done some work on the Air Force's proposals earlier, was selected to build the capsule.

The capsule was a truncated cone with a cylinder containing parachutes and a radio transmitter atop it. A jettisonable solid-fuel retro-rocket would slow the capsule for reentry; a convex "ablative" fiberglass heatshield attached to its base would then burn away. The capsule's attitude was controlled by tiny hydrogen peroxide thrusters. If something went wrong during liftoff, a rocket mounted on a tower atop the Mercury would jerk it away from the booster.

The President had decided to use military test pilots to man Mercury.

The Mercury Seven, announced in April 1959—John Glenn, Alan Shepard, Gus Grissom, Scott Carpenter, Walter Schirra, Deke Slayton, and Gordon Cooper—became instant national heroes before they actually did anything, rather to their own surprise. Although they were able, they were not from the top rank of military test pilots, who jeered at Mercury astronauts as just "spam in a can." The USAF had actually discouraged its best pilots from applying; it wanted them for its Dyna-Soar winged craft. NASA's publicity machine and the *Time-Life* empire, which gained the rights to the astronauts' stories, contrived to show them, and to some extent the Mercury project as a whole, in a misleading way. An intelligent group (average IQ 135), which included some interesting men and some odd-balls, was made to appear dull and uniform. In accordance with Henry Luce's prejudices, all were portrayed as typical small-town boys of middle-class backgrounds with ideal family lives—certain aspects of which (e.g., Cooper's separation from his wife) were ignored. In fact, their backgrounds were diverse and often differed from what the public was led to suppose. Glenn (a rock-ribbed Presbyterian in a profession and era when such commitment was suspect) and Grissom were both from working-class families. The astronauts might have been born in small towns, but not all had been raised there. Carpenter, the sole astronaut with a deep interest in space exploration for its own sake, came from a wealthy Boulder, Colorado family and was the son of a chemist. Shepard and Cooper came from military families, and Schirra's family had military connections; these were not typical middle-class backgrounds between the World Wars. It is a commentary on the changes in American attitudes that a decade later the fact that all were (or were supposed to be) typical middle-class white Protestants, which Luce doted on in 1959, would have caused grumbling, although it reflected no discrimination in the selection process, and that when Tom Wolfe tried to make them interesting in the book *The Right Stuff*, he did so by inverting their stereotypes from bland nice guys to hard-drinking womanizers—which some of them were. NASA's handling of Mercury, like much of its later public relations, seemed designed to make space travel as dull as possible. Over the protests of von Braun, it unduly played down the risks the astronauts faced.

In March 1959, NASA hoped for a manned Redstone flight in April 1960 and an Atlas orbital flight in September of the same year. (To test some features of the capsule, short-range unmanned flights would be made using a specially built "Little Joe" booster built of clustered Sergeant rockets.) In May Mercury, which already showed signs of slipping, got a DX priority.

The project took longer and cost far more than expected. A costly new tracking system was needed. In October 1958, von Braun had expected to have the Mercury-Redstone ready by the end of 1959; but work on it dragged far into 1960. It was basically a modified Jupiter C without upper stages, but it reverted to alcohol fuel (which was burned in the latest-model engine used in tactical Redstones) with some backup systems to increase safety. The abort-sensing and escape systems, which were intended to save the pilot if something went wrong, also posed unexpected difficulties. The main problem, however, was the capsule itself. Building it proved far more difficult than expected; it used titanium and nickel steels that were difficult to work with. The astronauts, each specializing in some aspect of the capsule or booster, rightly criticized the poor visibility and awkward exit from the capsule. Windows and a hatch that the astronauts could open themselves were installed. The astronauts wanted to be pilots, to control reentry, and they got their way here too, although McDonnell engineers had independently decided that this was desirable.

In mid-1960 it was still hoped that the capsule would fly before the end of the year. But MA-1, the first test launch of an Atlas carrying an unmanned capsule (on July 29), was a disaster. The Atlas exploded a minute after liftoff; the cause was never pinpointed. This set back orbital flights by six months.

The first unmanned Mercury-Redstone test was downright embarrassing. On November 21, the Redstone rose 4 inches; then its engine stopped and it fell back to the launch pad. Then the escape rocket fired, tearing itself away from the Mercury capsule, which stayed on the Redstone. Later the parachutes deployed; fortunately there was no wind, so they did not fill and pull the rocket over. It seemed that both the Redstone and the escape system had failed. MA-1 was bad enough, but the failure of the seemingly dependable Redstone shook everyone. Investigation showed that an umbilical connection that supplied power to the Redstone before and during liftoff had broken prematurely, causing the engine to cut off. Then the automatic sequences jettisoning the escape tower and deploying parachutes took place, just as they were supposed to after the end of powered flight! Although the Mercury-Redstone itself had not failed, and although it flew perfectly on December 19 and again (it carried a chimpanzee on January 31), von Braun's team insisted on a third test flight. The administration of the lagging Mercury program was widely criticized; its reputation with the public and the new President's advisers remained low. It was not at all clear, to those directly involved, that the American manned space program would go on.[8]

LONG-RANGE PLANNING AND
THE ORIGINS OF APOLLO

Neither NACA/NASA nor the Eisenhower Administration had endorsed any of the long-range plans submitted in 1958, although the Administration had bought the vehicle and engine projects that such programs would need.

It was clear that unmanned satellites—or research, weather observation, communications, and navigational aids—would be launched as far into the future as anyone could see; but there were no set plans for any manned efforts beyond Mercury or unmanned probes beyond the moon. (Venus probes using Atlas-Able were dropped when it was downgraded to a lunar launcher and proved unequal even to that task.)

In late 1958 and early 1959, the Jet Propulsion Laboratory developed tentative plans for circumlunar probes and flybys of Mars and Venus. It viewed them as a first step toward trips to the moon and the planets. The later conflict between advocates of manned and unmanned exploration was as yet hardly visible; JPL was enthusiastic about manned flight. It intended to launch its probes with Atlas and a new upper stage, Vega, developed in cooperation with General Electric.

The Administration, always open-handed toward unmanned exploration, readily authorized Vega in March 1959, but by the end of the year NASA realized that Agena and Centaur could do the job more cheaply. Vega was canceled. That ended JPL's role in propulsion; henceforth, despite its title, it was a center for developing instrument packages. By December 1959, it planned to send five Ranger impact probes to the moon, using Atlas-Agena B, in 1961–1962; they would take pictures on the way in and perhaps carry an instrument package designed to survive impact. It was hoped that beginning in 1962, Atlas-Centaur would send Mariner flyby probes to Venus and Mars. JPL's plan was integrated into an overall program that NASA adopted that same month. Such unmanned work was not controversial.

Administrator Glennan wanted and expected manned efforts after Mercury. In the spring of 1959, he formed a Research Steering Committee for Manned Space Flight under the engineer Harry Goett. The Committee was composed of representatives from NASA's centers and major divisions. Its members had long pondered follow-ups to Mercury (such as building a space station, conducting a circumlunar flight, or achieving a moon landing); but in the late 1950s it was generally assumed that all three would take place, probably in that order.

Interest swiftly concentrated on flights to the moon, although in the minds of people at that time that did not exclude a space station or other objectives. Circumlunar flights and moon landings both needed vehicles that were capable of reentering earth's atmosphere at escape velocity and would withstand much more heat than vehicles returning from earth orbit, but otherwise they were quite different tasks. A flyby or orbit around the moon was far simpler than landing on it, requiring less total rocket thrust and less complex equipment. (The abortive Soviet moon program planned to use different vehicles for each job.)

At its first meeting, the Goett group outlined nine possible objectives, including a manned maneuverable satellite, a manned spacelab, a moon landing, and landings on Mars and Venus. Max Faget, who represented the Space Task Group, and George Low, who nominally (but not actually) headed the manned space program and supervised the Space Task Group, proposed making a moon landing the next major objective. (Both men would play vital roles in the Apollo program.) The Committee's second meeting in June endorsed this, and the Committee dropped landings on other planets as a specific objective. It reviewed the major alternative methods to get to the moon and the major technical problems each would face. All would require storing fuels in space, developing a throttleable engine for the moon landing, and using fuel or solar cells for auxiliary power.

In August 1959, the Space Task Group's New Projects Panel recommended developing a three-man spacecraft capable of reentry at escape velocity, to serve as both a circumlunar craft and transport to and from a laboratory in earth orbit (but not yet for a moon landing). At the end of 1959, NASA's Program Planning Office recommended establishing a space station in the late 1960s, and landing on the moon (using Nova) in 1970 or after. The more cautious official long-range plan, adopted by NASA in December (but not endorsed by higher authority), envisaged introducing the Thor-Delta, Atlas-Agena, and Scout launchers in 1960 and putting up weather satellites and passive reflector communications satellites in that year. In 1961 there should be manned Mercury flights and the introduction of Atlas-Centaur and Ranger probes. Mars and Venus probes should follow in 1962, with Saturn flying the year after. Circumlunar flights, establishment of a space station, and Nova flights should start in 1968; a manned moon trip was envisaged for 1975 or so. Glennan regarded the latter as part of an orderly program in which scientific work would have first priority; he did not envisage a crash program to go to the moon. He encouraged NASA's designers and industry to start examining the moon problem.

Exploration of the three-person craft recommended by the Space Task Group continued; in mid-1960 Silverstein dubbed it Apollo. It became the manned payload for Saturn-class vehicles. Study contracts for Apollo were given to Convair, General Electric, and Martin in October. Apollo was to have a fourteen-day endurance—long enough for a moon voyage—but it was still assumed that a trip involving an actual landing on the moon would be made by some post-Apollo craft.

The Administration was far from endorsing a moon landing. The Presidential Science Advisory Committee's Man in Space Panel estimated that a moon landing would cost between $25 billion and $38 billion. That horrified Eisenhower; he accepted its advice that manned space flight was not justified on scientific grounds alone. NASA had to persuade him not to state flatly that there was no commitment to manned flights after Mercury. He followed the Bureau of the Budget's advice not to fund actual development of the Apollo craft, he limited work to research, and he cut back on funds for the upper stages of Saturn.[9]

SATELLITES

During 1960 the Americans tentatively began commercial use of near-earth space, with experimental weather observation and communications satellites. Tiros (Television Infrared Observation Satellite) was put up on April 1 by a Thor-Able; it could track large-scale weather systems. Operational weather satellite systems were put into orbit in 1966. On August 12, a Thor-Delta launched a passive communications satellite, Echo I—a 100-foot balloon of aluminized plastic, big enough to be seen easily by the naked eye, and readily reflecting radio waves. A Thor-Able-Star orbited Courier 1B, the first active communications satellite—capable of receiving and relaying messages—for the Army Signal Corps on October 4. It was successful but short-lived. The Bell System had already outlined a full-scale commercial communications satellite system; a series of experimental Bell and RCA active satellites, Telstar and Relay, were launched in 1962 by Thor-Deltas. They relayed occasional commercial programs. Syncom, an active satellite in geosynchronous orbit, was launched in February 1963 by a Thor-Delta with an extra stage. Full-scale commercial service was started during 1965–1966.

In 1960 the Air Force finally attained success with the Discoverer series of prototype recoverable reconnaissance satellites. They were also the first satellites to be put in polar orbits; Vandenberg Air Force Base had been developed precisely for polar launches. The returning Discoverer capsules were, if possible, to be recovered *before* they landed in the sea—specially equipped transport planes were to snatch them in mid-air. The true purpose of the Discoverers was heavily veiled, although the Soviets probably were not fooled; some of the recovery capsules contained nominal biological experiments in which insects and other life forms were to be exposed to space conditions.

Discoverer 1 was launched on January 21, 1959; the Thor-Agena put it in orbit but the satellite's stabilization system failed. The capsule of Discoverer 2, launched on April 13, apparently returned to earth but was not recovered. Ten more Discoverers failed; either the Thor or Agena failed, or the stabilization system failed, or the retro-rocket misfired, or something else went wrong. Only Discoverers 6 and 11's recovery capsules came down, and they were not found. On August 10, Discoverer 13 orbited successfully. The next day its capsule was recovered from the sea near Hawaii. On August 19, Discoverer 14's capsule, with the first high-quality photographs, was snared in mid-air by a C-119. The pilot received a Distinguished Flying Cross; the satellite system replaced the U-2, just in time. Discoverer 15's capsule was lost, but after that success was fairly steady, and improved boosters launched bigger Discoverers with a larger film supply. Ultimately thirty-eight Discoverers were launched through February 1963, twenty-six reached orbit, and twelve capsules were recovered.[10]

THE SOVIETS: MARS PROBES AND MEN IN SPACE

Late in 1958—perhaps only after the Americans clearly decided on Mercury—the Soviet leaders gave a final go-ahead to their own plans for manned orbital flights, using the R-7 and an improved version of the upper stage used to launch the Lunas. Korolev and others dismissed suborbital flights as unnecessary risks and a waste of time. Design of a manned satellite was finished by May 1959. Korolev would have liked to have it land in the sea. But Khrushchev overruled him; he wanted to be sure that cosmonauts landed within Soviet territory. Cushioning an impact on land, however, was difficult, so the designers decided to have the pilot eject during descent and parachute down. The Soviets were a bit embarrassed by this, and for many years they tried to hide the fact that their first cosmonauts landed separately from their spacecraft. (The rules governing international aeronautical records—which were not written with space travel in mind—insisted that to be counted as valid, a flight had to end with a pilot aboard.) The Vostok (East) spacecraft was a good design, although very heavy (over 10,000 pounds compared to only 3,000 for the Mercury). It was later adapted for the unmanned Cosmos photo-reconnaissance satellites and the Voskhod multimanned craft. If only because the Soviet engineers had more weight to play around with, it was safer in some ways than the Mercury, despite the cosmonauts' having to bail out. It consisted of a spherical cabin for the pilot, a separate instrument module, and a retro-rocket below it. Only the passenger module would land. It was weighted at one end to assume almost automatically the correct position during reentry; and it was coated completely with "ablative" material, unlike the Mercury, which had to be positioned carefully for reentry. The cosmonaut had supplies for a flight of ten days; he could last until the natural decay of the Vostok's low orbit led to reentry, and he stood a chance of survival even if his retro-rocket failed. He breathed an atmosphere of normal composition, unlike the Mercury pilots, who used pure oxygen (which, grim experience would show, was far more dangerous). But there was less for the cosmonaut to do; his craft was fully automated and, especially on the first missions, the cosmonaut was really just a passenger. In late 1959, twenty Soviet Air Force test pilots were selected for training; they were mostly younger than their American counterparts.

The first Vostok was launched, as a Korabl-Sputnik (*korabl* means "ship"), on May 15, 1960. But it did not return; its retro-rocket shot it into a higher orbit instead of slowing it down. A Korabl-Sputnik carrying two dogs, under TV observation, as well as rodents, insects, and plant life was sent into orbit on August 19 and was recovered the next day. The dogs and their companions were the first living things to return from orbit; the Soviets missed having the first recovery from orbit by a week. But another Korabl-Sputnik burned up on reentry on December 1. Solution of the problem evidently took some time; but two Korabl-Sputniks returned successfully in March 1961. The Soviets encountered a final hurdle: In a test of the landing system in February, the parachutist was killed. The hatch through which he ejected was too small. It was redesigned hastily; the Soviets were poised to put the first man into space.

The Soviets ran into serious problems with their interplanetary probes, which were to be launched by the R-7, with the improved second stage and a third escape stage. These plans fell afoul of a design flaw in the new escape stage, grossly unreliable electronics, and leadership blunders. The new stage usually would not fire in free fall. For the next few years, most Soviet interplanetary probes that reached orbit were stuck there, and the few that went to other planets suffered radio failure.

In October 1960, there was a launch window for flights to Mars. This seemed most convenient for Khrushchev, who was visiting New York to address the United Nations. He expected to reap great propaganda by getting at least one Mars probe underway; and although the Soviets were suffering more launch failures than the West realized, Khrushchev expected success. But two Mars probes, launched on October 10 and 14, apparently never reached orbit.

A third probe was available. Marshal Nedelin, head of the Strategic Rocket Force, which launched all Soviet spacecraft, would have preferred to pass up the launch window and wait until the apparent problem was solved. But he was under great pressure. A launch was attempted on the night of October 23–24. The R-7 simply did not fire. Routine "safing" commands were sent to shut off the vehicle's electrical systems. Normal procedures called for a long wait before engineers inspected the rocket; but Nedelin ordered them out immediately. He and his staff joined them. The lower stages had shut down properly, but the top stage had not; a timer started its engine on schedule. It blew up the R-7, killing up to 190 people, including Nedelin. The cream of the Strategic Rocket Force was wiped out. The Soviets tried to hide the disaster, reporting that Nedelin had died in a plane crash, but the news leaked out in a distorted form. Penkovskiy and other sources mistakenly reported that Nedelin and the rest had died when a nuclear-powered rocket exploded; there were other reports that a new ICBM had been involved.

The Soviets blundered ahead when a launch window opened for Venus. On February 14, a probe reached orbit, but the escape stage failed to fire. The Soviets covered up by calling the probe a new type of Heavy Sputnik. When they launched again the escape stage worked, sending Venera 1 on its way. But radio contact was lost two weeks later.[11]

Although the Soviets had their share of problems, most of the world was convinced that they were far ahead of the Americans. The Americans had detected the Van Allen belts and solar X-rays; introduced solar cells and made the first television pictures of earth; launched the first weather, communications, and polar-orbit satellites; and made the first recovery from orbit. But the Soviets had scored most of the *spectacular* firsts. They had launched the first satellite, were the first to reach escape velocity, the first to hit the moon, the first to see its far side, and the first to send animals into orbit and recover them. They were about to score one more success, with immense impact.

8

Humans in Orbit and Interplanetary Probes, 1961–1966

On April 12, 1961, the first human left earth for a flight into space. Major Yuri Gagarin rode Vostok 1 into orbit; after 108 minutes and just one revolution, he landed with no ill effects. Everything had gone according to plan. The flight was completely automatic; Gagarin's controls had been locked in case he went mad. He had a code in a sealed envelope that would enable him to unlock the controls in an emergency (the project directors thought a deranged man could not use the code), but he obeyed orders and left the envelope unopened. Gagarin had been selected as the result of Khrushchev's order that the first cosmonaut be a Russian of lower-class origin with no Jewish or Asian "taint." The father of his nearest rival, Gherman Titov, had been a teacher—a suspiciously bourgeois profession in Imperial Russia—and Titov was passed over on that account. Ironically, Korolev had preferred Gagarin, whom he deemed the smartest cosmonaut anyway. Gagarin, who seems to have been a decent man, became a hero throughout the Communist world. (Considering the sort of people usually held up for admiration there, this was all to the good.) Cosmonauts in general got movie-star treatment (even more than the Mercury seven) and kept it long after Americans seemingly lost interest in their astronauts.

In the West, Gagarin excited jealous rage. An amazing number of people tried to convince themselves that his flight had been faked or that he was the first survivor of many attempts in which cosmonauts had died.[1] The dominant reaction, however, was worry and a determination to catch up. Gagarin's flight, and other events, finally provoked the United States into deciding to go to the moon.

THE LUNAR DECISION

In late 1960 and early 1961, NASA planners had hardened in favor of landing on the moon. On February 7, a Manned Lunar Landing Task Group concluded that the job would need no new technical breakthroughs. It argued that Saturn and Nova would be built anyway, and it expected a manned space station by the late 1960s; a moon landing should be possible by 1968–1970. The new President was vaguely committed to do more in space, but it was far from certain that he would buy this as an objective.

The incoming Administration did not even contact NASA head Glennan, a Republican who expected to be replaced. Before his inauguration, Kennedy had appointed an ad hoc committee under Jerome Wiesner, who became his Science Adviser, to study the space and missile effort. Wiesner was strongly critical of NASA's orientation to manned flight and of its management, especially of the Mercury program. He urged Kennedy to distance himself from Mercury. Despite his statements during the campaign, Kennedy cared little about space travel and had in fact been scornful of it—unlike his despised Vice President, who was the real force in the Administration in favor of a massive space effort. Lyndon Johnson became chairman of the revived Space Council, which had been unimportant under Eisenhower.

Power-hungry and tricky, Johnson was also deeply patriotic, a genuine reformer, and in many ways a better man than his predecessor and successor in the White House. But the programs he carried out so energetically proved poorly thought out or downright mistaken, and many of the men he would inherit from Kennedy were incompetent and even disloyal. The failure of his Presidency and his unpopularity ensured that, although more responsible than any other politician for the flight to the moon, he would get no credit for it.

Early in the Kennedy Administration, Johnson helped secure the crucial appointment of James Webb as NASA's new administrator. Webb had shuttled for many years between government and the business world. An old New Dealer, he had been Truman's Director of the Bureau of the Budget and later Undersecretary of State. Later he had been a business associate of the powerful, corrupt Oklahoma Senator Robert Kerr (who apparently persuaded Johnson to back Webb) and a director of Douglas Aircraft. As director of a nonprofit educational operation, he had developed widespread contacts with scientists and was a close friend of the physicist Lloyd Berkner. Berkner had been the leading scientist candidate for the NASA job and was chairman of the National Academy of Sciences' Space Sciences Board. Unlike Wiesner, and perhaps most American scientists, he was an ardent proponent of manned space flight and was an important counterweight to the advice of Wiesner and the PSAC. At first sight Webb might have been an unpromising figure, a classic political finagler. But despite his association with Kerr, his reputation was safe and he was probably the best person available to direct NASA during the Apollo era. His wiles were devoted to getting the job done; and he tried to maintain a balanced program of unmanned exploration and work on "exotic" propulsion.

Webb's appointment in itself was a force for a big space program. On March 22, he met the President to justify increased effort along the lines of NASA's long-range program. He did not argue directly for a commitment to a moon landing; instead he focused on booster development— something even Wiesner did not oppose. Kennedy approved an increase of NASA's budget by almost $126,000,000 (to $1,235,000,000), designed to speed up Saturn, Centaur, the F-1, and nuclear rocket development. He did not approve more money for Apollo, which was still envisaged as a multipurpose craft, not necessarily intended for a moon trip. A decision on spacecraft development waited on the success of Mercury.

Gagarin's flight, although expected, nevertheless had a great impact; there was a strong U.S. reaction in favor of a bigger space program aimed at a moon landing. Even those who realized that the United States was stronger than the Soviets and even ahead in many aspects of space called for a dramatic effort to counter the evident blow to American prestige. Curiously, Kennedy at first resisted a speedup, grumbling privately that the U.S.S.R. was really a backward country and the fuss was exaggerated. But he decided to pander to the climate of opinion he had fostered yet despised privately. In a well-publicized meeting with Webb and others on April 14, he stressed his concern and asked if there was any area in which the Americans could catch up to the Soviets.

The Bay of Pigs fiasco hardened Kennedy's inclination to do something dramatic. He asked Johnson whether there was a chance to beat the Soviets at putting up a manned orbiting laboratory or going around or to the moon. He wanted to know the costs of an increased program, whether NASA was achieving the best possible results, and whether emphasis should be put on nuclear, solid, or liquid-fuel large boosters.

Johnson started a careful review; he conferred with NASA leaders at several levels, as well as General Schriever and others. All advised that there was no chance of beating the Soviets to a manned laboratory; but it might be possible to reach the moon first, for the Soviets were probably not far ahead in building the size of rocket needed. All recommended a moon landing, which might be done by 1967–1968.

On April 29, Johnson answered Kennedy's questions. He recommended a moon landing and accelerating all types of booster development. Johnson worked to mobilize a consensus, including congressional leaders of both parties, in favor of a bigger program. He pushed Webb on; Webb would have liked to wait another thirty days to get a NASA study's specific conclusions on how to reach the moon. On May 5, Johnson ordered the agencies involved to submit detailed recommendations by May 8, before he had to go overseas. Kennedy was already favorable to a moon program, but he decided to wait for the first manned Mercury flight.[2]

THE FIRST AMERICAN IN SPACE

Project Mercury had continued a rocky course. Mercury-Atlas 2 put an unmanned capsule into orbit on February 12, while a third successful unmanned Redstone flight was made on March 24. But on April 25, Mercury-Atlas 3 went off course and had to be destroyed. The Mercury-Redstone combination seemed safe enough, but as the day of the first manned flight neared, McGeorge Bundy and some prominent Senators (including J. W. Fulbright) urged postponing it and then launching in secret. Kennedy demanded, and got, repeated assurances that no great risk was being taken.

Early on May 5, after delays due to weather, Lt. Commander Alan Shepard entered his Mercury capsule, Freedom Seven. After holds due to weather and electrical and computer problems, the Redstone roared off at 9:34 A.M. Initially he found less vibration than he expected, but there was terrific buffeting as he passed the speed of sound. The escape tower was jettisoned and the autopilot worked as expected, but Shepard saw little through the small ports or the periscope—he had left a filter on it before launch to avoid being blinded by glare, and he was afraid to remove it lest his hand hit the poorly placed control that would abort his mission. He did glimpse part of the Florida coast and nearby islands.

Mercury capsules had two independent control systems, each of which operated in two modes. They could be left entirely up to the autopilot, or the pilot could use a semiautomatic system that controlled the same attitude-control jets. A different set of thrusters could be operated through either a purely mechanical "manual proportional system" or a "rate command" electrical system. Shepard tried all of them, once mistakenly leaving two systems on at the same time, and altered the attitude of the capsule along all three possible axes. The capsule tended to roll slightly clockwise because dirt had clogged a hydrogen peroxide tube. Reentry went well and the main parachute popped open within sight of the recovery carrier, *Lake Champlain*, 15 minutes and 302 miles from Cape Canaveral. Shepard had reached a peak velocity of 5,134 miles an hour and a height of 116 miles. The capsule was quickly recovered by helicopter.[3]

That afternoon Kennedy announced that he planned a faster, bigger space program. The next day (May 6), officials from NASA, the Defense Department, and other areas backed Johnson's recommendations for an intensive, but not crash program for a moon landing in 1967, ahead of the Soviets. (Defense representatives suggested an interplanetary flight as an alternative that would offer more scope to beat the Soviets). No one knew, or even pretended to know, what the Soviets actually planned. Other elements of a broad space program, including a nuclear rocket, were discussed.

The recommendations Johnson gave the President on May 8 stressed manned space flight as a contribution to national prestige. Kennedy never consulted the PSAC as a body, although Wiesner took part in the meetings that led to Kennedy's decision. Wiesner made clear his lack of enthusiasm for the moon project and that the PSAC would not recommend it on scientific grounds; its justification must be political. He and Kennedy carefully avoided putting the PSAC in a position in which it would have to oppose or support a decision to go to the moon. On May 10, Kennedy approved the proposed program. At NASA's suggestion, he changed the target date for a moon landing from 1967 to "within the decade of the 1960s."

In his announcement of May 25, Kennedy made it fairly clear that prestige and Cold War politics were the decisive elements in his decision. He remarked, "If we are to win the battle for men's minds, the dramatic achievements in space which occurred in recent weeks should have made clear to us all, as did the Sputnik in 1957, the impact of this adventure on the minds of men everywhere who are attempting to make a determination of what road they should take." He noted that "no single space project in this period will be more exciting, or more impressive to mankind, or more important for the long-range exploration of space; and none will be so difficult or expensive to accomplish."

Later, in 1962, asked to justify the expense, he would comment, "Why does Rice play Texas?"—a revealing flippancy.[4] No one genuinely interested in space travel would have compared it to a football game—which, after all, does not cost billions of dollars. Ironically, President Eisenhower, who was really interested in space exploration, had recoiled from a major manned space effort for the honorable reason of sparing the economy. And he would not spend large sums purely for prestige. Kennedy did not really care about space, but he and his advisers had a different view of what the economy would stand and were quite willing to throw money about for prestige. At least at the presidential level, the great adventure was launched for the meanest of motives.

THE VOSTOK FLIGHTS

Somewhat later in 1961, the Soviets would finally decide to go to the moon, too. Both sides plunged ahead with more flights with existing equipment, and both developed, for differing reasons, interim craft—Voskhod ("sunrise" or "upward trip") and Gemini to fill the gap between Vostok and Mercury and the lunar craft—as well as bigger boosters. While the Americans worked on the Titan and Saturn series, the Soviets developed a huge new booster—eventually called the "Proton" after the first satellite it put up, and the "D-booster" in the West. Comparable to the Saturn IB, but even more powerful and looking like an enlarged R-7, it consisted of a cluster of six parallel stages around a central core, with two upper stages fueled with nitrogen tetroxide and hydrazine. It could put 44,000 pounds into low-earth orbit. But the Proton, still used for commercial satellites, was never reliable enough for manned flight. A smaller satellite launcher was developed from the R-9 ICBM; it was a Soviet counterpart of the Titan. The Soviets made a mistake that was ultimately important to their lunar program: They never developed hydrogen-fueled upper stages comparable to Centaur or the S-IV series.

Although the Soviets had exploited their program for political purposes all along, they had—except for the Mars 3 disaster—generally conducted it prudently. But politics intruded increasingly. Khrushchev, wanting to make a big impression during the Berlin crisis, insisted that the next Vostok flight do something big. Against Korolev's wishes, he insisted that it stay in orbit a full day; Korolev feared its liquid-fuel retro-rocket might not function after so long in zero gravity.

Gherman Titov was launched on August 6 and landed the next day. Unlike Gagarin, Titov took control of the craft and changed its attitude. Also unlike Gagarin, he suffered from motion sickness after a few hours in orbit. (Cosmonauts seem to have been more susceptible to space sickness than the Mercury astronauts, possibly because their bigger cabins offered more opportunity for subtle visual disorientations, which triggered this reaction to weightlessness.)

The next Vostok flights were even more spectacular; they may have been timed to distract the West's attention from the Cuban buildup and to show that the Soviets were still ahead of the Americans. Vostok 3, carrying the first non-Russian cosmonaut, Andrian Nikolayev (a Chuvash), went into orbit on August 11, 1962. Nikolayev had been up just under a day when Vostok 4, with Pavel Popovich (a Ukrainian) was launched. It was inserted into an orbit so close to that of Vostok 3 that it was within visual range of it. This group flight successfully conveyed the false impression that the Soviets could rendezvous in space. (The United States was not even capable of two space missions at the same time.) In fact, the Vostoks were quite incapable of the real maneuvering needed; the mission at most showed the skill of the Soviet launch crews and ground guidance. Both Vostoks landed on August 14.

Another group flight, in 1963, completed the Vostok program. On June 14, Vostok 5, flown by Valery Bykovskiy, went into orbit. Two days later, Khrushchev uncorked a new spectacular, which had been planned since 1961. Vostok 6 carried a woman, Valentina Tereshkova, a factory worker and sky diver. She was merely a passenger, and the craft remained on autopilot. The orbits of the two craft did not match as closely as those of Vostoks 3 and 4; Vostok 5 seems to have gone into a higher orbit than intended. Tereshkova became spacesick but stuck it out; her flight, originally planned to last one day, was extended to three. Bykovskiy landed after a record five-day flight. The Soviets made much of Tereshkova's flight as demonstrating their enlightened treatment of women, and they noted that she had flown longer than any Mercury astronaut. This did remove any worries that women could not endure space flight (or were better at it than men). But the Soviets themselves never took their egalitarian pose seriously. None of the other three women trained with Tereshkova flew. Indeed, the male officials and cosmonauts, and eventually Tereshkova herself, openly jeered at the idea of more women cosmonauts, and none flew until the 1980s. Tereshkova married Andrian Nikolayev—possibly it was arranged or forced—and became a propaganda spokeswoman. But the marriage failed and her personality was not really suited for the latter role.

Korolev wanted to launch a seven-day Vostok mission and considered sending up a modified Vostok for a rendezvous and docking mission, but Khrushchev's demand that the Soviets must seem to be ahead of the United States in every way and at every moment forced him to take another, less useful course.[5]

THE MERCURY FLIGHTS

NASA carried out one more suborbital flight. Virgil "Gus" Grissom's capsule was modified a great deal, with an explosive jettisonable side hatch and a better control system; he wore an improved space suit. He was to be left free to make observations through the windows that had replaced the tiny ports. Launched on July 21, after the usual irritating delays, the flight itself went well. Grissom was getting ready to leave the capsule—he had actually asked the recovery helicopter to wait a bit while he jotted down some data—when the explosive hatch blew unexpectedly. Grissom had just removed a safety pin but had not hit the plunger to actuate it. The sea was rough and poured in. Grissom barely got out and nearly drowned as water entered a valve in the suit. A helicopter got to him just in time; the capsule sank in deep water. The episode was never explained satisfactorily. It was widely supposed that Grissom had panicked and set off the explosive mechanism at the wrong moment. But apart from other things, everyone else who used the plunger hurt his hand, which Grissom did not, so this is highly unlikely.

It was time to go on to orbit. Tests of the Mercury-Atlas, however, had fallen far behind schedule and had been erratic. The first had blown up, the second flew well, and the third had been aborted. An unmanned capsule was launched successfully on September 13; MA-5, which carried a chimpanzee, followed on November 29, but the capsule had problems with attitude control. Nevertheless, the capsule and chimp returned in good shape.

John Glenn, who was the sole Marine among the astronauts and who had a spectacular war record, was chosen for the first orbital flight. He was to try to test the effectiveness of visual observation in space (looking for the smallest possible landmark on earth and tracking the Atlas booster after his capsule separated from it), judge the effect of the occultation of stars by the atmosphere, and study weather patterns. If he did not suffer space sickness, he would try to induce it. After repeated delays due to leaking fuel tanks (the Atlas actually had to be taken apart and reassembled) and weather, MA-6 lifted off at 9:47 A.M. on February 20, 1962. Glenn was inserted into an orbit with a peak of 159 miles and a low of 100 miles; that was low enough that if his retro-rockets failed, orbital decay should bring the capsule, Friendship 7, back in eighteen hours. Glenn had enough oxygen to last for twenty-eight hours; he was to stay up for three orbits if possible.

Glenn found he could not make himself sick no matter how hard he tried. Over the Pacific, he encountered the first mystery of manned space flight. Thousands of glowing specks that looked like fireflies flowed past him; they seemed to him to be self-illuminated and not coming from his capsule.

Glenn had problems with attitude control. Early on he found that the attitude indicators on his control panel were wrong, but he was able to orient himself by eye. Later, however, the capsule started drifting to the right. Finding that one of his thrusters had gone out of action, Glenn overrode the autopilot and tried other modes, finally shifting to the "fly-by-wire," semiautomatic mode. All this diverted him from his observations.

Unknown to Glenn, ground control was gravely worried. Telemetry indicated that his heatshield and landing bag (which cushioned impact with the sea and kept the capsule afloat) were no longer locked in place. If the instruments were right, only the straps holding the retro-rocket pack to the capsule kept the heatshield in place. Ground control decided to keep the retro-rockets in place after they fired, instead of jettisoning them as usual. There was one problem, however. If one of the three rockets did not fire, or if not all the rocket fuel was burned, they would ignite on reentry and probably shove the capsule out of the proper attitude. Glenn had other problems with equipment that did not work too well. He was told of the possible problem with the heatshield just ten minutes before reentry, although he apparently had deduced what was going on from the nature of questions from the ground. The retro-rockets fired properly, but Glenn had a bone-rattling ride down and an uncomfortable moment when he thought that his heatshield was coming apart. But it had all been a telemetry error. The rocket package made the capsule unstable, and Glenn had used so much fuel maintaining his attitude earlier that his thrusters ran dry. He hit the Atlantic 40 miles from the target area but was quickly picked up by a destroyer. Hot and dehydrated, but basically in good shape, he returned to a hero's welcome, which he parlayed into a political career.

Scott Carpenter, who flew the next mission on May 24, was given a long list of tasks. He was to release and observe a tethered, multicolored balloon to determine the reflective properties of different colors in space and obtain drag measurements; observe the behavior of liquids in zero gravity; check the visibility of a ground flare; and take pictures of weather systems and the "airglow" (light generated in the upper atmosphere by chemical reactions). His flight started almost routinely, and he went into the scientific program with zest. He managed to track his Atlas booster, but he could not see the flares shot off below, although he found that he could see surprisingly small objects on the ground. He took the planned photographs, and released the balloon, but it did not inflate.

Carpenter had quickly turned his capsule around for reentry with a minimal use of fuel, but during later planned maneuvers he repeatedly and accidentally actuated both automatic and manual systems, using much fuel. On his last orbit, he refrained from trying to control his attitude and just drifted to conserve thruster fuel. Contrary to what had been feared, he was quite comfortable. He had observed and photographed Glenn's fireflies, but he decided that they were related to his capsule.

On his last orbit he accidentally hit his capsule's hatch, which seemed to make fireflies stream by. Further taps on the hatch and wall had the same result; it was later concluded that the fireflies were bits of ice or frozen thruster fuel coming off the heatshield. These observations caused Carpenter to start reentry preparations late. When he started to get the capsule into the right attitude, he found that the automatic system was misbehaving. Moreover, his electronic horizon scanner was not working properly; he had to check the real horizon and determine his attitude by looking out the window. Constantly switching between the brightness outside and the dim cockpit was difficult. And, once again, he had both "fly-by-wire" and manual systems on simultaneously. The capsule was still not aligned properly when Carpenter fired his retro-rockets, three seconds late. The rockets themselves were not as powerful as they were supposed to be. Only then did Carpenter find that he had both control systems on. Ignoring his untrustworthy instruments, he used the remaining fuel sparingly but still ran out on reentry. He missed the planned recovery area by 250 miles and was feared lost; but he was picked up after three hours. Although publicly maintaining that Carpenter had done well, many at NASA condemned him privately and made sure that he never flew again. Some at NASA falsely insinuated that he had panicked. In fact, while Carpenter had made mistakes, he was also a convenient scapegoat for an overcrowded schedule and the equipment failures that had caused most of his problems.

NASA tacitly recognized that it had not all been Carpenter's fault in its arrangements for the flight of Walter Schirra. This was a long-endurance flight to be extended to seven orbits, if possible. The Mercury had to carry more oxygen, as well as lithium hydroxide to absorb CO_2, and ways had to be found to conserve electrical power and thruster fuel. At Carpenter's suggestion, a switch was installed to discourage use of the more powerful thrusters until they were needed for fast maneuvers. Schirra was to focus on running the capsule and was given few experiments needing his participation. MA-8, carrying Sigma 7, blasted off on October 3, 1962. The Atlas fired longer than expected, putting Schirra into the highest orbit—peak 176 miles—attained during Mercury. Schirra performed efficiently. His flight was threatened by a sudden rise in temperature in his space suit during his first orbit. He was nearly ordered down, but he managed to control the problem. Otherwise he suffered less from equipment problems than other Mercury astronauts. After seven orbits and the most successful Mercury flight, he landed in the Pacific in sight of the recovery carrier.

Earlier plans to have a Mercury capsule stay up for a day or more were now revived. The capsule had to be modified considerably; heavier batteries and more oxygen, water, and thruster fuel had to be carried. To compensate for this, the "rate command" electrical control system and the almost useless periscope were junked.

Gordon Cooper went into orbit in Faith 7 on May 15, 1963. Unlike Schirra, he performed a fair amount of observation and experiment. An attempt to eject a tethered balloon failed again; Cooper did eject a small flashing beacon which proved unexpectedly difficult to see. He found that pumping water in zero gravity also proved unexpectedly difficult. He made extensive observations of zodiacal light and the airglow and photographed the horizon and weather phenomena. He had a comfortable ride until his nineteenth orbit, when his instruments started giving false indications. On the twentieth orbit he lost all attitude readings, and on the next orbit the autopilot went out. He had to perform all attitude changes guided by eye, using the clumsy, fuel-wasting manual control system. But he had enough time to get ready, and reentry was remarkably smooth. Once again the capsule was recovered quickly.

Webb decided to end the Mercury program; it had cost far more money ($400 million) and time than had been expected. NASA put a good face on the results, stressing the experience gained and the lesson that humans could withstand space conditions.[6] It did grumble, however, that much hardware had failed to meet specifications or had malfunctioned.[7] The blunt fact was that important systems of the Mercury capsule had proven unreliable; space travel was still in an experimental and highly dangerous stage.

PROJECT GEMINI

As early as 1959, there had been proposals for an advanced or Mark II Mercury capable of longer flights. The decision to go to the moon, and the growing likelihood that doing so would require a rendezvous of different craft in space, made it desirable to have an interim program, Gemini, for longer flights and developing rendezvous techniques. With Gemini, the United States caught up with, and began to surpass, the Soviets in manned space flight.

The Gemini spacecraft (NASA dropped the term *capsule* during the latter part of the Mercury program) emerged during 1961; a contract was given to McDonnell to build it in December. It looked much like Mercury, but in fact it was modified greatly. Carrying two men, it was over twice as heavy (8,000 pounds), and its systems were rearranged to make them more accessible for maintenance. It would use new fuel cells to provide electrical power (they also provided barely drinkable water), enabling it to stay up for fourteen days. Instead of having an escape tower to pull the whole craft away from the booster in case of disaster, the Gemini crew had airplane-type ejection seats. The "reentry module" had an offset center of gravity to provide maneuverability during descent; advised by an onboard computer, the pilot could steer it by rolling it. An "adapter module," which would remain in orbit, carried retro-rockets and an orbital attitude and maneuvering system (OAMS) far better than Mercury's attitude control system. It enabled the craft to change orbit to some extent, and if the retro-rockets failed it could be used to reduce speed enough for a safe reentry. Gemini was to be lofted by a Titan II ICBM; rendezvous and docking would be practiced with Agena upper stages in orbit. Once coupled to the Agena, the Gemini could alter orbit to a greater extent than the OAMS allowed. It was originally hoped to fly as early as March 1963, and some suggested that by docking with a Centaur, Gemini could make a circumlunar flight in 1965. James Chamberlin, the head of the Gemini program, even suggested using Gemini to land on the moon (using the never-built Saturn C-3 to put it in orbit around the moon; the astronauts would enter a tiny landing craft to reach the moon's surface). This was the first fully developed version of "lunar orbital rendezvous," the mode used for the actual trip.

But getting Gemini into earth orbit proved hard enough. It fell farther and farther behind schedule, with rising costs. There were clashes with the Defense Department over the Titan II; getting it "man-rated" or safe enough to carry the crew, proved more difficult than expected. The Agena "target vehicle" also presented difficulties, as did the fuel cells. The first Geminis had to use conventional batteries. A "paraglider" system (which resembled modern hang-gliders and was designed to give the Gemini pilot greater control during descent and even make it possible to come down on hand) did not work well and was dropped.[8]

Khrushchev's desire to beat Gemini led to the two dangerous Voskhod flights. The United States was planning a two-person craft; therefore, Khrushchev wanted a three-person flight first. Korolev and his assistant, Konstantin Feoktisov, left work on a moon craft to make the Vostok a three-seater. It could not carry ejection seats for three people, so it was altered so the crew could land with it. An additional large retro-rocket would cushion the impact. To squeeze three people aboard, the reserve parachute was discarded and the people were jammed into lightweight couches without space suits. This worked only because one of the crew members was very small. The crew had no way out if the flight was aborted or the cabin ruptured. After one unmanned test flight, Voskhod 1 was launched on October 12, 1964 and was crewed by Vladimir Komarov,

Boris Yegorov, and Feoktisov. The gamble worked; they landed the next afternoon. Khrushchev was deposed the day after, but one more Voskhod mission (albeit of a more reasonable sort) was flown under his successors. It was designed to beat the Americans to what was awkwardly called Extravehicular Activity (EVA), or a spacewalk. Voskhod 2, launched on March 18, 1965, carried Pavel Belayev and Alexei Leonov and a collapsible airlock to let Leonov leave the craft in orbit.

Spacewalks proved more dangerous than anyone expected. After a few minutes outside, Leonov found it impossible to get back in. His primitive space suit had swelled up. Dangerously close to the limits of his backpack oxygen supply, he had to reduce the pressure in his suit to a dangerous level. After several minutes of contortions, he barely managed to get back inside. Voskhod 2 landed the next day, after its autopilot fouled up and the pilot took over manual control; it came down 1,300 miles off course in the Urals.[9]

THE GEMINI FLIGHTS

Five days after Voskhod 2 and after two unmanned flights, Gemini 3, carrying Gus Grissom and John Young, lifted off. This was basically an engineering test flight, limited to three orbits; no attempt was made at rendezvous. But it would be the first manned flight in which a craft would change orbit, and it carried interesting experiments to study radiation and zero-gravity effects on cells. A third experiment tried successfully to inject water into the plasma around the descending craft (to eliminate the radio blackout previously experienced during reentry). Gemini 3 went more smoothly than any Mercury flight. Grissom used the OAMS to change orbit three times; the last put Gemini 3 in an orbit so low that it would reenter soon even if its retro-rockets failed. The "reentry module" developed less lift than wind tunnel tests had predicted and got off course; the crew had an unpleasant wait in the sealed capsule. Grissom understandably refused to open a hatch until the Navy secured a flotation collar around his craft.

NASA had seriously considered a spacewalk on Gemini 4 for months, and the crew slated for the mission had fought hard enough for one that they had secured vital preparations for that step. But there was strong opposition to a spacewalk as premature. If not for the desire to vie with the Soviets, a spacewalk probably would not have been scheduled so early in the program. Even NASA's highest levels were divided, but Webb was persuaded. Other goals for Gemini 4 (which had been formulated earlier) were (1) an attempt to close with the spent second stage of its Titan booster, and (2) a longer flight (four days) than the Americans had yet attempted. Originally a week-long flight had been expected, but with fuel cells still unavailable conventional batteries would have to be used.

James McDivitt and Edward White lifted off on June 3, 1965. Right after reaching orbit, McDivitt tried to rendezvous with the Titan's upper stage. But the necessary techniques were not understood at NASA. Judging relative positions by eye, McDivitt tried to catch up with his target by thrusting toward it, without success. This just drove Gemini 4 into a higher orbit, in which it moved slower relative to its target (which stayed in a lower orbit). It fell farther behind the Titan stage. The right way to handle the rendezvous was to reduce speed and drop to a lower orbit, which would let the craft close in on the target. Applied at the right moment, a burst of speed would close the gap.

On the third orbit, White went on a spacewalk. Unlike the Soviets, he depended on an umbilical connection with the Gemini for oxygen. There was no airlock; the whole craft had to be depressurized to let him out. He carried a "hand-held maneuvering unit," usually called a "zip gun," which squirted a jet of oxygen to let him move and maneuver. It worked well, but he soon used up its oxygen supply. There were some dangerous moments when White tried to return and reseal the hatch, which had been hard to open in the first place. Fortunately, he was an unusually strong man, but he was utterly exhausted by the effort.

For the next two and a half days, the crew photographed the areas they passed over and performed experiments, which were generally successful. Reentry proved more difficult than expected; the computer failed (in a way never explained) and could not provide the data the pilot needed to use the Gemini's lift capabilities. But the Gemini 4 landed surprisingly close to the desired point. It had been a partial, if dangerous, success.

Gemini 5 (manned by Gordon Cooper and Charles Conrad) was supposed to rendezvous with an Agena, but one was not ready in time. Instead the Gemini itself would eject a target pod with a flashing light and a radar beacon and transponder, and practice joining up with it. Gemini 5 finally had fuel cells, and it was to stay up eight days.

Gemini 5 lifted off on August 21. The new fuel cells did not work properly; soon after reaching orbit, they lost the pressure needed to function properly. Cooper feared total failure and had to reduce power consumption, preventing a try at rendezvous with the already ejected pod. Finally the fuel cell pressure stabilized at a low but acceptable point, and ground control decided to let the crew stay in orbit. The crew practiced a phantom rendezvous with an imaginary vehicle (a point in space specified by ground control) and carried out all but one of the planned experiments.

Toward the end of the mission the OAMS became undependable, but the crew stayed up the full eight days. Coming down, however, they missed the recovery area widely. Although this was due to a mistake in programming the Gemini's computer, NASA thought Cooper was partly to blame. He never flew again.

Gemini 6 (manned by Walter Schirra and Thomas Stafford) was finally to rendezvous with an Agena. Sound rendezvous techniques had been worked out; Edwin "Buzz" Aldrin, perhaps the smartest man in the astronaut corps, played a central role in this. But on October 25, the Agena broke up in flight. The mission was postponed and replanned. Gemini 7 (manned by Frank Borman and James Lovell) would fly first, with supplies for a fourteen-day flight and major medical experiments. Then Schirra and Stafford, whose craft depended on batteries and had an endurance of only two days, would be launched to rendezvous (but not dock) with Gemini 7. Some NASA engineers had urged this for many months; the Agena flop enabled them to sell the idea to the higher-ups within three days. This rendezvous posed formidable problems for those preparing the rockets on the ground, and some changes had to be made to Gemini 7.

Borman and Lovell got off easily on December 4; for the first time the astronauts removed their space suits (which were a newer, better design). Meanwhile Gemini 6-A was readied hastily. On December 12, Schirra and Stafford tried to lift off, but the Titan's engines stopped just after ignition. By the rules, the crew should have ejected, because their instruments showed that the Titan had actually left the ground and was about to crash back into it. But Schirra sensed that the Titan had not really moved and stayed his hand. The men stepped out of the Gemini instead, saving the mission. A speedy investigation found that the problem was caused by someone having left a dust cover on the Titan engine's gas generator. The booster was readied hastily again; on December 15, it flew successfully. After six hours of maneuvering, Gemini 6-A joined up on Gemini 7, using surprisingly little fuel. Schirra practiced further maneuvers around Gemini 7, and he landed the next day in the first really controlled reentry. Borman and Lovell remained in orbit despite trouble with thrusters and fuel cells, and they landed on December 18. They showed no more ill effects than men who had been up just four days; adjustment to weightlessness (which later proved debilitating over much longer periods) had taken place.

The Gemini program had finally accomplished rendezvous, but not yet docking, with another vehicle; and spacewalks were not yet safe. There was so much trouble with the Agena that substituting another, inferior docking target was considered; there was even talk of cutting short the program and in effect passing the buck to Apollo. Intensive work finally seemed to solve the Agena problem, which stemmed from the fact that the modified Agena that was used had to be able to fire its engines five times rather than twice, as was expected of the standard Agena D.

Gemini 8 (manned by Neil Armstrong and David Scott) was to combine both docking and an EVA; better equipment for the latter was now ready. On March 16, 1966, a target Agena reached orbit 180 miles above the earth. Gemini 8 lifted off forty-one minutes later. Not quite six hours later, Armstrong closed in on the Agena. After careful checks, he crept up on it and docked with it. The major aim of the Gemini program had been achieved; but disaster almost followed triumph. The joined spacecraft started rolling; the crew could not bring them under control. At first they thought the Agena was at fault and hastily uncoupled from it. Things became even worse; the Gemini whirled wildly. One of its thrusters was jammed, spewing out valuable fuel. Using a last-ditch mode of attitude control, the separate reentry attitude control system, they landed as soon as possible, in the Pacific instead of the Atlantic. Engineers examining the craft found that the mission had been undone by a simple electrical short; modifications were made so that the episode could not be repeated.

Gemini 9 was to compare optical versus radar methods in arranging rendezvous. Some engineers hoped to discard radars and save weight on the Apollo craft and the lunar landing craft by having the crews depend on their eyes, optical sights, and lights. (The astronauts had no such confidence in themselves.)

The Atlas sending up the next Agena went out of control, so NASA substituted the alternative Augmented Target Docking Adapter (ATDA) vehicle developed by McDonnell. A simple target incapable of changing orbit, it was launched on June 1, 1966. Although signals suggested that the launch shroud covering the ATDA's docking port had not been jettisoned properly, Gemini 9 (manned by Thomas Stafford and Eugene Cernan) was launched on June 3. They rendezvoused with the ATDA in just over three hours—only to find that the shroud was indeed jammed in place. That ended the possibility of docking.

On June 5, Cernan left the Gemini. Working in a space suit again proved exhausting, and he found that every little movement of his fingers changed the position of his whole body. His faceplate fogged and his suit over-heated. He did most of what had been planned, but prudently he did not cut loose from the Gemini (he wore a backpack oxygen tank) when he could hardly see what he was doing. Stafford and Cernan managed to do almost all the assigned experiments and landed almost at the planned point on June 6.

Gemini 10 (manned by John Young and Michael Collins) was given even more to do. To make up for past failures, there would be a dual rendezvous. It would dock with a newly launched Agena, use it to move to a higher orbit, and rendezvous with the Agena used by Gemini 8—if the crew could find it. The Agena was out of power, and would be hard to find without its transponder. Collins was to leave the craft and do useful work. Discarding the cumbersome backpack, he would depend on an umbilical connection to the Gemini.

On the afternoon of July 18, the Agena and Gemini 10 were launched. Young docked with the Agena nearly six hours after launch; an hour after that, the Agena engine kicked the joined craft into a much higher orbit— the highest yet reached by a manned craft. Collins popped his hatch for his first EVA, photographing stellar ultraviolet radiation. He had to stop when both men's eyes began to burn due to a malfunction in their suits. On their third day aloft, they undocked from their Agena and docked with Gemini 8's target. Collins then emerged to collect experimental packages from his own craft and the Agena. Despite better equipment, the EVA still proved awkward and time-consuming. On July 21, Gemini 10 landed after the first fully successful mission.

Gemini 11 (manned by Charles Conrad and Richard Gordon) was launched soon after its Agena target on September 21. Simulating the type of rendezvous to be used on the moon trip, Conrad and Gordon docked with the Agena right off the bat. Using little fuel, they alternately practiced docking and undocking. In an exhausting spacewalk (despite improved gear), Gordon strung a tether from the Agena to the Gemini. The joined craft then flew to an unprecedented high orbit (peak 850 miles). Then the astronauts undocked from the Agena to practice tethered flight, which proved unexpectedly tricky. They efficiently carried out almost all planned experiments and landed right by the recovery ship on September 15.

The last Gemini mission, flown by James Lovell and Buzz Aldrin and launched on November 11, 1966, essentially duplicated Gemini 11, with more emphasis on EVA (which had been studied carefully). Some new restraints and guides were installed to help an astronaut on a spacewalk. Lovell and Aldrin docked despite radar failure, but the Agena's engine proved undependable, so no shift in orbit was made. An experiment in tethered flight went well, as did Aldrin's EVA. Despite problems with their fuel cells, they flew the full mission before landing on November 15.

The Gemini program had cost $1,147,000—more than twice what was expected. It did not contribute much directly to work on Apollo, for the two programs tended to develop concurrently rather than in succession;

Apollo's design was settled by the time Gemini flew. But Gemini provided valuable experience in maneuvering, rendezvous in space, and the use of fuel cells on long flights.[10] During Gemini the United States had finally caught up with the Soviets in the ability to put heavy loads into space using Saturn and Centaur.

After great delays, the Centaur upper stage had been perfected. It had already been seventeen months behind schedule when the first Atlas-Centaur blew up in May 1962. The General Dynamics engineers had assumed that a thin bulkhead between the oxygen and hydrogen tanks would prevent the oxygen from warming up the colder hydrogen, but their techniques to prevent or detect hydrogen leaks were inadequate. Centaur's management (a group NASA had taken over from the Air Force and only loosely supervised) was much criticized. NASA finally turned over Centaur to Silverstein and the Lewis Laboratory. Centaur flew successfully in November 1963, but the next flight failed. Centaur was not really reliable until 1966. It could put 10,700 pounds into low-earth orbit. Saturn, with an even bigger payload, developed more smoothly. The first Saturn I, with dummy stages above a live first stage, was launched on October 27, 1961. The first S-IV hydrogen-fueled second stage flew on the fifth Saturn I launch, in January 1964. Saturn I was basically a development vehicle, used only to carry a few Pegasus micrometeorite-detector satellites and to test Apollo components. The Saturn IB, with uprated engines in a lightened first stage and an S-IVB second stage with a single new J-2 engine, flew in February 1966. It could put 20 tons into orbit. Not a single Saturn I or IB failed; it was a great credit to von Braun's team, whose reliability, rather than originality, made it the mainstay of the Apollo project.[11]

PROBES TO THE MOON

Unmanned probes to the moon and the other planets attracted less attention than manned flights, but they were of greater scientific interest. Moreover, what they found determined the course of manned exploration.

With the decision to send men to the moon, NASA extended the already planned Ranger program from five to fifteen flights and decreed that collecting data for Apollo had precedence over data of more scientific importance. Rangers were to take TV pictures of the moon before crashing into it. The most complex probes yet to leave earth, they had to align themselves on two axes, to keep an antenna pointed toward earth and solar cells facing the sun while rotating to maintain an even temperature. After lengthy delays, an Atlas-Agena launched the first Ranger on August 22,

1961. The Agena's second "burn," intended to send Ranger 1 from earth orbit to the moon, failed. Ranger 2, in November, flopped for the same reason. NASA was not too dismayed; the first two Rangers were considered engineering test models. But Ranger 3, the first fully instrumented probe (launched on January 26, 1962), missed the moon and went into orbit around the sun. An attempt to have it transmit pictures of the moon as it passed by failed; its antennas were not oriented properly. In April 1962, Ranger 4 launched properly, but its master clock failed; it did not carry out its program and hit the far side of the moon without transmitting anything. In October Ranger 5's solar panels failed and the dead probe missed the moon by 450 miles. Washington finally lost patience, Congress began an investigation, and NASA conducted its own inquiry. JPL had remained a semiautonomous operation, run for NASA by Caltech, and NASA had long held that JPL's internal organization lacked a proper focus on programs. NASA's board of inquiry condemned JPL's design, execution, and testing. There were indications of misappropriation of funds and even sabotage. JPL conceded that there had been a lack of close program management while its best people had gone to the Mariner interplanetary probes, and that there had been design flaws and poor construction.

Ranger was redesigned drastically. All scientific instruments were dropped to provide space for backup systems; only the television system remained. Ranger 6, launched January 30, 1964, hit the moon—but its TV system failed. There was another congressional investigation, and Webb used the situation to put JPL under closer control. NASA renegotiated its contract with Caltech, and JPL was reorganized; Alvin Luedecke, who had recently retired as General Manager of the AEC, took the new post of General Manager of JPL. JPL's field of responsibility was narrowed; Ranger's follow-on programs, Surveyor and Lunar Orbiter, were to be built by Hughes and Boeing, respectively.

But Ranger finally triumphed. Ranger 7, launched on July 28, 1964, hit the Mare Nubium three days later and worked perfectly. Ranger 8 crashed into the Mare Tranquillatis in February 1965; the last Ranger landed in the crater Alphonsus a month later. The last six Rangers were canceled. The Ranger pictures showed the moon to be even more heavily cratered than had been supposed, supporting the idea that lunar craters were meteoritic in origin; but otherwise the terrain seemed smoother and more gently rolling than had been expected.

The Soviets, after tribulations comparable to Ranger's, won the race to soft-land instruments on the moon. In early 1963, they had renewed their Luna probes, but the first two either never got into orbit or missed the moon. In March 1965, another probe failed to leave earth orbit; in May Luna 5 crashed instead of braking to a landing. Luna 6 missed the moon the next month. In October Luna 7's retro-rockets fired too soon and it crashed. Two months later, Luna 8's engines started too late. On February 3, 1966, Luna 9 successfully landed in Oceanus Procellarum; the Soviets reported that the soil seemed porous but firm.

The much bigger and heavily instrumented Surveyors were delayed by the problems with the Centaur. Moreover, Centaur's expected payload declined, forcing reductions in Surveyor's weight. The difficulty of building Surveyor was underestimated at first. Hughes had not had a space project before and mismanaged it for a time, although Surveyor's final success rate was far better than Ranger. Surveyor 1, originally scheduled for mid-1963, landed in Oceanus Procellarum on June 2, 1966. It worked splendidly, taking 21,000 photographs of the surrounding terrain and confirming Soviet reports of the soil. Surveyor 2 tumbled wildly and crashed into the moon in September 1966. Surveyor 3 landed in the Ocean of Storms in April 1967 and made tests of the physical qualities of the soil, scratching small trenches. Contact with Surveyor 4 was lost just before it was to land in July 1967. The heavier Surveyor 5 landed in the Mare Tranquillatis in September. It carried an instrument capable of a limited chemical analysis of lunar soil; it sprayed alpha particles on the soil and analyzed the reflections received. It suggested that the soil was probably a basalt and that the moon was not an unchanged primitive object utterly unlike earth. Surveyor 6 performed a similar soil analysis in the Sinus Medii. Under control from earth, its "vernier" engines fired, jumping the probe a few feet from its original site. Surveyor 7 landed in the more rugged Tycho highland area, showing that the soil there was somewhat different. Surveyor produced a vast amount of data on the moon; although too late to affect Apollo's design, it confirmed that the design was reasonably safe.

The Soviets also beat the Americans in putting a probe into orbit around the moon. Luna 10, launched on March 31, 1966, carried a magnetometer to measure the moon's nearly nonexistent magnetic field, but no camera. Lunas 11, 12, and 14 were also successful lunar satellites. The Americans joined in with a successful and more useful series of Lunar Orbiters, launched by Atlas-Agenas from August 1966 through 1967. They carried cameras to map the moon (as had Luna 12). The first three surveyed the projected Apollo landing sites, leaving the rest to examine other areas. The Lunar Orbiters mapped most of the moon and uncovered an unexpected and important fact. Oddities in their orbits and those of the

Lunas indicated irregularities in the moon's gravitational field, due to concentrations of mass ("mascons") under the maria basins.[12]

TO THE PLANETS

It has been estimated that in the first half of the 1960s, the Soviets put at least twice the effort into unmanned lunar and planetary probes as did the United States. The lunar effort was well rewarded, but the Soviets' efforts to reach Mars and Venus piled up a series of flops even worse than the early Rangers. Thanks to continued failures of their escape stage and electronics, all twenty-six attempts failed.[13] The first exploration of the planets was done by the Americans; they would be the first to reach Venus, the "most maddening of planets."[14]

Mariner had to overcome serious trouble. By the summer of 1961, it was clear that Centaur was far behind schedule; any probes to earth's neighbors in 1962–1964 had to be launched by the less powerful Agenas. Mariner A, the original version of the Venus probe (Mariner B was the Mars version), was redesigned hastily, using many components from Ranger. The new Mariner R weighed 447 pounds, only a bit more than one third of the original version. JPL, in cooperation with Lockheed, lightened the Agena itself.

A pair of probes were ready for the launch window for Venus in the summer of 1962. On July 22, the Atlas-Agena carrying Mariner 1 went off course due to a tiny mistake in programming its guidance computer and had to be blown up. On August 27, Mariner 2 was launched successfully but barely overcame another guidance malfunction.

Mariner 2 carried just six instruments: microwave and infrared radiometers, a magnetometer, and charged particle, plasma, and micro-meteorite detectors. The most critical items, in relation to Venus, were the magnetometer (which would measure the planet's magnetic field) and the radiometers (which were to determine its surface temperature). The crucial question was whether the microwaves detected coming from Venus in the 1950s were actually produced by high surface temperatures or, as many believed, by some phenomenon in its upper atmosphere. If the latter was the case, a microwave radiometer scanning the disk of Venus from nearby should show "limb-brightening" (that is, the edge of the disk, where the atmosphere appeared thickest to the spacecraft, would show greater intensity), while if the surface was hot, the radiometer would show "limb-darkening" (the edge would show lesser intensity). Moreover, the radiometer would check radiation on two different wavelengths, one of which was absorbed by water vapor; if no microwaves of that wavelength were picked up, it would indicate that there was a lot of water vapor in Venus's atmosphere.

On December 14, Mariner 2 passed Venus at a range of 21,598 miles; its instruments were activated by a signal from JPL. The future of space exploration—perhaps much of the future of the human race—depended on what the instruments found. The microwave radiometer performed three scans of Venus—first its dark side, then the boundary between the light and dark areas, and then the day side. The scans all showed "limb-darkening"; the microwave radiation came from the hot surface of the planet. Analysis showed that Venus was even hotter than earth-based measurements had suggested—about 800°F. No Van Allen belts or magnetic field were found; evidently the planet rotated slowly if at all. (Later radar measurements from earth, confirmed by Mariner 10 in 1974, showed that Venus spins slowly in a retrograde direction; its day is 243 earth-days long—longer than its year!) Together with the microwave measurements, the infrared measurements suggested a very dense atmosphere with little water vapor.

Even though only a few astronomers had believed that Venus was habitable, most had assumed that it was more earth-like than this. It was not just uninhabitable, but fantastically difficult to explore. Why two planets so similar in size and not too differently situated had evolved so differently seemed hard to explain. Some continued to think there was something wrong with the observations (or the generally accepted explanation of them) and insisted that the microwave emissions were produced by some strange effect in the ionosphere and had nothing to do with surface conditions. The planet might have a magnetic field and Van Allen belts pinched by the solar wind and forced down into its upper atmosphere. Venus, or part of it, might be earth-like after all. Further probes, however, confirmed the dismal picture drawn by Mariner 2. Mariner 5 and Venera 4, the first successful Soviet interplanetary probe, reached Venus in October 1967. Mariner 5, bigger than Mariner 2, flew by with instruments capable of measuring the density and composition of the atmosphere; it showed that the atmosphere was overwhelmingly composed of carbon dioxide, and the air pressure at the surface was ninety earth-atmospheres. Venera 4 actually entered the atmosphere; most of it burned up, but a small, strong capsule descended under a parachute. Its transmissions stopped before it landed but confirmed the picture of Venus as hell. The Soviets continued to send probes there (the Americans concentrated on Mars). Venera 7 actually reached the surface on December 15, 1970, resisting and reporting the incredible conditions for half an hour. Even then, some in the West wondered if the Soviets were faking; but in 1978 a new series of American probes, Pioneer Venus, provided independent confirmation.[15]

MARINER 4 AND MARS

With the success of Mariner 2, the Americans turned to Mars. The Martian Mariners had to travel farther from earth and the sun, and they needed a better communications system and more solar panels. Unlike the Venus probes, they carried a television camera to examine Mars's surface through a telescope, as well as a magnetometer and additional detectors for micrometeorites, cosmic rays, solar plasma, and any Van Allen belts. And there was a radio occultation experiment to measure the thickness of Mars's air by its effects on a radio beam passed through it.

Mariner 3 was launched successfully on November 5, 1964, but a fiberglass shroud that protected the probe in the first stage of flight failed to come off, rendering it useless. A better metal shroud was substituted hastily on Mariner 4; it was launched on November 28. There were problems with the sensors (which were to ensure that the probe would orient itself properly), but these were overcome. On July 14, 1965, Mariner 4 passed Mars. Surprisingly, it found no Van Allen belts and almost no magnetic field. It transmitted twenty-two pictures of Mars's southern hemisphere; three proved useless, but the rest showed a heavily cratered, rather moon-like terrain. The occultation test showed that Mars's surface atmospheric pressure was probably under 10 millibars instead of the 60 to 80 expected; it was comparable to that at 90,000 to 100,000 feet above the earth.

A few astronomers had predicted that Mars would be heavily cratered, but the results produced general shock; instead of being a little earth, Mars seemed like a bigger moon. Mariner 4 itself did not disprove the existence of life on Mars, but made it less likely. With such a thin atmosphere, Mars would be far more difficult to explore. It would be hard if not impossible for winged spacecraft to glide to a landing; or planes to fly; people would have to wear space suits when outside. Successive, better-equipped Mariners in 1969 and 1971 showed that the first reactions had been slightly exaggerated; Mars was a bit less like the moon than had been first thought. Only the southern hemisphere was heavily cratered, and even the craters showed signs of erosion. There were signs of geological activity such as vast volcanoes, and there might have been free water in the past. But these Mariners also indicated that Mars's seasonal color changes—the traditionally accepted evidence for life there—were probably due to the redistribution of dust by seasonal wind changes. There was still some possibility of life; the 1976 Viking probes did not entirely settle the question. Although the predominant interpretation of the experiments they performed was that they indicated that there was no life on Mars, some insisted that the results were ambiguous.[16]

The first interplanetary probes were great feats, but their results were deeply disappointing (except, perhaps, to a few geologists). Few had really expected to find a habitable Venus or intelligent life on Mars, but earth's neighbors proved duller, more lifeless, and harder to explore than anyone had supposed. Any encounter with other life—much less intelligence— would probably have to wait for interstellar, not interplanetary, travel. If humans ever settled Mars and Venus, it would only be after they were "terraformed" by incredibly vast engineering projects. Had those planets proved more interesting, the development of space travel would have been vastly different. Finding even a Venus on which a protected human could walk, or clear proof of life on Mars—much less a habitable Venus or cities on Mars—might have given an irresistible impetus to exploration beyond the moon. Some of the programs described in the following chapters might have had a different course.

9

The Other Road—
Wings toward Space

Like some other aspects of the modern world, space travel was produced by the convergence of two originally independent courses of development. It did not grow solely out of the building of bigger and bigger ballistic missiles and satellite launchers, as is widely assumed. It was also a product of the growth of aviation—the development of rocket-powered research airplanes designed to fly ever higher and faster. The latter element may be the distinctive American contribution to space travel, for it was limited largely to the United States; but it has been strangely downplayed, or ignored, even in the United States. The two courses of development are converging in the development of "aerospace planes," wholly reusable winged spacecraft that are capable of taking off and landing like conventional aircraft and that fly to orbit using a combination of rockets and "scramjets" (supersonic combustion ramjets), scooping up atmospheric oxygen to feed the engines on the way up. Such vehicles are under development as the X-30A and the projected National Aerospace Plane.[1]

The development of rocket research planes in the United States was sparked by researchers interested in building higher-performance aircraft. But some of the proponents of space flight, between the world wars, had envisaged it as growing directly out of aviation. Charles Lindbergh, one of the few persons prominent in the development of aviation who was also involved in early rocketry, may have seen it in this light; Korolev and Goddard were aware of this possibility and were interested in rocket planes. Some Austrians (Max Valier, Franz von Hoefft, and Eugen Sanger), who were loosely connected with the main group of rocket enthusiasts in

Germany, formed a Viennese school, which (in contrast to most in the VfR) believed that space flight would grow out of building rocket-powered planes, rather than vertically launched ballistic rockets. They were wildly optimistic about the ease with which such machines could be built. But the Germans shunned Valier, the leader of the group, for his addiction to occultism and for publicity stunts such as building rocket-powered cars. Valier later died in an accident in 1930.

THE "ANTIPODAL" ROCKET BOMBER

The much more sober aeronautical engineer Eugen Sanger (Valier's successor as leader of the Viennese school) and Irene Bredt (Sanger's student and later his wife) envisaged a research craft approaching an aerospace plane, the Silver Bird. In 1936 they went to work for the Luftwaffe in Germany; they had little or no contact with the Peenemunde group. While doing useful research on propellants, they reworked the Silver Bird into an offensive weapon, an "antipodal" rocket bomber. It would be a slim, flat-bellied dart 91 feet long, with a 50-foot wing span, powered by a 100-metric-ton-thrust engine burning diesel fuel and liquid oxygen. It would be launched by a huge rocket-powered railborne sled. As it left the sled its own engine would fire, kicking it to a speed of 13,500 miles an hour and a height of 90 miles. As it reentered the atmosphere, the pilot would hold it at such an attitude that it would skip off the denser layers of air, bound back into space, and repeat the maneuver several times. At one low point, it would drop a 660-pound bomb; New York was envisaged as the main target. It would land halfway around the world from its European base, presumably in Japanese-controlled territory near Australia, to refuel for a return mission.

Unfortunately for the Allies, in 1942 the Nazis rejected Sanger's proposal. It would have been an even bigger waste of resources than the V-2, even if (which was very unlikely) it had been ready for use in the war. The rocket bomber faced formidable problems. Building an engine more than three times as powerful as that of the V-2 would not have been easy, although Sanger built a combustion chamber for it in 1941. Materials to meet the stresses and heat involved (later research indicated that they would be worse, during the skips, than the Sangers thought, and this threw grave doubts on whether the whole idea was practical) would have to be developed. The elaborate launcher would be vulnerable to bombing, and by the time the bomber was ready the landing area in the "antipodes" was likely to be in Allied hands. (Sanger considered an improved bomber that could skip all the way around the world back to Germany.) In any case, it was an absurdly costly way to deliver one high explosive bomb.

After the war, however, the victors, especially the Soviets, found the Sanger proposal very interesting. With atomic weapons, a small bombload was no longer quite so useless. (The payload of Sanger's design was too small to deliver existing atomic bombs, but it might be increased, and later bombs would be smaller.) Developing a guidance system for unmanned missiles then seemed very difficult; a piloted rocket bomber would not need one. Although the rocket expert Grigori Tokaty-Tokaev warned that Sanger's concepts were far from realization, Stalin wanted the Sanger plane built. His son Vassili and Tokaty-Tokaev went to Germany to find the Sangers and bring them back. The search failed; the French got to them first. They worked for the French and wrote about space flight until Eugen Sanger's death in 1964, but they never obtained backing for a major development project.

In the early 1950s, German engineers in the U.S.S.R. worked on what was apparently a testbed vehicle for a modified, unmanned version of the Sanger concept, designated the R-15. Reports that the Soviets were building a full-scale "antipodal" rocket bomber were common in the late 1950s and 1960s. The Soviets seemed to have had a continuing interest in the concept but never put a major effort into it; it was eclipsed by ICBM development. They worked on a winged reconnaissance craft capable of reaching orbit, the Lapotok (which resembled the American Dyna-Soar), but it was canceled in 1960.[2] Variants of Sanger's ideas, strongly advocated by Walter Dornberger, led a sort of halflife in the United States and had ultimately blossomed into that abortive project.

The popular prophets of space flight in the 1950s, like von Braun and Clarke, did not envisage the full-blown aerospace plane and regarded the Sanger proposal as an unpleasant military footnote in the development of rocket technology. But they expected that the manned upper stages of earth-to-orbit ferry rockets would be winged, reusable vehicles. Only the wish to get people into space as soon as possible and the availability of a well-understood ballistic missile nose-cone technology led the Americans and Soviets to concentrate on capsules that would reenter like warheads and land using parachutes. It was clear even then that this approach was inherently limited and inadequate. It would never be able to return a really big payload from space. Landing on the ground (as the Soviets did) was jarring; landing in the sea (as the Americans did) involved the danger of sinking (as happened to Grissom's Mercury capsule) and the further danger that complex and costly recovery efforts would be disrupted by the weather. Either way, the capsules would be too battered and scorched to be used again. The amount of control the astronaut exercised during reentry and landing was limited. Winged craft would be far more controllable, have far more margin for error, require less effort in recovery, and allow far more flexibility in planning missions. But Mercury and Vostok marked a deemphasis on development of such craft, which had been underway for some time.

THE X-PLANES

During World War II, NASA's predecessor (the National Advisory Committee on Aeronautics) and the armed services became interested in developing high-speed research planes. Contemporary wind tunnels could not reproduce the effects of speeds between Mach 0.7 to 1.3; only actual flights could investigate the supposed sound barrier. NACA would have preferred a jet-powered research plane, but the Army Air Force rightly insisted that in the near future only rocket engines were powerful enough for supersonic flight.

No one liked rocket planes. They were tricky, allowed only brief flights, and required launching from a bomber, a mother ship, in mid-air. But they would have to do. Fortunately Reaction Motors was already building a 6,000-pound-thrust rocket engine, the XLR-11 (which burned alcohol and liquid oxygen), for the Navy for rocket-assisted takeoffs for bombers. It served to power the early rocket research planes. In March 1945, the bullet-shaped, straight-winged Bell X-1 was ordered. A whole series of X-1s (ranging through the X-1E) was eventually built. A parallel Navy-NACA project, the jet-powered Douglas D-558-1 Skystreak, would investigate high subsonic speeds. In August, after engineers evaluated data on swept wings captured in Germany, a second phase was added to the Navy project. Three swept-wing D-558-2 Skyrockets would be built, in several versions, using pure jet, mixed jet and rocket, and pure rocket propulsion and using the same rocket engine used in the X-1s. Only the pure rocket versions would reach really high speeds.

The X-1s and the Skyrockets proved spectacularly successful, although the X-1s were plagued by fires and explosions. An X-1, flown by Chuck Yeager, became the first plane to pass the speed of sound on October 14, 1947. The sound barrier was a myth; the real problems were at higher speeds. A. Scott Crossfield, flying a Skyrocket, became the first man to fly past Mach 2 on November 20, 1953, reaching a speed of 1,291 miles an hour. A few weeks later Yeager flew the X-1A to Mach 2.44 (1,650 miles an hour). The planes set altitude records.

Operational jet fighters soon flew regularly at Mach 2, but the rocket planes had been the only way for designers to get the needed data ahead of time. The jet-powered Douglas X-3, whose development started in 1945, had been designed for long flights at Mach 2 but proved a complete failure. Long delayed, it proved grossly underpowered and almost impossible to control when finally flown in 1952.[3] If research was to stay ahead of operational requirements, rocket power had to be used, despite its limitations and difficulties. Indeed, the Americans were approaching altitudes at which jet engines would not work at all.

THE X-2

Despite their powerplants and performance, the X-1s and Skyrockets had conventional structures built of familiar materials like aluminum and magnesium. The next-generation research plane, the Bell X-2, was something different. Begun in late 1945, just a few months after the X-1, the X-2 (two were built) was a swept-wing plane designed to reach Mach 3.5 and heights of up to 130,000 feet. The main aim of the X-2 was to investigate aerodynamic heating, for it would fly fast enough to cause serious heating by friction with the air. It had to be built of exotic materials. The X-2's fuselage was built of K-Monel (a nickel-copper alloy), and its wings and tail surfaces were built of stainless steel. It was powered by an advanced new rocket engine, the Curtiss-Wright XLR-25, with 15,000 pounds of thrust. Unlike previous engines, this would be throttleable; it had a complex new turbopump system. Like the X-1s and pure rocket D-558-2s, the X-2 would be air launched. Unlike them, it substituted skids and a small nosewheel for conventional landing gear. Instead of an ejection seat, the pilot would bail out using an ejection capsule; the whole front end of the plane would be blown off in an emergency. Some of these new features posed staggering problems.

The story of the X-2 is interesting, not for what was achieved but because it shows just how badly a project of this sort can go.

The first X-2, minus powerplant, was rolled out of the factory as early as 1950, but the engine (and powered flight) was long delayed. On May 12, 1953, while on a captive test flight over Lake Ontario that was designed to test methods of topping off its liquid oxygen tank, X-2 number 2 exploded. The pilot, Jean Ziegler, was killed, along with a man on the B-50 mother ship. The X-2 fell into the lake; the B-50 barely staggered home. The blast was wrongly attributed to an electrical malfunction touching off vapors in the propellant tank section, and it led to time-consuming modifications of the remaining X-2. Glide tests showed that the X-2 had poor directional control and serious problems with its landing gear; there were several crashes. Time was running out on the program; it suffered great cost overruns as well as delays, and it had to meet a deadline for powered flight of December 31, 1955. The project directors took risks they would normally have avoided to get in under the deadline. The X-2 caught fire on its first powered flight on November 18, 1955.

The project was allowed to go on after repairs, but it was discovered that the plane needed further modification. On August 8, the X-1A had exploded and had to be jettisoned from its B-50 carrier. The investigation of its loss revealed the real cause of the explosions that had destroyed the X-2 in 1953, and the X-1D and X-1 number 3 in 1951. The leather gaskets used in the rocket planes for sealing joints carrying liquid oxygen were impregnated with a material—tricresylphosphate—that is sensitive to shocks at low temperatures; it could blow up if struck sharply. All material of this sort had to be replaced.

The X-2 resumed flying in March 1956. It reached Mach 2.5 in May, but it was clear that its performance would fall short of expectations without further modifications. By extending the rocket nozzles, launching from greater heights, and taking every measure to cram more propellant into the tanks, Colonel Frank Everest flew at Mach 2.87 (1,900 miles an hour) in July. On September 7, Iven Kincheloe climbed to 126,000 feet, where the X-2's control surfaces were useless—they had no air to grip. Both men had great difficulty controlling the X-2 at high speeds even lower down. Crossfield considered their successes remarkable, and they may have been lucky. The problem of "inertia coupling," in which instability around one axis triggered instability around another axis and which had nearly killed Yeager on his Mach 2.44 flight, had not been solved. Moreover, the X-2's instruments apparently lagged behind in their responses. On September 27, Milburn Apt, another capable pilot, reached Mach 3.2 (2,091 miles an hour), but then the X-2 went out of control. The survival capsule did not work well and Apt was killed.

The X-2 only flew about twenty times and cost three lives. The Air Force later conceded that the program in its later stages was rushed and not well run. It set speed and altitude records but generated little data on aerodynamic heating.[4]

The X-2 was a failure.

THE X-15

The X-15 program had its share of ups and downs but proved far more successful than the X-2. It originated in June 1952, when NACA's Committee on Aerodynamics called for greatly increased research on

flights between heights of 12 and 50 miles and at hypersonic speeds—
Mach 4 through 10. It envisaged a tentative effort to look further into flights
up to orbital velocity. The latter was a big departure for a conservative
organization that had shied away from talk of space flight.

Some people opposed a new piloted research plane, arguing that it was
just too dangerous and that an unmanned vehicle should be built. But
NACA went ahead. By May 1954, NACA had worked out the preliminary
design characteristics for a new air-launched craft designed to fly a ballistic
trajectory, beyond the earth's "sensible atmosphere." The pilot would
experience two or three minutes of weightlessness before reentry and
would be flying high enough that conventional aerodynamic surfaces
would provide no control. "Ballistic controls," small hydrogen peroxide
rockets, would be needed. NACA decided that no combination or clustering
of existing rocket engines would be adequate to power the X-15; a new
engine was required. It further chose the structure and materials for the
craft. On reentry the X-15 would encounter far higher temperatures than
the X-2. One possible approach was to insulate most of the craft so that
only exposed surfaces would have to take the heat; that way most of its
structure could be built of relatively light conventional materials. Much
later this approach was used in the Space Shuttle, with newly developed
materials. But in 1954 there was no sure way to insulate the plane, and
even if one were developed it would involve more danger in an experimental craft and hamper the accurate measurement of heat transfer rates,
which was a major objective of the whole project. A hot structure, in which
the whole X-15 would be heat resistant, had to be built. A new nickel-
chrome steel alloy, Inconel-X, was chosen for the X-15's wings and
fuselage. Since the temperatures of various parts of the X-15 would vary
greatly, the thermal stresses on it would be considerable, especially on the
wings. It was expected to reach heights of 250,000 feet or more and speeds
of up to Mach 6.6.

Whether the X-15 was a spacecraft has been questioned; some deemed
it an airplane, others just a bridge to true spaceships. Inasmuch as it left
the limits of the atmosphere (usually defined as a height of 50 miles)
several times, it is hard to avoid concluding that the X-15 *was* a spaceship,
albeit a primitive, short-range one. Only the fact that the first Vostok and
Mercury flights preceded the first X-15 flights over 50 miles by a few
months prevented the general recognition of this. Indeed, in some ways
the X-15 was more of a true spaceship than Mercury or Vostok; it was
fully controllable and capable of flying over and over again—not a capsule
retired after each flight.

In July 1954, NACA reached agreement with the armed forces on the project; they would finance the X-15 jointly while the Air Force would control administration and NACA would make the technical decisions. In January 1955, bidding was opened for the X-15 contract. The aircraft companies were only moderately interested; experimental planes were not profitable. In July 1955, North American Aviation narrowly beat out a design proposed by Douglas. Ironically, North American had changed its mind and tried to get out of the competition, fearing that the X-15 would hamper its work on new fighter planes. Learning that it had won, North American offered to go on if allowed an extension of the agreed-on schedule; the government, not wishing to reopen the whole issue (which would cost further time anyway) graciously agreed. That was very fortunate for North American, for the fighter projects were later canceled. The X-15 may not have been profitable in itself, but the experience it provided helped the company (later Rockwell International) secure the contracts for the Apollo spacecraft, the Saturn V moon rocket, and the Space Shuttle. Whether this was always as fortunate for the space program is perhaps less certain.

North American's managers could not be accused of foresight. They regarded the construction of the first spaceship as a minor sideline. They did form a team of specialists in each phase of design and fabrication under the direction of the company's Advanced Design Section, led by Charles Feltz. That way the regular work of the plant would not interfere with the X-15 (or perhaps the other way around). An unusual feature of the project was the important role of the ex-NACA test pilot, A. Scott Crossfield. An engineer, he was fascinated by the X-15 and left the security of NACA to work for North American on this one project. As its test pilot, he would make the X-15's first flights, and he had considerable influence on its design. He persuaded the designers and the Air Force not to include an escape capsule of the sort used on the X-2. If something went wrong, he insisted, it was safer to stay in the X-15 until it was going low enough and slow enough for a conventional ejection seat to work.

The X-15's development was hampered by the lack of data on speeds through Mach 3.5 that the X-2 should have supplied. But the loss of the X-2 inspired the redesign of the X-15's tail. There were major questions about the working of the ballistic controls; attempts to test them on the modified X-1B had not worked well. There were doubts, too, about whether the combination of the X-15 and its B-52 mother ship would be stable. The X-15 was too big to be carried under the belly of the B-52 (substituted for the B-36 when the project was well advanced) like earlier rocket planes. It had to be tucked under a wing. Major problems had to be overcome in fabricating the X-15 itself. Inconel-X, hardly used before, was hard to shape and weld. Special tools and techniques, including "chemical milling," using acids had to be developed. The liquid oxygen and fuel tanks, of stainless steel, were also hard to make. Nevertheless, the ship was completed in a remarkably short time. The first of the three X-15s built was rolled out of the factory in October 1958. It was an all-black, dart-shaped craft, 50 feet long, with stubby wings little longer than its drooping horizontal stabilizers. It had big, wedge-like vertical tail fins; the ventral fin (which was later shortened and, still later, not carried at all) had to be dropped prior to landing. The innovative wedge shape of the fins solved the instability problem that had destroyed the X-2. An interesting accompaniment of the X-15 was the most elaborate flight simulator yet designed; it was later used to help train the Mercury astronauts.

For the X-15, Reaction Motors developed the XLR-99, which was the most advanced and powerful throttleable rocket engine yet built and which burned ammonia and liquid oxygen to generate 57,000 pounds of thrust. Ammonia (a second choice after hydrazine, which was not yet considered ready for use when the XLR-99 was designed) was slightly more potent than kerosene, by then the conventional rocket fuel, but had never been used much. Reaction Motors found out why the hard way. It proved hard to burn and caused combustion instability. The XLR-99 fell farther and farther behind schedule. North American offered to have its Rocketdyne Division supply an engine, but the Air Force forbade this lest it interfere with work on missile powerplants. NACA decided early on that the XLR-11, a pair of uprated X-1 engines supplying 16,000 pounds of thrust, would be used on the first flights of the X-15 if the XLR-99 was not ready.

By 1957–1958, North American had become more interested in the X-15. There were serious proposals to develop it into what would unquestionably be a spacecraft. North American engineers proposed a super X-15, launched on an Atlas missile or a Navaho booster for a 9,000-mile suborbital flight. That would require strengthening the X-15's skin and providing better air conditioning, but proponents argued that if started in late 1957 it could be ready by 1960. There was even a proposal to beat the Soviets by putting the existing X-15 into orbit; the pilot would bail out on the way down. But this meant the loss of a valuable craft and was rightly rejected. Later there were proposals for a completely redesigned X-15B, carrying two pilots, to be put into orbit by a multistage booster built around clustered Navahos or Titan missiles. The time required for this, however, put such proposals out of court as rivals for the nascent Mercury project, and the scheme appeared competitive with Dyna-Soar, which was specifically intended as a winged orbital vehicle.[5]

On March 10, 1959, the first X-15 made its first captive flight, suffering a small fire when an auxiliary power unit failed. On June 8, Crossfield left the mother ship for the first glide flight. An apparent landing instability proved due merely to the fact that the controls did not respond fast enough. More power was applied to the controls, and that cured the problem. Ground tests with the XLR-11 disclosed many problems with the old X-1 engines and the X-15's own tanks and plumbing, delaying the first powered flight by a month. X-15 number 2 finally made the first powered flight on September 17, reaching Mach 2.11 (1,393 miles an hour). An alcohol fire developed when a turbopump casing ruptured just before landing, but the ship was repaired in record time. On the fourth rocket flight, on November 5, the engine exploded due to an ignition failure in the proven XLR-11, forcing an emergency landing in which the X-15 was further damaged when the nosewheel strut did not function properly. It returned to the factory for repair, but it became clear that there was no fundamental defect in the X-15.

X-15 number 1 began flying under power; it and the repaired second plane began performing fairly reliably with the XLR-11, flying an average of every ten days. Air Force and NASA pilots began taking over from Crossfield. Neil Armstrong, who ten years later would be the first man to set foot on the moon, was the backup for Joseph Walker, the chief NASA pilot. On August 4, 1960, Robert White of the Air Force set a speed record of Mach 3.31 (2,196 miles an hour) in X-15 number 1; on August 8 Walker set an altitude record of 136,000 feet.

The XLR-99 had finally arrived and was installed in X-15 number 3 at Edwards Air Force Base. On June 8, Crossfield conducted a static ground test of the new engine. After a first test at full power, he checked the ability to stop and restart the engine. When he restarted it, an explosion destroyed the rear half of the X-15. Crossfield was lucky to survive; only thick concrete bunkers, recently installed, saved the ground crew. A stuck ammonia relief valve had caused the blast. X-15 number 3 had to be largely rebuilt; it returned to service in December 1961.

Crossfield flew X-15 number 2 with the XLR-99 on November 15, 1960. The worst bugs were out of the X-15, and Crossfield had shown its ability to fly at low altitudes and speeds. By the end of the year, the X-15s were turned over to the NASA-military team. On March 30, 1961, Walker tested the Mercury astronauts' spacesuit on a flight in X-15 number 2 to 169,600 feet, the highest flight yet. Record-setting flights were frequent over the next few years.

Curiously, just as the long-awaited main powerplant let the X-15 program attain its goals, it began fading from public consciousness. It had received much publicity in the late 1950s but was overshadowed by the Mercury flights. Even its most spectacular achievements were mentioned, it at all, only briefly in newspapers that gave headlines to Vostok and Mercury. It had been fashionable, earlier, to declare that the X-15 was the first spaceship, but in 1961 and after, it apparently fell to the status of a mere aircraft, perhaps since it could not reach orbit (although the first Mercury flights did not orbit the earth either). The incomprehensible public-relations line taken by NASA and the Kennedy Administration also contributed to the X-15's growing obscurity. They chose to play up the Mercury flights, in which the United States merely trailed the Soviets, rather than the X-15, in which the United States was exploring new territory with little Soviet competition. Although eight of the twelve men who flew the X-15 took it over 50 miles up and were considered astronauts, they remained little known to the public. (Ironically, even Tom Wolfe's famous book, *The Right Stuff*, which tried to set the record straight, wound up overwhelmingly stressing the Mercury flights.)

On November 9, 1961, White flew X-15 number 2 to Mach 6.04 (4,093 miles an hour), reaching the X-15's design speed. On April 30, 1962, Walker reached 246,700 feet in X-15 number 1. On July 17, 1962, White flew the rebuilt X-15 number 3 to 314,700 feet; this was the first flight over 50 miles up, beyond what NASA considered the limits of the "sensible atmosphere." White was the first X-15 pilot to be awarded astronaut's wings. On August 22, 1963, Walker took X-15 number 3 to 354,200 feet—over 67 miles up. This proved to be the peak altitude attained by the X-15.

The spectacular flights that stretched the X-15's performance to its limits were only a small part of the program. More important was the day-to-day gathering of data, largely on heating and aerodynamics. There were many modifications to the X-15; after September 1962, the ventral fin was usually discarded. The need for a piloted vehicle was amply demonstrated; it has been calculated that, had it been remotely controlled, the X-15 would have crashed on thirteen of its first forty-four flights. As it was, it remained dangerous. On November 9, 1962, John McKay of NASA, flying X-15 number 2, ran into exceptionally bad luck. A throttle control failed and the engine stuck at only 30 percent of full thrust. McKay could not dump his fuel, and the X-15 was badly overweight when he touched down. The landing gear collapsed and the X-15 flipped over. McKay was badly hurt and never recovered fully.

It was clear that the craft would have to be rebuilt. NASA decided to modify it as well, into the more advanced X-15A-2. It would carry two huge drop-tanks under its belly to provide propellants for a longer burning time; they would be dropped as it passed Mach 2 and could be reused after landing by parachute. The fuselage and landing gear were lengthened to let the X-15A-2 serve as a flying testbed for a "scramjet" engine. To protect the fuselage during long flights within the atmosphere, it was covered with "ablative" coatings that would be mostly used up on each mission.

The X-15A-2 first flew on June 25, 1964. On October 3, 1967, William Knight flew it to Mach 6.7 (4,520 miles an hour), slightly faster than planned, carrying a dummy "scramjet" engine—the last step before carrying a real engine. But the "ablative" coating did not work quite as expected and the X-15A-2 was badly damaged. Tremendous heat developed and the dummy engine was torn off. The X-15A-2 was retired.

Less than six weeks later, X-15 number 3 was lost. On November 15, Michael Adams flew it to 266,000 feet. As he came down to 230,000 feet, he apparently misread an indicator as meaning that he was in a roll rather than a sideslip. His reaction pushed the X-15 into a spin. At 120,000 feet he recovered from the spin, nosing over into a steep dive. But a design flaw in the quasi-automatic control system special to the X-15 number 3 caused violent "pitch oscillations"; the nose whipped violently up and down. Adams never regained control, and the X-15 tore apart in mid-air.

It was characteristic of the one-eyed public view of space matters that, while the fire that killed three Apollo astronauts in January 1967 caused headlines around the world and elaborate investigations, Adams's death aroused little interest. The *New York Times* put the story on page 14.

The crash aborted a proposal to turn X-15 number 3 into a delta-wing craft with an improved engine, capable of reaching speeds up to Mach 8. It would have been mainly a testbed for "scramjets."

The last X-15 flew a few more missions but was near the end of its useful life. It was retired in December 1968; in all the X-15s had flown 199 times. The program had cost about $300 million, a bargain as aerospace projects go, and had demonstrated successful hypersonic flight within the atmosphere and piloted, winged reentry from space. Much data, some of it unexpected, was collected on reentry heating. The X-15 had tested successfully the use of ballistic attitude controls and transition between those controls and conventional aerodynamic surfaces. No less than twenty-seven major advances were credited to the X-15. Much that it had done was immediately relevant to the space program; it had tested insulation used in the Saturn V and navigational devices used in the Apollo craft.[6]

DYNA-SOAR (X-20)

John Stack, one of the participants in the X-15 program, later suggested that, if not for the shock of Sputnik, the United States probably would have orbited an astronaut in a winged vehicle by 1968. Even before Sputnik, there was a nascent program, Dyna-Soar, that promised to do just that.

There had been some interest in the Sanger "antipodal" bomber in the late 1940s and 1950s. Not surprisingly, given its work in rocket planes, Bell Aircraft was a center of this. Bell, not the government, took the initiative. Beginning in 1952, Bell proposed a "boost-glide" vehicle, Bomi, a manned reentry craft to be launched by one or two expendable rocket stages for bombing or reconnaissance missions with ranges of up to 10,000 miles. The Air Force doubted that the proposed craft could overcome the reentry heating problem and generate the lift Bell claimed, and it was more interested in using it for reconnaissance rather than attack missions. In 1954 Bell, and other manufacturers, gained study contracts to work on the concept. During 1955–1956, Bell and the Air Force began envisaging a global-range vehicle and the Air Force became more interested in a bomber version, RoBo. For a time three different systems were under study by the aircraft companies, the Air Force, and NACA: RoBo, Brass Bell (a reconnaissance craft), and Hywards (a purely research vehicle). On October 10, 1957, all three programs were consolidated into one three-stage project, Dyna-Soar (a contraction of Dynamic Soaring). Step I, basically the old Hywards plan, would develop a piloted test craft to explore speeds and altitudes beyond those planned for the X-15. Step II would produce an operational reconnaissance and bombing craft with a range of 5,000 miles. Step III would be a craft capable of reaching orbit.

There was a strong competition for the Dyna-Soar I test craft. The contractors actually proposed longer-range vehicles than the Air Force had asked for. Some proposed a craft to go to earth orbit and return; others a "boost-glide" vehicle flying about the earth as a high-speed glider. As competition between the finalists proceeded, the Air Force envisaged orbital flights by late 1963 and a weapons system in the late 1960s. During 1959 there were bitter arguments about what booster should be used to launch Dyna-Soar, while Herbert York tried to cut back the program to a purely suborbital research effort; he later deemed Dyna-Soar nonsensical. The Air Force fought him off, but making Dyna-Soar a weapon became increasingly remote. It was hard to see what offensive or reconnaissance function it could perform that could not be done more simply by ICBMs or unmanned satellites.

Boeing won the Dyna-Soar contract in November 1959. By late 1961, after many changes in plans, it was decided that a Titan IIIC would put Dyna-Soar in orbit. The final schedule for the program, after many slippages, called for a piloted mission in 1966. Ten Dyna-Soars (called X-20s from late 1962) would be built.

The X-20 was a one-person craft with short delta wings and twin wing-tip rudders; it was built mainly of steel alloys, with molybdenum sheets covering its lower surfaces and ceramics covering the nose and the leading edges of the wings. A "water wall" between its inner and outer shells took care of the heat. Landing after a single long glide, the Dyna-Soar had evolved from the Sanger concept to something more like von Braun's A9/A10. (NACA/NASA engineers were leery of the Sanger "skip" concept.) It would go into space atop a "transtage" that would let it change orbit and would be discarded before returning to earth. The X-20 proper was an unpowered glider; it carried only a solid-fuel rocket to kick it away from the booster if something went wrong during launch and act as a backup retro-rocket.

But it never passed the mockup stage. The Kennedy Administration seemed uninterested and redirected funds away from it in 1961. The ultimate purpose of building a weapon had become nebulous. The Air Force finally made its objective a defensive weapon to protect U.S. reconnaissance satellites, but the Administration was not concerned with this. The continual slippage of the project schedule also made it less interesting. The X-20 would carry only one man and a payload of just 1,000 pounds; the cheaper Gemini, carrying two men into orbit, would fly earlier. Although the X-20 involved a greater technical advance and had more potential for developing a dependable transportation system, the Secretary of Defense canceled it on December 10, 1963. Instead the military would get a Manned Orbiting Laboratory, basically a Gemini with an accompanying service module. After much money was wasted, this program too was canceled; McNamara may have intended it merely as a device to placate the Air Force and perhaps never intended to see it carried out.

The muddled nature of the Dyna-Soar program, its excessive delays, and the lure of the more quickly accomplished capsule approach drove winged spacecraft into the shadows for some years. NASA and the Air Force concentrated research on small "lifting bodies," which were bluntly shaped vehicles with small, upturned airfoils—a cross between the ballistic and winged reentry approaches. The first of these, the Northrop HL-10 and M2F1, which flew at low heights and speeds, were succeeded by the X-23A, X-24A, and X-24B, built by Martin. Three small X-23A un-manned models were fired into space by Atlas missiles in 1966–1967 and survived reentry. The X-24A was a scaled-up manned version of the X-23A to test the "lifting-body" approach at relatively low aircraft speeds. It flew successfully from 1969 to 1971 and was later rebuilt as the differently shaped X-24B.

This program, carried out on a small budget, provided data useful to the development of hypersonic planes and the Space Shuttle; but it is notable that the latter proved much closer in design to the canceled Dyna-Soar. The Shuttle owed more to the X-15 than to the Mercury, Gemini, and Apollo capsules. As the Apollo astronaut Frank Borman later noted, "Ships like the *Challenger* borrowed very little if anything from the entire Apollo program. They were experimental craft designed for research in areas Apollo hardly touched."[7]

10

The Road Not Taken— Nuclear Propulsion

The main line of development of space travel, up to the present, has been the perfection of larger and more efficient chemically fueled rockets. But in the 1950s and 1960s, Americans explored nuclear propulsion. Perhaps only a series of flukes—and decisions that were downright perverse— prevented gigantic advances in space flight.

Using nuclear power for spaceships had been an attractive idea ever since the early twentieth century. Leo Szilard, the scientist most responsible for the American atomic bomb project, once indicated that he had decided to concentrate on nuclear research in 1932 because only atomic energy could "enable man not only to leave the earth but to leave the Solar System."[1] Many argued that only nuclear power would make inter- planetary flight possible, or at least an economic proposition. Robert Bussard, one of the most important proponents of the nuclear rocket, observed that space flight stretched chemical fuel technology "to the utmost"; "a multiple stage chemical rocket system as massive as a small naval cruiser is presently required to send two or three men to the Moon with safe return. Such a course is reasonable only if the job must be done and there is no other way to do it."[2]

The development of nuclear reactors and bombs seemed to make nuclear propulsion an immediate possibility. With one exception (which will be discussed later in this chapter), there was no way to use nuclear energy *directly* for propulsion; the heat generated by a nuclear reactor had to be converted to run some form of engine.

THE NUCLEAR REACTOR ROCKET

One possibility was to use a reactor to generate electrical power to run the ion rockets conceived by Goddard and actually built on a small scale by Soviet researchers between the world wars. But ion rockets could only be used in a vacuum and with their small thrust were not likely to be practical and useful until humankind was well established in space. To be of value in the near future, nuclear reactors had to be used to heat a propellant (or, more exactly, working fluid) that would be expelled through a rocket nozzle. The higher the temperatures the reactor developed, the greater the exhaust velocity. Potentially, the most potent reactors would run so hot that their cores were molten or even gaseous. Gaseous-core reactors might attain a specific impulse (the measure of the effectiveness of a rocket fuel or engine) as high as 3,000 to 7,000 seconds. (The absolute limit of chemical propulsion was under 600 seconds.) But such reactors were technically far distant, and it would be hard to prevent the costly and dangerous loss of fissioning reactor fuels through the rocket exhausts; the contamination problem meant that they could only be used well out in space. Although the so-called light-bulb or closed-cycle type of gaseous-core reactor might avoid that problem, even studying the problems inherent in this sort of reactor was difficult.[3] Only solid-core reactors, running at much lower temperatures, were likely to be practical in the near future; but since they developed a specific impulse as high as 1,300 seconds, they still offered higher performance than chemical combustion.

Right after World War II, many expected that nuclear power would soon be in widespread use. Although those who were best informed were the least optimistic about the prospects for nuclear power in general, even some who were otherwise pessimistic expected early applications to rockets.[4] But it did not turn out that way. For all its advantages over chemical fuels—the ability to generate enormous power in a small space and get along with just one propellant—the nuclear rocket faced great difficulties. For all its power, a nuclear engine would weigh considerably more than its chemical counterpart. Control was a serious problem; nuclear reactors were slow to start up and shut off, while a rocket engine has to start quickly and stop sharply. A rocket reactor ran under more severe conditions than any other type; operating at high temperatures, it would suffer severe thermal stress as its structure heated up, and severe pressures as propellant flowed through it. The best propellants and reactor materials were liable to be antithetical; the reactor parts had to be protected from direct contact with propellants. Often costly, unfamiliar materials that were hard to work with would be needed. The nuclear rocket's exhaust nozzle had to run at higher temperatures than that of a chemical engine. Shielding against radiation would exact a heavy penalty in weight. Radiation damaged organic materials, like lubricants, that were usually used in rocket engines; this forced the development of substitutes.

EARLY EXPLORATIONS

Some of these problems became apparent in the first examinations of the nuclear rocket. Some scientists working on the Manhattan Project, notably Richard Feynman, may have thought of the nuclear rocket during 1944; the concept was widely discussed after the war ended. The von Karman report of the Army Air Force's Scientific Advisory Board was unenthusiastic and concluded that the nuclear rocket would be hard to develop, competitive for still scarce fissionable materials, and lacked a clear military need. Nevertheless, the Air Force showed some interest, commissioning analyses of the nuclear rocket at RAND and North American Aviation, as a subsidiary element of early work on the Navaho missile. A North American study concluded in February 1947 that liquid hydrogen would be the best propellant for a nuclear rocket, while graphite, an allotropic form of carbon that had the peculiar property of gaining strength over a wide range of high temperatures, would be the best material for constructing reactors. But it reacted with hydrogen, so some kind of coating or cladding, probably of metallic carbides, would be needed to protect it. The North American engineers even delivered a preliminary design of a nuclear-powered ICBM, which, with modifications, could launch a satellite. A study at Johns Hopkins commissioned by the new Atomic Energy Commission reached parallel conclusions but warned that development would be long and costly, would use too much nuclear fuel, and required more data on the materials involved. The Air Force concluded that a nuclear rocket was unnecessary or premature. But it was interested in nuclear-powered planes. Desultory, small-scale study of nuclear rockets went on at Oak Ridge, Tennessee, as a sideline of the nuclear plane effort. But interest gradually trailed off.[5]

REVIVAL

In 1952–1953, a single physicist, Robert Bussard, revived official interest in the nuclear rocket. By then production of fissionable materials had expanded vastly; scarcity of fuel was no longer a major roadblock as it had been in 1946–1947. Bussard had long been interested in space travel. When he joined the Aircraft Nuclear Propulsion Program in 1952, he embarked on a major study of the nuclear rocket. His July 1953 report dealt with them as powerplants for missiles, but it seems clear that he regarded this as a stalking horse for space flight. He concluded that nuclear engines would be more efficient for missiles for all but the smallest payloads and shortest ranges. Published in the secret *Journal of Reactor Science and Technology* in December 1953, his report interested John von Neumann and Eugene Wigner of the Teapot Committee, among others. Von Neumann actually arranged a small program of research on the necessary reactor materials at Oak Ridge. Interest in nuclear rockets grew at the AEC's Los Alamos and Livermore laboratories, some private contractors, and the Air Force Research and Development Command. Urged on by ARDC, in late 1954 the already interested AEC authorized six-month feasibility studies of the nuclear rocket at both Los Alamos and Livermore. The Air Force's Scientific Advisory Board had formed an ad hoc Committee on Nuclear Missile Propulsion; in February 1955, it advised starting nuclear rocket development immediately.

Los Alamos soon decided, as had Bussard, that only solid-core reactors were a practical bet; but Los Alamos held that Bussard had oversold the case for nuclear-powered missiles. It concluded that a nuclear-powered ICBM would not really have an advantage over a chemically fueled one, although it pondered using a boosted "air duct" device to burn reactor-heated hydrogen with atmospheric oxygen in the first phase of flight, which might restore the vanished advantage. Further study suggested that that idea was impractical, but that a nuclear upper stage atop a first-stage chemical rocket, probably a Navaho booster, would still provide a big payload advantage over purely chemically powered ICBMs. In March 1955, Los Alamos and Livermore submitted parallel reports, including preliminary reactor designs. They made clear that nuclear rockets were a good possibility, although it was likely that as far as missile propulsion was concerned they were now but a backup for the Atlas and Titan. Both labs formed permanent nuclear rocket divisions.

PROJECT ROVER

On November 2, 1955, the AEC approved parallel programs at both laboratories to demonstrate feasibility, with the Air Force as the ultimate user of a nuclear rocket. The Nuclear Rocket Propulsion Program (usually called Project Rover, although that code name was allotted only in 1957) then came under the Missile Projects Section of the AEC's Aircraft Reactors Branch and the Air Force Propulsion Laboratory at Wright Field. Both AEC labs concentrated on graphite reactors; Los Alamos envisaged an engine using ammonia (although its performance would be far inferior to that of hydrogen, it would be easier to use in a military missile); Livermore envisaged a more ambitious engine using hydrogen and capable of delivering a big load to earth orbit. In April 1956, the Defense Department set a target date for 1959 for the development of the nuclear rocket. In the following months, Aerojet and Rocketdyne received USAF contracts to develop nonnuclear components for the project—primarily nozzles and turbopumps for liquid hydrogen. A search for test sites in Nevada began. Late in 1956, the program ran into its first heavy weather. Budget problems had forced a general review of all military projects. The interservice Special Weapons Project Group formed a special committee under General Herbert Loper to examine the nuclear rocket. It concluded that a nuclear-powered ICBM was not really needed, but that work on nuclear propulsion should go on for space work. But the 1959 target date for a demonstration of feasibility was unrealistic; the date should be pushed back to 1960–1962. In January 1957, the Defense Department cut back support and stretched it out; ground tests were expected by 1963, and flights in 1968. In March rocket work was concentrated at Los Alamos; Livermore was assigned Project Pluto, the nuclear ramjet, instead.

After Sputnik interest in nuclear rockets revived. Two prominent Democratic members of the Joint Congressional Committee on Atomic Energy (JCAE), Clinton Anderson and Henry Jackson, were strong proponents of it; they urged, unsuccessfully, that it get a DX priority. Anderson became the project's leading congressional backer and kept it going for several years in the late 1960s, when the Executive Branch would otherwise have ended it.

A Democratic Administration might well have reacted to Sputnik by launching a Manhattan Project type of effort to get a nuclear rocket; in some ways, it is strange that even the Eisenhower Administration did not do so. But the PSAC was skeptical of early success, while Herbert York was hostile to nuclear propulsion. NASA also tended toward a cautious approach. Anderson wanted the AEC to be given overall control of the nuclear rocket; he was not too happy when responsibility for the non-nuclear side of the project was transferred from the Air Force to NASA in October 1958. He was also unable to prevent the Administration from cutting the budget for it in 1959.

The JCAE consistently favored more funds and a more aggressive approach, siding with AEC against NASA. There was an incipient dispute over development approaches between NASA and the AEC. The AEC favored faster, more aggressive development with concurrent, parallel approaches to problems. It did not worry much if a particular test failed;

failure might teach more than success. Reliability could wait. The AEC approach derived from its emphasis on weapons development. Speed was desirable, but lives were not immediately at risk. (Bombs, and reactors for that matter, were tested at a distance by remote control.) Although the pressure of competition with the Soviets would erode this approach during the 1960s, NASA followed NACA in minimizing risk taking and stressing reliability all along. In aircraft development, lives were at stake at an early stage, and a test should succeed before the next step was taken. The difference was not acute in the late 1950s, for NASA did not then want a closely controlled centralized program. The JCAE, disliking the existing loose arrangements, pressed for a joint AEC/NASA office under a single manager, like the AEC/Navy organization under Admiral Rickover that had run the spectacularly successful nuclear submarine program. In August 1960, NASA and the AEC duly formed a joint Space Nuclear Propulsion Office (SNPO). Anderson wanted an AEC man—preferably Colonel Jack Armstrong, who headed the Missiles Projects Branch of its aircraft propulsion project and who was regarded as a young Rickover. But NASA opposed him and secured the appointment of Dr. Harold Finger of its Lewis Laboratory, who had managed the NASA side of Rover since 1958. Although capable, he was no Rickover but was a cautious man of the conventional NACA/NASA mold.[6]

In early 1959, before the SNPO was formed, NASA's leaders made an important decision: Any nuclear engines would be started in orbit or near orbit to minimize the risk of an accident and the spread of radiation. But they also seem to have decided that a powerful single-stage-to-orbit system was not really needed. The decision was adhered to, although studies suggested that even the worst possible accident would contaminate only a small area. A test on January 12, 1965, in which a Kiwi-B reactor was destroyed deliberately, indicated that people 1.5 miles from a worst possible accident should be safe.[7] In any case, it was increasingly unlikely that the type of reactors on which development focused could power a lower stage. There was, however, general confidence in the late 1950s and after that a nuclear rocket would fly by 1970.[8]

KIWI

Early in 1957, the Rover directors settled on a two-phase reactor development program, Kiwi, which would take place at an elaborate test facility to be built at Jackass Flats in Nevada. The Kiwi-A reactors— ultimately three were tested—would prove the basic feasibility of the nuclear rocket, establish testing procedures, and supply data on reactor functioning and materials—especially for designing fuel elements. The A reactors would use only hydrogen gas at low power levels. The higher-power Kiwi-B series—five were built—would use liquid hydrogen and (it was hoped) be actual prototypes for a flyable engine. (With space work now the objective, hydrogen had replaced ammonia.) The design of Kiwi-B proceeded concurrently with work on Kiwi-A.

The first Kiwi-A reactor, assembled in 1958–1959, was based on the preliminary design Los Alamos had produced in 1955, scaled down from 1,500 megawatts to 100 megawatts. (In a flight reactor, 1 megawatt of power should translate into 50 pounds of rocket thrust.) Gas would be fed in under pressure (a turbopump system was still under development) to a reactor consisting of stacks of fuel elements—flat uncoated plates—in a cylindrical core, moderated by heavy water and cooled by regular water. The Kiwi-A reactor did not resemble a real engine.

In April 1959, during a checkout of the flow-control system, the bellows that pumped the hydrogen gas leaked and caused a bad fire, delaying actual operation. In July 1959, Kiwi-A finally went critical, reaching a power level of 78 megawatts. Despite the failure of a part in its core (which caused the reactor to get hotter than expected) and severe erosion of the unprotected fuel elements, the test proved that a nuclear rocket could work. Two more Kiwi-A reactors, A-prime and A-3, tried out elements of the Kiwi-B design. On October 10, 1960, one reached 100 megawatts. But both reactors lost material from their cores, revealing that their core designs were not structurally sound—an ominous sign for the Kiwi-B series.

Kiwi-B was to reach 1,000 megawatts for five minutes, using hexagonal fuel elements of a graphite-uranium mixture with various protective coatings. The neutron reflector around the reactor, and the pressure vessel containing it, were to be of flight weight. Perhaps most importantly, it would use liquid hydrogen. After cooling the rocket nozzle, the hydrogen would be fed into the top of the reactor, flowing through longitudinal passages in the fuel elements where it would be heated. It was hoped that Kiwi-B would be followed quickly by Kiwi-C, which would add a working liquid hydrogen turbopump. It would be a "breadboard engine," using all flight-type equipment but arranged for convenient test purposes rather than in the exact layout of an operational engine. But the core failures of Kiwi-A-prime and A-3 forced a major redesign.[9] Meanwhile the Rover project had given up a dramatic alternative to the graphite reactor approach embodied in Kiwi.

THE DUMBO ALTERNATIVE

As we noted, in 1959 NASA decided to use nuclear engines only on the upper stages of multistage vehicles. The original hope for single-stage nuclear rockets taking payloads to orbit or beyond was put off. Safety considerations aside, this decision was enforced by the nature of the reactors being developed. Their thrust-to-weight ratio would be low. Although useful and important, they did not solve the basic problem of space travel—moving things from earth to orbit economically.

But another line of development might solve that problem: an all-metal, laminar-flow reactor. This concept, called Dumbo, had been developed at Los Alamos, outside the Nuclear Rocket Division, by Bruce Knight, B. B. McInteer, and E. S. Potter in 1957. It envisaged a very different structure and fuel elements, to heat hydrogen to much higher temperatures in a very short space. In Kiwi-type graphite reactors, the propellant flowed longitudinally down through the fuel elements in a path parallel to the rocket's thrust. In Dumbo, the hydrogen flowed upward from the base of the reactor into a space around a set of hollow tubes, which contained both moderator and fuel elements—but in separate layers, instead of being mingled as in the graphite reactor. The hydrogen flowed through pores in the layer of zirconium hydride moderator that formed the outer surface of the tubes, through a thin nickel screen, and then through the fuel element proper, which formed the inner surface of the tubes and was made out of very thin plates of uranium dioxide and tungsten cermet, cladded on both sides by pure tungsten. Inside the tubes, the heated gas flowed down and out the exhaust. Hydrogen within the reactor underwent laminar flow instead of the turbulent flow of the graphite reactor, and the reactor's geometric factor—the increased contact area between propellant and the fuel elements heating it—was vastly greater, while the fuel elements themselves were less affected by heat. The result was a far better thrust-to-weight ratio. Dumbo's chief problem was making its fuel elements; tungsten was hard to work with and costly. Nevertheless, good progress seems to have been made and fuel elements were tested successfully at full-power conditions.

It is still not entirely clear why Dumbo was canceled. Tests of a Dumbo reactor were originally scheduled for mid-1960. But early in 1959, it was dropped from the test schedule in favor of Kiwi-A-prime. In the fall of 1959, work on Dumbo was halted, purportedly because there was not enough money to try both Dumbo and Kiwi and the latter was believed more certain to work. It has been reported, however, that those in charge of the program did not understand the Dumbo concept. They ordered that the planned test use the same exhaust nozzle as Kiwi-A, which forced use of too low a rate of fuel flow for Dumbo to work properly. Since Dumbo's predicted power would then be no better than that of the Kiwis, there seemed no justification for incurring the trouble and cost of using tungsten.[10] Dumbo's cancellation left Rover oriented toward space-to-space propulsion and dependent on the acceptance of large-scale space missions after Apollo—building a moon base or trips to the planets.

NERVA AND RIFT

Although the 1960 Democratic platform called for a major nuclear rocket program, the Kennedy Administration was divided on whether to follow through. A PSAC subcommittee studying nuclear rockets was split. Trevor Gardner and the representatives and friends of the Los Alamos group strongly favored nuclear propulsion. But many, led by Jerome Wiesner, opposed emphasis on nuclear propulsion. The issue of nuclear propulsion did not stand on its own; it was associated with the question of whether there should be a big space program oriented toward a long-term effort beyond a moon landing—something Wiesner and many others did not favor. Stanislaw Ulam, a member of the subcommittee, felt that some members (chemists) were simply biased in favor of chemical fuels or afraid of nuclear energy. The subcommittee recommended reducing the nuclear rocket to a minor effort. Lyndon Johnson and Senator Anderson opposed this; Gagarin, the Bay of Pigs, Johnson, and public pressure then led Kennedy to favor a major manned program (at least through a landing on the moon) and, by association, Rover. On May 25, 1961, Kennedy authorized development of an operational engine, NERVA (Nuclear Energy for Rocket Vehicle Propulsion) and a flight-test vehicle, RIFT (Reactor in Flight Test). At this early date it was optimistically hoped that RIFT would fly by 1966–1967 as an upper stage on a Saturn rocket, and even serve on the moon rocket if something went wrong with its chemical counterpart. In July 1961, Aerojet became the prime contractor for NERVA. It made most of the nonnuclear engine components, while Westinghouse built the reactor.

Choosing an industrial contractor triggered a fight over the direction of the program. The AEC, which had wanted an industrial contractor brought in much earlier, favored a decentralized program run mainly from Los Alamos; NASA now wanted a highly centralized program run from Washington, and it got its way. This was a formula for success contrary to that followed by most of the successful projects chronicled in this book, and it was particularly doubtful since the central problems of the program involved nuclear engineering.

In May 1962, with work on a reactor prototype apparently well underway, Lockheed got a contract to build ten RIFT vehicles to serve as third stages on Saturn Vs. Only four were to fly, and just three would fire their engines. RIFT influenced the Apollo project and the design of the Saturn V, whose diameter was determined by the expected dimensions of the nuclear stage. Some facilities at Cape Canaveral were designed to handle the nuclear version of the Saturn.[11] But the program had begun to go awry.

KIWI-B

Several versions of Kiwi-B—B1, B2, and B4, which varied chiefly in core support design—were planned. B4 was the favored design. Delays were imposed by design changes after experience with the later Kiwi-As, labor disputes, unexpected difficulties with the changeover to liquid hydrogen, and problems with developing turbopumps, flow-control systems, and nozzles. A test cell equipped for liquid hydrogen work was not ready in time, so an older one was modified to do the job. Meanwhile, Kiwi-B1A was tested using hydrogen gas, to try out some components. An explosion during a checkout in November 1961 caused more delays. In December, Kiwi-B1A finally went critical, although its power was limited to one third of the design level. As it reached the planned peak, proving some of the new design features, a leak in the interface seal between the rocket nozzle and the reactor pressure vessel caused a serious fire. The test cell had to be modified to improve safety. Still more problems followed. Structural problems with the B2 design were found; and the B4 went critical prematurely as it was being assembled. Its fuel elements had absorbed moisture from the air, changing their nuclear properties, and modifications had to be made.

Rover returned to the B1 design for a first test on liquid hydrogen. It was already known that its core design was deficient; the test was run to gain experience using liquid hydrogen and try out some nonnuclear components. On September 1, 1962, the B1B reactor reached a level of 900 megawatts but then its core failed; some fuel elements spat out of the exhaust nozzle. Since the design was going to be discarded anyway, this caused little worry; nonnuclear items and the test gear had worked well. Indeed the test was a great success in terms of maintaining control over a damaged reactor.

No such comfort could be drawn from the test of Kiwi-B4A on November 30. It reached 600 megawatts when there were flashes of light from the nozzle as reactor parts shot out. The test was stopped quickly; 90 percent of the parts in the core had been broken.[12]

The cause of the failure was soon diagnosed correctly as a flow-induced vibration of the reactor core caused by a weak lateral core support. But it sparked a major crisis for the project, already six months behind schedule; in October its enemies in the PSAC had attacked RIFT as premature and pressed for a lower level of funding, although the project was stoutly defended by Webb and Anderson. The latter inspired a presidential visit to Los Alamos and Jackass Flats. Unfortunately, the visit took place the week after the B4A failure, which was a godsend for the critics. At Los Alamos, Kennedy heard arguments for and against Rover by Harold Finger and Wiesner. Wiesner argued that the nuclear rocket was technically premature and in any case was worthwhile only if a moon base and/or a Mars trip were planned. NERVA should be reduced to a low-level effort and RIFT stopped. En route to Nevada, Kennedy decided to delay RIFT pending the outcome of the next hot reactor run. More funds would be provided if tests succeeded by July 1963.

The fate of the program was thus likely to turn on one test. Over the opposition of Los Alamos, which was sure it already knew the cause of the B4A failure, Finger imposed the more cautious NASA approach. He insisted on an elaborate step-by-step policy of component testing and "cold-flow" testing of reactor designs which involved tedious studies of hydrogen passage through specially instrumented Kiwi-B reactors without fissionable fuel. They proved that Los Alamos had been right. A new B4D reactor was tested at full power, 1,000 megawatts, on May 13, 1964. It performed well, but the test had to be stopped prematurely when the nozzle ruptured. B4E, with the same core design but an improved coating for fuel elements that increased their lifetime, was tested successfully in August and restarted in September. Some at Los Alamos maintained that Finger merely wasted a year and a half showing that they had been right all along. Given the stakes the political leadership had put on a single reactor run, it is arguable that Finger had little choice even had he not preferred this approach. His caution did not prevent major cuts in funding. In December 1963, President Johnson was under strong pressure to cut the federal budget. He was presented with three alternative funding levels for Rover— $300 million for a full-scale, flight-oriented program; $200 million for a lesser level; and $150 million for research work with no plans for a flight engine. Wiesner and the Bureau of the Budget wanted even deeper cut. Johnson chose the $150 million level; RIFT was canceled. NERVA continued as a ground-based technology development project. No flight test or mission for the engine it developed would ever be scheduled.

As James Dewar, the historian of Rover, has observed, the termination of the flight objective presaged the post-Apollo turn against the space program in general.[13]

Nevertheless, the project still aimed at a 250,000-pound-thrust engine. Ironically, in technical matters it had crossed the hump just as its support slipped. Westinghouse was building a series of NERVA experimental reactors (NRX) based on the Kiwi-B4 design; NRX A-4, the first "breadboard" engine, was tested successfully from December 1965 to March 1966; the last NRX ran well for an hour at full power.

Meanwhile Los Alamos designed a series of 5,000-megawatt Phoebus reactors with bigger cores operating at higher temperatures and improved fuel elements. As an intermediate step, a Phoebus 1 series of smaller reactors of up to 1,500 megawatts would gather data for the full-scale Phoebus 2 series. Phoebus 1A reached full power in June 1965, but was damaged when its hydrogen supply was exhausted unexpectedly and the reactor core overheated. The accident was caused by a faulty hydrogen tank gauge deranged by radiation. This, and a lesser problem with NRX A-3 in April 1965 (also caused by a fault outside the reactor) seem to have been the only troubles with the post-Kiwi tests. In contrast with its earlier phases, the program advanced smoothly. A Phoebus was tested at 4,200 megawatts in June 1968.

But an attempt in 1967 by the Administration and the JCAE to get more money for Rover failed. In 1968, over Webb's opposition, the budget was slashed and the objective scaled back. The NERVA II 250,000-pound-thrust engine was dropped; only the first-step 75,000-pound NERVA I would be built. Contemporary observers thought that Webb was lucky to have kept Rover alive at all. The budget was slashed again in early 1970, although the NERVA XE engine, in full flight configuration, had been tested successfully at 55,000 pounds of thrust in September 1969. Fuel element lifetimes had been extended considerably.

Rover was close to an operational engine. It was hoped that NERVA I would power a ferry between lower earth orbit and "geosynchronous" orbit. But it was not to be. NASA found it hard to get money even for an earth-to-orbit shuttle, and in 1971 it effectively sacrificed nuclear propulsion for it. Some thought this a mistake because it merely antagonized some of NASA's strongest congressional supporters and because the shuttle-NERVA combination could have been sold. But Senator Anderson, Rover's strongest backer, was in his last year in the Senate and in poor health; and the Nixon Administration, despite strenuous efforts by Representative Barry Goldwater, Jr. did not care. Rover ended in early 1972. It had, however, contributed much to technological development.

Very difficult problems—notably making reliable long-lasting fuel elements and rocket nozzles—had been solved. Much was learned about working with graphite, beryllium, and Hastelloy X, the alloy used for the nozzle. The nuclear rocket effort had promoted the technology of handling liquid hydrogen and contributed much to Apollo and the Space Shuttle.[14]

The technology necessary for maintaining a moon base or any sort of manned deep-space exploration had been set aside. One commentator has written of the mishandled nuclear rocket program: "This is not a scientific or engineering failure. It is a political failure of the first magnitude."[15] Ultimately the nuclear rocket was revived by the Strategic Defense Initiative; it explored an upper stage powered by a new type of "particle-bed" reactor. The collapse of the U.S.S.R. disclosed that the Soviets too had worked on a nuclear rocket, possibly one able to take off from the earth's surface.

Several factors led to the abortion of the first nuclear rocket effort. Its transfer from the Air Force to NASA may have been unfortunate. Although it is hard to document or pinpoint, there seems to have been a bias within NASA (not shared by Administrator Webb) against nuclear or other "exotic" forms of propulsion; it is doubtful whether such a bias existed or would have developed in the Air Force. At best, in NASA nuclear propulsion was one project among many, and a long-range one at that. Had the USAF kept responsibility for nuclear propulsion, while NASA got the rest of the space effort, a desirable competition might have resulted. The Air Force probably would have favored the more daring pace the AEC wanted; the hiatus from 1962 to 1964 would not have occurred. The nuclear rocket is not the only episode suggesting that it is not always desirable for all development projects in a particular field to be centralized under one agency or even totally centralized themselves.

Yet perhaps the true turning point of the project was internal: the choice in 1959 to drop Dumbo. That decision automatically made the nuclear rocket less important. If successful, Dumbo would have been a direct (indeed unbeatable) competitor for the big, essential job of boosting large loads from the earth to space. Kiwi-NERVA, by contrast, was of value only to a big post-Apollo program. The third turning point of the program was the failure of Kiwi-B4A and the delay that followed. The hiatus and "cold-flow" testing proved unnecessary. No criticism need attach to Harold Finger for the course taken. Given the irrational political insistence on having one test decide everything, he had little choice. The NASA approach was really enforced from above. But the near halt in testing and the long slippage in dates for a flight test undermined the program and set it up to be cut in 1963. In the end, however, the nuclear rocket was the victim of the failure to plan ahead or agree on a long-range post-Apollo effort. The Kennedy Administration did not care, and President Johnson could not muster the necessary support.

ORION: PROPULSION BY BOMB

A bizarre idea to use nuclear energy for spaceships appeared at about the same time as the reactor rocket: propulsion by nuclear bombs. (This is often called, perhaps euphemistically, the nuclear "pulse rocket.") In December 1944, Stanislaw Ulam (a brilliant mathematician then working at Los Alamos) and Frederick de Hoffman pointed out that a spaceship could be propelled by successive small nuclear blasts. Debris—plasma or gas from an explosion at the right distance—hitting a properly designed "pusher plate," attached to the ship's tail by shock absorbers, would shove it along. Ulam and F. Rennes made some preliminary calculations in a memorandum circulated at Los Alamos in 1947, but there was little interest in the idea for some years. The scarcity of nuclear fuel, and weapons research (to which Ulam made notable contributions; he was at least coresponsible with Teller for the H-bomb) prevented following up the idea. But a physicist, Lew Allen, demonstrated that it was not obviously impractical; the right materials could survive very close to a nuclear explosion. At Eniwetok, Marshall Islands, in the Pacific, small steel balls withstood a 20-kiloton blast just 10 meters away.

In 1955 Ulam and Cornelius Everett published a paper on the concept. They envisaged a test craft hurled by a first-stage chemical booster to high altitude, where it would use a series of nuclear charges ranging from the equivalent of 30 tons of TNT to 1.5 kilotons.[16] This proposal sparked interest and even the development of a rival internal nuclear pulse system, somewhat more like a rocket. Small blasts inside a huge steel chamber would expel water or liquid hydrogen through a nozzle. Like a rocket engine, the blast chamber would be regeneratively cooled by the propellant. The internal system, designated Helios, was studied by the Livermore Laboratory and Dandridge Cole of the Martin company for some years; there was even a design concept for a huge 73,000-ton Helios-powered ship with delta wings for return to earth. But it became clear that the Helios engine would be very heavy and offered much lower performance than the external system; its performance was rated at a specific impulse of 1,400 seconds—external systems offered 2,000 to 6,000 seconds.

The external pulse concept, dubbed Orion, attracted attention after Sputnik. In April 1958, ARPA allotted $2,330,000 to work on it. Theodore Taylor, a brilliant nuclear weapons designer, became project engineer; he was soon joined by the able and imaginative physicist Freeman Dyson.

Dyson later remarked that even in 1958 he had seen that chemical rockets would cost too much and do too little.

The Air Force took over Orion from ARPA in 1960; NASA had little interest in it. At first it progressed nicely. The principal problem was finding the right shape for the "pusher plate" and protecting it from "ablation" by successive blasts. Other problems were shielding the crew and designing shock absorbers. Taylor devised much better bombs ("pulse units") than originally expected—"shaped charges" buried in polyurethane plastic which would greatly increase the amount of debris hitting a "pusher plate." Designers created a satisfactory "pusher plate" and a system to spray protective grease on it between blasts. A high-explosive powered test vehicle, called Hot Rod or Put-Put, reached heights of 200 feet. But the project ran into increasing difficulties at higher levels. Work on Orion involved a big jump; going further required nuclear explosions; and a full-scale vehicle would be expensive. The Air Force found it hard to find a mission for Orion. Some officers contemplated space battleships armed to stop Soviet ICBMs, and maybe deal with unfriendly Martians and Venerians, but they could not get anyone to buy the concept. That left interplanetary exploration—now a NASA monopoly. There was much dislike of bringing nuclear bombs into space; and Dyson detected a general disinterest in radical propulsion ideas. Herbert York opposed Orion; in 1970 he wrote that he was still not sure "whether the Orion idea was utter nonsense or was simply grossly premature."[17] The government interpreted the 1963 treaty banning nuclear tests in the atmosphere and space as forbidding Orion and was unwilling to seek modification of it. (It could have argued that explosions in an Orion system were not covered by the treaty anymore than laws governing the use of explosives apply to the explosions in the pistons of internal-combustion engines.)

Oddly, what might seem to be the most obvious objection to Orion (or at least Orion launchings within the atmosphere)—that its "pulse units" would produce fallout—played little role in the opposition to the project. Study suggested that it would not be nearly as bad as might be supposed. Dyson estimated that an Orion program would add only 1 percent to the fallout from bomb tests, producing an average of one tenth to one cancer death per flight. (He later deemed even that unacceptable.) A NASA study in 1963 suggested that a surface-based flight to Mars would, at worst, produce contamination equivalent to that of a 1-megaton bomb test—on the unrealistic assumption that all fission products were trapped in earth's atmosphere. By using fusion, instead of fission explosions, fallout could be reduced further and almost eliminated if fusion explosions could be produced without a fission trigger.[18]

Several designs for Orion-powered vehicles were produced. But by 1965, with no military mission, the Air Force could no longer keep Orion. NASA refused to take it, because it would need a risky and costly course of in-flight development, contrary to its usual emphasis on ground-based development, and it was unlikely that the test ban would be amended to allow actual flights. Orion ended after the expenditure of $11 million.[19] It has been well said that Orion "was so promising that it seems only by chance, politics and extraordinary circumstance that today nuclear pulse powered spaceships are not zipping with ease through the Solar System."[20] Indeed, with the possible exception of the ion rocket, the pulse system was the only system in prospect that offered the possibility of interstellar flight.

11

To the Moon

In May 1961, the United States had decided to land men on the moon. It was now clear that the Apollo spacecraft would take them there; it gave its name to the whole effort. But it was not yet clear just *how* to get there. The question of method, or mode, was the crucial issue of the project. It determined how big a rocket was needed and whether an additional spacecraft or particular techniques would be required. In turn, the question of rocket development influenced the mode decision, since it was expected (wrongly it turned out) to be the pacing item in the project.

The choice of mode had major implications for the exploration of the moon and the development of space capabilities after Apollo. It led to sharp disagreement between NASA's field centers and its Washington headquarters. Unlike the Manhattan Project, to which it was often compared, Apollo was executed by an already existing bureaucracy, with some special offices superimposed. The Apollo Program Office in the Office of Manned Space Flight in Washington (which should not be confused with the Apollo Spacecraft Program Office at Houston, which dealt with the Apollo spacecraft proper) oversaw a relatively decentralized program. James Webb later considered that to be one of the keys to its success. The Marshall Space Flight Center (von Braun's team) would develop the launch vehicle; the Space Task Group at Langley, Virginia, which later in 1961 became the Manned Spacecraft Center at Houston, would develop the Apollo and any other spacecraft needed. Most of the work was done by private industry under their supervision. Coordinating the centers and

deciding who they should report to in Washington, were the main organizational problems of Apollo.

There were at least half a dozen possible modes for lunar flight, but only
three had a real chance of being chosen:

1. "Direct ascent," which was apparently the simplest, involved
   launching a huge vehicle straight from earth. Its upper stage or
   stages, carrying the Apollo spacecraft, would land on the moon
   and fly back to earth. It should be noted that at an early date it was
   decided that, even with direct ascent, a flight to the moon should
   be made in two steps. First the lunar vehicle would enter a
   "parking orbit" around earth. Then it would accelerate to escape
   velocity ("translunar injection"). This gave a longer "launch
   window" than a one-shot launch from a site on earth, at the cost
   of more weight for the launch vehicle to ensure a longer life for
   vital systems. (It cost the Saturn V a weight penalty of nearly a
   ton and a half.) "Direct ascent's" most obvious drawback was that
   it needed the biggest rocket of any mode; probably a Nova would
   be required. By the same token it meant the biggest leap forward
   in rocket power. Less obvious drawbacks were that it involved
   hauling all the fuel and equipment needed during the trip all the
   way to the moon, and backing a large vehicle down to its surface.

2. "Earth Orbit Rendezvous" (EOR) involved a launch from orbit
   around the earth. Either a lunar vehicle would be assembled in
   space by combining two or more upper stages placed in orbit, or
   an empty lunar vehicle would be put in orbit and then refueled by
   a tanker stage. It could use a smaller launch vehicle; two of the
   projected advanced Saturns should be enough. EOR, however,
   required multiple launches, developing capabilities of rendezvous
   in space, and either assembling vehicles there or transferring fuel
   in zero gravity, with then unknown difficulties.

3. In "Lunar Orbit Rendezvous" (LOR), the mode finally used, the
   Apollo spacecraft would be launched from earth, as in "direct
   ascent," to an orbit around the moon. It would stay there, and a
   separate landing craft would descend to the moon; after it returned
   it would be left in orbit around the moon. By reducing the weight
   that had to go all the way to the moon and back, LOR made it
   possible to use an advanced Saturn rather than a Nova. But the
   drawbacks were numerous. Another spacecraft had to be developed, in addition to the Apollo, along with rendezvous techniques.

There was less chance of surviving a mishap in a rendezvous around the moon than in earth orbit. And just two men, not three, would reach the moon's surface. Although the Americans eventually chose LOR, and the Soviets a combination of EOR and LOR, it initially attracted little interest. Buzz Aldrin, the astronaut most expert in orbital mechanics and rendezvous, later recalled that he and most people at first thought LOR bizarre.

There were at least three other possible modes. One involved rendezvous and refueling in transit between earth and moon. Another was "lunar surface rendezvous." A vehicle designed to return to earth would land unmanned on the moon, along with one or more tankers. Then explorers would land in one craft, transfer to the return vehicle, and fuel it for a trip home. JPL liked this plan, but no one else did. A variant of this, jovially called the "poor slob plan," would park a man on the moon without a way to return him. He would be supplied by unmanned rockets until a vehicle capable of a round trip was built! Private industry proposed this, as a way to beat the Soviets, but NASA did not take it seriously.

Until 1961 NASA had inclined toward EOR, which von Braun backed consistently. But the Space Task Group at Langley became interested in "direct ascent." The Manned Lunar Landing Group study, the main official examination of the issue before Kennedy's decision, concluded that both modes were practical. A new group, the Fleming Committee, formed on May 2 amid the process leading to the decision for Apollo, favored "direct ascent." But NASA's leaders wanted more options; another group, the Lundin Committee, was asked to provide them. It took note of LOR, but it favored EOR as the fastest, safest way to reach the moon. But no choice of mode was made.

A NASA-Defense Department Planning Group was to choose a big booster to fill both the needs of Apollo and the military (which, it turned out, had no interest in the matter). It wrangled over the mode issue. Most members wanted EOR, using two Saturn C-4s. (The C-4 was to have a first stage with four F-1 engines and a second stage with four J-2s.) But its chairman, Nicholas Golovin, backed by the Space Task Group, favored "direct ascent" and building Nova, as well as an advanced Saturn. (Von Braun and his team also wanted Nova eventually but maintained that it would take too long to build to reach Kennedy's deadline.)

Arguments dragged on for three months, but no real decision was made before a reorganization of NASA supervened. Moreover, other decisions overtook those supposed to determine mode and booster. In September NASA chose the big government-owned Michoud plant at New Orleans to build the boosters for Apollo. It was near Huntsville, and boosters could go by water to Cape Canaveral. But although it could handle the advanced Saturns, its roof was too low for Nova—which would require rebuilding Michoud or a whole new plant. That, and the time factor, strongly favored a Saturn and some sort of rendezvous. In November Milton Rosen, the new Director of Launch Vehicles and Propulsion, formed yet another committee to reach a final decision on mode and booster; but it reported quickly. Again, there was a split between chairman and majority. Rosen still wanted "direct ascent" and Nova, but most members favored EOR, while noting LOR as an alternative. Rosen finally recommended building the Saturn C-5, but with a critical difference. Originally, the C-5 had been envisaged as having four F-1s in its first stage, five J-2s in its second stage, with a modified S-IVB (from the Saturn IB) with one J-2 as its third stage. Basically, it was the C-4 with a more powerful second stage and third stage. Rosen, however, insisted on adding a fifth F-1 to its first stage. He pointed out that it could be mounted where the heavy crossbeams carrying the original four F-1s joined. Von Braun's team typically had made them stronger than needed. After strenuous arguments, Rosen won over the von Braun group. The C-5 (later the Saturn V), with five F-1s, was approved on December 21, 1961. Boeing quickly got a contract to build the first stage, and North American the second stage, under NASA supervision at Michoud; Douglas would build the S-IVB at its California plant. The fifth engine was one of the crucial decisions of the program. As several times before and later, von Braun had been overruled or persuaded to change; but the excellence of his work made possible improvements he had not envisaged.

Von Braun was overruled yet again on mode. The decision to build the C-5 had not settled, but strongly affected, the mode issue. Some thought "direct ascent" marginally possible with the C-5, and it was still possible that Nova could be built, too. But the C-5 made some sort of rendezvous likely. By late 1961, it appeared that EOR must be the mode, but the old Space Task Group, now the Manned Spacecraft Center, pushed LOR. In 1959 and 1960, early studies of lunar landing modes, at Vought Aircraft and by some engineers at Langley, had independently suggested LOR— apparently in ignorance of earlier suggestions going back decades. John Houbolt, a Langley engineer, fought for LOR during 1961, at first with little success. But the higher-ups at NASA kept it increasingly in mind. Houbolt stressed the simplifications and weight savings of putting the lunar landing functions in a separate craft. Critics like von Braun stressed the danger of a rendezvous around the moon and doubted the weight saving. Building a separate landing craft, after all, involved duplicating functions, too—in crew arrangements, propulsion systems, and instrumentation. Whether weight would be saved in the end was questionable. Critics rightly doubted the accuracy of Houbolt's figures and thought his idea of the instruments the crew would need for the landing absurdly simple. But Faget (the Apollo spacecraft designer) and even advocates of "direct ascent," like Gilruth and Rosen, were increasingly impressed with the difficulty of landing a big vehicle on the moon. Faget's ideas of how to do that became increasingly awkward and complex. While still pushing for "direct ascent," Gilruth was increasingly impressed by LOR; as "direct ascent" became unlikely, the Manned Spacecraft Center swung over to it. Brainerd Holmes, the Director of the headquarters Office of Manned Space Flight, remained undecided; he wanted a consensus at the rival field centers. In January 1962, he assigned his new deputy, Joseph Shea, a systems engineer, to reinvestigate the mode issue and get the centers together. Shea concluded that, while Houbolt's figures were overoptimistic, LOR would work, but it needed further study. Vought got a contract to do this; it demonstrated that the lunar landing craft would be heavier than had been thought, perhaps too heavy for the C-5. But further consideration led Washington to back LOR. Only von Braun's center held out, but Holmes and Shea decided to win him over gradually rather than just order him into line. Time was wasting, especially if a special landing craft had to be built, and the indecision was starting to harm other aspects of the project. Von Braun gradually warmed to LOR; perhaps he simply decided that since no one was ready to enforce a decision, he would have to be the reasonable one. Finally, on June 7, he swung over to LOR. He had decided, he said, that it had the best chance for success within a decade and splitting the functions of the Apollo and the landing craft would simplify development and management. Shea's staff produced a study showing that LOR would cost less than other modes and be completed six to eight months sooner.

Sluggishly and reluctantly, NASA had decided; but it had to defend its decision against outside pressure. North American, which was building the Apollo craft, wanted it to land on the moon and disliked LOR. (It was unlikely to be chosen to build the landing craft and, already full of contracts, it was finally excluded from bidding.) The PSAC weighed in with contradictory arguments. Some members liked EOR as safer and having more growth potential for future space work. But its main thrust, led by Wiesner, was in favor of an alternative NASA had already studied as a backup to LOR—"direct ascent" with a Saturn V and a lightened spacecraft with a two-man crew, using liquid hydrogen instead of the less powerful storable fuels for the moon landing. But NASA insisted that liquid hydrogen would have to be used for the return too, with unacceptable complications. It also insisted that the PSAC alternative would take longer and cost more. The arguments became bitter; von Braun, ironically, wound up defending LOR to the President. Wiesner finally gave up in November 1962.[1] On November 7, Grumman Aircraft, which had never worked on space projects before, won the contract for the landing craft—the Lunar Module (LM). It was a happy choice; Grumman proved the best of NASA's contractors and made up much of the time lost by the shambling decision on mode.

That decision had a major impact on the future. Despite the time wasted, it is generally agreed that it made it possible for the Americans to beat the Soviets to the moon. But it also had a price tag. It reduced the effective expeditions to the moon to just two men each. One consequence was that a scientist, rather than a man with test pilot background, reached the moon only on the last Apollo flight. It also, as the PSAC and von Braun foresaw, produced a specialized and limited vehicle. EOR would have encouraged capabilities for building space stations and assembling deep-space craft in orbit; "direct ascent" would have forced development of an enormous booster, perhaps with similar results. A Nova could have put 200 tons into earth orbit—six times the payload of the Space Shuttle.

THE APOLLO/SATURN V SYSTEM

Thus in the last part of 1962, the pattern of the project was set. The Apollo spacecraft and Lunar Module would be launched by the three-stage Saturn C-5/Saturn V. The F-1-powered S-IC first stage (burning kerosene and oxygen) and S-II and S-IVB upper stages (with J-2 engines burning hydrogen and oxygen) would put the S-IVB and the payload in earth orbit. Then the S-IVB would launch the Apollo-LM combination to the moon. In transit, the Apollo would separate, turn around, and dock with the LM (which had been launched underneath it) and pull it away from the spent S-IVB. The Apollo spacecraft's own 20,500-pound-thrust engine (in its Service Module), burning hydrazine and nitrogen tetroxide, would burn to put it in orbit around the moon. Moving from the Apollo Command Module to the LM, two men would descend to the moon, using a throttleable descent engine (up to 9,870 pounds of thrust) that burned the same fuels as the Apollo's powerplant. When the time came to return, the spent descent stage would serve as a launch platform for the LM, which would fire a simple, 3,500-pound fixed-thrust ascent engine using the same fuels. (The ascent engine was also a backup if the descent engine failed on the way down.) Returning to lunar orbit, the LM would dock with the Apollo. The crew would transfer back to the Apollo and jettison the LM. The

Apollo's engine would return it to earth. Before reentry, the Service Module would be jettisoned. Only the Command Module would land. In effect, the Saturn V/Apollo-LM combination was a six-stage rocket, the LM alone comprising two stages. Grand as it was, it was also the ultimate demonstration of the impossibility of the chemically fueled multistage rocket as a basis for economical space travel. A 3,100-ton vehicle was needed to land just 16 tons on the moon and return a vehicle weighing 6.5 tons to earth. And not one item of the system could be used again!

Work on the LM had finally gotten underway when Apollo hit heavy weather, externally and internally. Congress and most people, and probably (despite what is often said) most scientists, had favored it in 1961. In 1963 it became popular to utter doubts. Some Republicans, following Eisenhower's lead, objected to the cost; others, including Barry Goldwater, wanted a big space program oriented to earth orbit and military needs. Some prominent scientists—notably the physicist Philip Abelson, the editor of *Science*, and the mathematician Warren Weaver—argued that the money ought to be spent on other scientific matters or on education. Some of their arguments were impressive, but they failed to ponder the actual likelihood of money "saved" from Apollo being spent on such alternatives.

They had little chance to stop Apollo; it was too far along. Abelson and others finally saw this, and by 1965, while not necessarily changing their minds, they turned to other things since most of the money Apollo would take had already been spent. But the episode indicated what would happen when the question of a large post-Apollo space effort came up.

Within NASA, there had been growing quarrels over running and financing Apollo. In 1962–1963, Holmes wanted an even more overwhelming priority for Apollo (which already took 75 percent of NASA's budget) than it already had, threatening to starve all scientific (as opposed to technological) work. Webb defended a balanced program and strongly advised the President against any such step, which Holmes insisted would only follow Kennedy's own mandate. Webb and Holmes also split on management questions. NASA's field centers then conducted projects under each and any of the directorates at headquarters in Washington. Holmes wanted to have all field centers working on Apollo report only to him. Webb would not agree. The two men finally broke over a supplementary budget request that Webb opposed. In September 1963, Webb replaced Holmes with George Mueller. An electrical engineer like Holmes, he also had a Ph.D. in physics. (Ironically, within the Apollo program, he favored engineering considerations over scientific ones even more than Holmes.) Mueller had worked as a systems engineer for Space Technology Labs and had much experience in ICBM and space work.

NASA was reorganized; and Mueller got what Holmes had been denied—simplifying lines of authority between NASA program offices and centers. Mueller was much more ready to dominate the centers than Holmes. He put the able Air Force general Samuel Phillips, who had run the Minuteman program, in charge of the Apollo Program Office. Holmes's former deputy, Shea, took over the Apollo Spacecraft Program Office in Houston. The new regime was more vigorous than the old. Mueller soon enforced a critical decision for "all-up testing." Studies had indicated that at the present rate of progress, there would probably be no landing on the moon before 1971. Mueller sharply cut the number of Saturn I flights and decreed that, instead of incremental testing of each stage of the Saturn IB and Saturn V, each vehicle would be tested "all-up," with all live stages and a spacecraft the first time off. And the third launch, not the seventh, of each vehicle would be manned. Mueller argued that it was not just the sole way to beat the deadline, but a more realistic process; and computerized checkout systems could replace much of the step-by-step method. Von Braun balked at first, but later admitted that Mueller had been right and that without "all-up testing" the moon flight could not have been made in 1969.[2]

SATURN V

Developing the Saturn V probably was not the worst problem of the Apollo program. Still, the difficulties were formidable. Although it did not involve great technical breakthroughs, the mere scaling-up in size of basically conventional equipment proved daunting. Fortunately some crucial components—the F-1 and J-2 engines and the S-IVB stage—had already been well underway before the decision to go to the moon. Under von Braun, the Saturn V Program Office (ably headed by Arthur Rudolph) used techniques such as PERT that had been developed in the Polaris program. PERT proved useful but was finally phased out in 1967. Rudolph was a highly capable engineer, but unlike von Braun's other associates he was an "old" (pre-1933) Nazi; in 1984 he was forced to renounce his U.S. citizenship for having falsely denied knowing of crimes committed at Nordhausen.

The F-1 was tested as early as April 1961, with a thrust well above the designed level; but making it reliable took years. Its mere size had required new test facilities. Fabricating a thrust chamber required specialized metallurgic research and the development of a new brazing process, and a special furnace to join the tubes that composed it. A system was developed to operate its controls using its own fuel instead of a separate hydraulic system. Designing a turbopump to supply it with fuel was difficult, and new materials had to be developed for it. Above all, there was combustion instability, which destroyed several engines and worried NASA; in 1963 Holmes even pondered starting work on another engine lest the F-1 prove incurable. The engineers were reduced to detonating bombs in the combustion chamber to induce the instability under controlled conditions. Finally, during 1963–1964, a lengthy "cut-and-try" reworking of the fuel injector reduced the instability to within safe limits. The S-IC stage that carried the F-1s itself needed new techniques.

Ironically, the Michoud plant, which had helped dictate the choice of Saturn over Nova, had to be modified to handle it, and much special equipment, such as "electromagnetic hammers," had to be developed for use there. Welds of unprecedented length were needed for its fuel tanks. Transporting the huge stages required a fleet of special barges. The hydrogen-powered upper stages also presented complex problems (chiefly the J-2 engines and insulating the hydrogen tanks). Douglas engineers working on the S-IVB devised their own insulating material and a complicated way to line the tanks with it. An exotic method of "explosive forming" was developed for making parts for the big oxygen tanks. Despite the success of the Douglas engineers, North American chose a different approach for the S-II stage, which led to much trouble, as did welding its tanks. The Marshall Center, which worked well with Boeing and Douglas, encountered much friction with North American over the S-II. Von Braun and others were exasperated with its workmanship and management; von Braun made North American replace its man in charge of the program. There were other problems; in 1967 von Braun grimly noted that the H-1 engines for the Saturn IB had arrived with dirt in them and other problems. Still, von Braun maintained standards at Marshall, and it was not the Saturn V that proved the stumbling block of the program.[3] Other problems with North American overshadowed those with the S-II and the engines and led to Apollo's greatest crisis.

THE APOLLO SPACECRAFT

Martin, General Electric, and Convair submitted preliminary designs for the Apollo craft just before Kennedy decided to go to the moon. But the Space Task Group had never planned to use any of them, except as a check on an in-house design devised mainly by Max Faget. Faget's design consisted of two modules. The Command Module, or crew cabin, was a rounded cone; the Service Module contained propulsion systems, fuel cells, and life-support systems. Had "direct ascent" or EOR been used to go to the moon, additional stages would have been attached for the lunar landing and takeoff; when LOR was chosen, the Apollo was modified to dock with the Lunar Module. One difficulty in designing the Command Module was that on reentry it would be going too fast to depend on a simple heatshield; it had to be wrapped entirely in "ablatives" with provisions for vents for its attitude-control thrusters.

The craft would still be built by private industry, however, and choosing a contractor proved controversial and not too satisfactory. When bids were reviewed by NASA's Source Evaluation Board in October 1961, Martin and North American were the prime candidates. North American, however, already had plenty of work on the engines. The Board preferred Martin, despite the intervention by higher-ups who insisted on adjustments to the criteria used that had favored North American. Yet their decision was reversed by Webb and his associate administrators; North American got the job. For many years there were strong suspicions that Lyndon Johnson's corrupt crony Bobby Baker and Senator Kerr had fixed the selection; Baker was known to have connections with North American, which allegedly promised to place some Apollo work in Oklahoma. It seems, however, that many in NASA had disagreed strongly with the Evaluation Board from the start. Webb and others were swayed by Gilruth and others, who argued that North American's experience with the X-15 and allegedly superior key personnel made it a better choice.

Experience would cast doubt on the wisdom of that argument. Many at NASA were unhappy with North American's performance. In its first year or two, its work on Apollo was understaffed with inexperienced people; there was much waste and delay. Shea, head of the Apollo Spacecraft Program Office, was deeply discontented. Things did not get much better. In December 1965, Shea and von Braun's representatives drew up a report, signed by General Phillips, warning North American's president of dissatisfaction with the handling of the Apollo and the S-II. Both lagged behind schedule, exhibited degradations in performance, and vastly increased costs. Now both programs seemed overmanned, and some technical problems had not been resolved. A limited shakeup resulted at North American.[4] But it took three dead men to change things.

THE APOLLO FIRE AND AFTERMATH

Realistic people expected deaths in space travel; some U.S. and Soviet astronauts had already died in flying accidents. It was a surprise that the first to die in a spacecraft would die on the ground. On January 27, 1967, Gus Grissom, Edward White, and Roger Chaffee were in Apollo 012, atop a Saturn IB at Cape Canaveral, simulating the first manned Apollo earth-orbit flight (which was scheduled for February 21). There had already been a lot of trouble with 012. The three men were in spacesuits, in an all-oxygen atmosphere such as would be used in space, behind a locked hatch. A fire began at 6:31 P.M. White could not open the complicated hatch before he and the others were overcome; flames bursting from the ruptured side of the Command Module forced away the men in the next room, and the rescue workers found their gas masks inadequate. By the time they opened the hatch, the crew was long dead. Badly (but not fatally) burned, they had been asphyxiated by toxic gases.

Some of the problems at North American had already leaked out, in a distorted form, before the fire. Now there was an explosion of criticism of NASA and North American. Senator Fulbright and others actually urged canceling the whole Apollo program.

Webb promptly convened a Review Board under Floyd Thompson, Director of the Langley Research Center, which included the astronaut Frank Borman and Max Faget. It was, absurdly, immediately attacked as a coverup because it was overwhelmingly composed of NASA personnel, with a North American representative as well. But some of the NASA representatives were from outside Apollo, while other elements—from the PSAC and the Inspector General of the Air Force—were unlikely to be overfriendly to NASA. Nor was Borman likely to whitewash conditions that had killed his friends and endangered him and his surviving, and highly upset, colleagues. Apollo 012 was studied; the nearly identical 014 was taken apart for comparison; and 017, the next in line, was examined carefully. The results were shocking. The wiring had been done badly; and workmanship in general was poor. A wrench was found embedded in 012's wiring! There had been far too much use of easily damaged teflon insulation on wiring, and flammable materials like nylon. The investigators were shaken by experiments that showed how explosively such items burned in pure oxygen. A Bureau of Mines expert failed to find the immediate cause of the fire because things were so bad that it could not be pinpointed. Probably a short-circuit in the troublesome Environmental Control Unit, caused by insulation being scuffed off a wire, ignited leaking glycol coolant, which in turn set fire to nylon netting and velcro.

In a preliminary report on February 25, the Board recommended replacing the flammable materials, establishing firebreaks, and replacing the inward-opening hatch with a more easily opened hatch that swung outward. Its final report, in April, indicted the use of an all-oxygen atmosphere on the ground, the extensive distribution of flammable materials in the cabin, the use of vulnerable wiring and plumbing, and inadequate provisions for escape and rescue. It bluntly reported many deficiencies in design, engineering, manufacturing, and quality control.

Webb had managed to get the first congressional investigation to operate in closed session, but later open testimony embarrassed NASA and North American. NASA's bitter enemy, Senator Walter Mondale, publicized the Phillips report and charges made by Thomas Baron, who had been a quality control inspector for North American at Cape Canaveral. Baron had compiled a record pointing to poor workmanship and many other problems. He was fired in January 1967 for leaking his story to the press. Although Baron and the more violent critics were embarrassed when his supposed informants repudiated his greatly exaggerated claims, even North American conceded that half his charges were true. The astronauts' widows sued North American and received an out-of-court settlement for $650,000. (Mrs. White never recovered from her husband's death and later committed suicide.)

There was a terrific shakeup at NASA and North American. Joseph Shea, who suffered a nervous breakdown, was replaced by George Low as head of the Spacecraft Program Office. Management of industrial safety was altered throughout NASA. Webb made North American fire Harrison Storms as head of its Space Division. His replacement, William Bergen, an engineer from Martin, brought in other ex-Martin executives as well. Eventually almost all the top management was new; and they helped to restore North American's reputation. But it was not only the management that had been at fault; Borman, sent out with a team to oversee modifications to the Apollo, found much drunkenness among workers at the plant. This was curbed with the aid of union leaders. Although many liked to recall Apollo and the 1960s as a sort of golden age of patriotism and national excellence, these revelations suggest that things were already very different from the high morale of the "missile-gap" era.

There were considerable changes to the Apollo. The new hatch was much heavier, and the Command Module needed a bigger parachute to handle the load. The CM was modified to have a safer nitrogen-oxygen atmosphere on the ground, switching to pure oxygen in flight. A mixed atmosphere in space too would have been still safer, but the greater cabin pressure and weight would have forced total redesign of the Apollo and Lunar Module. Nylon was replaced by teflon, fiberglass, or beta fiber; all aluminum oxygen lines and solder joints were replaced by stainless steel with brazed joints (or when that was impossible they were covered with flame-resistant insulation and the soldered joints were armored). Emergency oxygen masks were added to protect the crew from fumes. Although Grumman's work was excellent, the LM too was modified to reduce fire hazards—delaying it another three or four months. The delay imposed by the fire allowed attention to some lagging items: Mission simulators, the navigation and guidance system, and computers had time to catch up. The scientific exploration of the moon actually benefited, for there was more time to devise appropriate instruments.[5]

THE LUNAR MODULE

Developing the Lunar Module proved complex and frustrating. It was actually more of a departure than the Apollo; no one had ever designed a vehicle to fly only in a vacuum, and it took time for the full implications to sink in. Its design took two years to finish. Obtaining adequate visibility for both landing and rendezvous proved tricky. (They needed two different radar systems.) The LM's low acceleration let the astronauts fly it standing up, which did help the visibility problem and allowed lightweight materials to be used. But the LM grew heavier and heavier, threatening to get too big for the Saturn V and imposing bigger requirements on its own engines. The final weight of the Apollo-LM combination approximated the weight originally calculated for a "direct ascent" vehicle. The ascent engine, subcontracted to Bell, although not trouble-free was the simplest engine developed during Apollo. But the descent engine, developed by Space Technology Labs, proved the trickiest. It suffered from rough burning and melting of the throttle mechanism. Originally scheduled for the fall of 1966, the first LM reached Cape Canaveral in June 1967, still full of bugs. The delays, and rivalry with the Soviets, caused a change in plans.[6]

THE SOVIETS AND THE MOON RACE

Contrary to a widespread belief in the West, which was not exploded until the Gorbachev era (although it never had any foundation), there was a real race to the moon, neck and neck until the last lap. Ironically, it may have been the Americans who fired the starting gun. The Soviets formally decided to land on the moon only after Kennedy's declaration.

The Soviets' program was hampered from the start by two serious errors. Korolev could not overcome the opposition of Glushko, the now conservative Soviet propulsion authority, to developing liquid hydrogen as a fuel. And, by a narrow margin, the Soviets underestimated the Americans, assuming that whatever Kennedy said, the Americans could not reach the moon before 1970 or later. They clung to this assumption with great tenacity.

Already, in 1960, the Soviets had decided to build an enormous booster, the N-1, that was comparable in sheer size to the Nova and would put heavy loads into earth orbit. With thirty engines, its first stage developed 12 million pounds of thrust, but the fact that its upper stages used oxygen and kerosene gave it an effective payload less than the Saturn V's. But Korolev seems to have distrusted the N-1. His lunar plans revolved around assembling a vehicle in earth orbit with smaller boosters. He devised a whole "Soyuz (union) complex" of spacecraft for the job. Soyuz A, which weighed nearly 13,000 pounds and was the manned component, would carry three men. Its design appears to have been inspired by the 1960 General Electric design for Apollo. It consisted of three modules: an equipment module containing retro-rockets, fuel, and solar-powered panels; a descent module in which the crew rose to and from the earth's surface; and an orbital module, a larger cabin and workshop used in space. Soyuz B was a "rocket block," a separate propulsion system that could be mated with Soyuz A; Soyuz V was a tanker. All could be launched by an improved version of the Vostok booster. For circumlunar missions, a Soyuz B would be put in orbit with dry tanks. Then Soyuz A would dock with it and then rendezvous with three or four Soyuz Vs to fuel. The mission would thus need five or six successful launches in close succession and a whole series of rendezvous. Korolev hoped to pull off a circumlunar flight—probably a simple "loop" around the moon rather than insertion into orbit around it—in 1966. With the addition of a lunar landing module and more tankers, an improved version of this system would put men on the moon in 1970. But Korolev and his colleagues were diverted to Voskhod, which cost them much time. Although tests of Soyuz B (called Polyot) in November 1963 and April 1964 apparently succeeded, his plan was discarded as too complex in 1964. Soyuz A, now called just Soyuz, would be built—later versions still fly to and from the Russian space station—but B and V were canceled. Khrushchev may have considered canceling the lunar effort in late 1963, but he did not do so; his successors fastened on a different plan. However, based as it was on the ideas of a man with a proven record of success, using proven rockets, Korolev's scheme might have beaten the Americans; and the Soviets would have been well advised to stick with it.

Korolev's influence may have sunk with Khrushchev; while he still worked on the spacecraft, the new plan depended on boosters built by the bureau of his rival Vladimir Chelomei. Politics intervened once more, fatally. In bad health ever since his imprisonment, Korolev needed surgery in January 1966. The Minister of Health insisted on operating on such an important personage himself, although he had not operated for years. He found an undiagnosed tumor; although it was treatable, the job was too much for the surgeon. Korolev died on the table. The Soviet program did not recover from the loss; his replacement, Vasily Mishin, lacked his influence and inspiration.

The new moon plan still depended on Soyuz, but on different boosters. A lunar flyby would be made in 1967 for the fiftieth anniversary of the Bolshevik coup, using a stripped-down Soyuz called Zond or L-1, carrying just one man, and launched directly from earth by the new Proton booster. A landing would follow, possibly as early as 1969, using a different system. An N-1 would put its third stage in orbit, with an L-3 lunar module (built around a modified Soyuz orbital module), a mission module, and a lunar braking stage. A Proton would launch a heavy L-2 Soyuz, carrying two cosmonauts, to dock with this assembly. The third stage of the N-1 would then send the vehicle to the moon. It would go into orbit around the moon; just one man would descend to the surface. A long succession of mishaps delayed and then wrecked these plans.

SOYUZ, PROTON, AND N-1

Soyuz, already delayed, did not work well. An unmanned test in November 1966, called Cosmos 133 and described as a scientific satellite, went badly. The heatshield failed and the craft was badly damaged on reentry. In February 1967, a second unmanned test, Cosmos 140, was attempted but the main control thrusters broke down and the parachute lines were damaged on reentry. In March and April, two orbital tests of the circumlunar version of Soyuz, Cosmos 146 and 154, suffered serious troubles. And in the same period two lunar probes went awry, demonstrating the unreliability of the Proton. Despite the unmanned Soyuz's poor performance, the Soviets put Vladimir Komarov into orbit in Soyuz 1 on April 23. Soyuz 2, carrying three men, was to rendezvous and dock with him. But one of Komarov's solar panels did not work, and his attitude controls went awry. Soyuz 2 was canceled immediately. Komarov stayed in orbit longer only because he could not stabilize his craft properly for reentry. Both his guidance computer and thrusters were apparently not working properly when he finally came down on April 24. The Soyuz plunged out of control, and he was killed. Along with the trouble with the Proton, that ended Soviet hopes for a circumlunar trip in 1967.

In March 1968, the Soviets began new tests of the circumlunar craft with the Proton. After orbital tests as Cosmos 186 and 188, a modified Soyuz with a heavier heatshield, Zond 4, was flown successfully out to the orbit of the moon (but opposite its position) and back. Zond 5, in September, looped around the moon carrying animals and plants, and landed in the Indian Ocean. It was a clear prelude to manned flight; the

Americans rushed to beat it. In October a successful manned Soyuz orbital mission was finally flown. Soyuz 2 was sent up unmanned; then Soyuz 3, carrying Georgi Beregovoi, went up to rendezvous with it. Zond 6 rounded the moon in November and landed in the U.S.S.R.; this required a tricky reentry path. The Soviets apparently still insisted on landing a man, if possible, inside their territory. The next Zond, in January 1969, failed when the still undependable Proton blew up. The Soviets now largely abandoned talking about going to the moon. (They had been open enough about it in the previous two years.) But they still nursed hopes of beating the Americans; they still thought that the latter were unlikely to succeed before mid-1970.

But the third leg of the Soviet moon plan now failed. On February 21, the first N-1 failed when its engine cut off prematurely. On July 3, the second disappeared in a spectacular explosion on its launch pad. The Americans landed on the moon three weeks later; that was the end of the Soviet lunar program. The Soviets later decided to use the N-1 as a booster for a space station, but it failed again in June 1971 and November 1972. In contrast to the successful Saturn series, the N-1 was a total flop such as no one could have predicted.

The Soviets shifted their manned operations to space station work and fell back on a program of unmanned lunar exploration, with creditable achievements. They had developed an unmanned probe able to collect moon rock and return it to earth. Luna 15, launched by a Proton, failed and crashed into the moon in July 1969. Luna 16 landed on September 20, 1970, and brought back a tiny sample of 101 grams. Luna 17 landed a Lunokhod, a camera-equipped remote-controlled vehicle, in the Sea of Rains in November 1970; it operated during lunar days until October 1971. Luna 18 crashed; Lunas 19 and 22 were successful lunar-mapping satellites. Luna 20, landing in February 1972 in the Sea of Fertility, returned 50 grams of soil to earth. Luna 21 landed a second Lunokhod in January 1973; Luna 23 another sample-and-return mission, failed when its drill-arm did not work. Luna 24, in August 1976, the last human-launched vehicle to return from the moon, brought back 170 grams of soil.[7]

PROVING APOLLO AND SATURN

In September 1967, NASA settled on a tentative schedule for the remaining steps to the moon. But it wanted to skip a step, if possible. On November 9, a complete Saturn V, with an unmanned Apollo craft, was launched as Apollo 4. (At their widows' request, the mission Grissom, Chaffee, and White never flew became Apollo 1; the next numbers were omitted, for reasons never made clear.) The flight went off without a hitch. The S-IVB was restarted successfully. The Apollo then cut loose. Its own engine sent it into an even higher orbit and fired again to ram it into a successful reentry at escape velocity. Apollo 4 seemed to mark the project's recovery from the fire and preceding blunders.

Launched on January 22, 1968, Apollo 5, another unmanned flight, used a Saturn IB to test the lunar module in orbit. The always reliable IB worked well, as did the LM—in most respects. But in maneuvers its descent engine shut down prematurely. That was due to errors in programming the LM's computer rather than a fault in the engine itself, and a pilot could have overridden it, but it forced some changes in the mission. Ground tests showed problems with the ascent engine and the windows and ribs of the LM. It became clear that it was unlikely that a manned LM could fly in 1968.

Fortunately, von Braun and George Low had insisted on at least one more unmanned test of the Saturn V. This flight, Apollo 6, launched on April 4, was a near disaster, although NASA pretended otherwise. The Saturn V exhibited "pogoing" (the lengthwise oscillation that had afflicted other big rockets) so violent that an astronaut might have been hurt. Moreover, two engines in the second stage shut off prematurely. The third stage reached orbit but could not be restarted. The Apollo's own engine sufficed for most of the planned maneuvers; but the mission could hardly be deemed a success.

The engineers at Marshall and the contractors soon found that two independent problems were involved. The "pogoing" was due to the resonance of some of the F-1s with the structure of the rocket. The engines were "detuned," and "shock absorbers" of helium gas were injected into valve cavities to prevent a repetition of the problem. It was found that the fuel lines going to the igniters of one of the second-stage J-2 engines had broken; the fuel valves had then shut automatically to stop the malfunctioning engine. Due to a crossed wire, the signal to shut off the oxygen to that engine went to another engine, stopping that one too! The ignition line of the S-IVB's J-2 had held up just long enough to reach orbit but had failed too, preventing a restart. Study showed that vibrations from the propellant flow caused the breaks; this had never happened on the ground because the cold of the liquid hydrogen had liquified air around the critical point in the lines, damping the vibrations. In space, this protection was absent.

Fixing the problems proved easy, but it took a lot of nerve to decide, just two weeks after Apollo 6, that the next Saturn V would be manned unless further developments dictated otherwise. This clearly violated the rules followed earlier in manned space flight; the race with the Soviets was inducing downright recklessness. (The blunders that led to the fire had not been caused, at least directly, by skimping on safety to save time.)

In August 1968, a drastic new step was taken to speed up the program. It had originally been planned to have the next Saturn V put up the LM as well as the Apollo and practice rendezvous and docking in earth orbit. But the LM would not be available soon; and well-founded intelligence indicated that the Soviets planned a circumlunar trip. George Low proposed having Apollo 8 go into orbit around the moon in December. He quickly won support from NASA's lower administrators; but Mueller and Webb needed persuading. They soon came around. This has been widely considered the most daring decision of the whole program; but arguably it was less so than the decision to man Apollo 8 at all. Von Braun observed that once that was decided on, it did not matter how far Apollo 8 went. There was a new element of danger, however. Earlier, it had been expected that any mission to lunar orbit would take the LM along. Should the Apollo's own Service Propulsion System fail, the LM's descent engine could be used to return to earth. Now, everything depended on one engine. If it failed, three men would be stranded around the moon.

While Apollo 8 was readied, the reliable Saturn IB finally launched the first manned Apollo. The mission Grissom and his comrades were supposed to have flown in 1967 was performed by Walter Schirra, Walter Cunningham, and Donn Eisele. Schirra was angry at being launched through high-altitude winds, but the flight went well, showing that the problem with the J-2 had been fixed. The vital Service Propulsion System was tested amply. An attempt to practice docking with the S-IVB stage, however, failed. As on Gemini 9, the device that was supposed to open up did not do so. The crew had a miserable time; they suffered from bad colds (worse in weightlessness than on the ground) but conducted their tasks despite electrical problems and landed on October 22. The go-ahead was given to Apollo 8.[8]

RECONNOITERING THE MOON

Apollo 8, carrying Frank Borman, James Lovell, and William Anders, lifted off smoothly on December 21. After a bit over two hours in orbit, the S-IVB stage fired again. Apollo 8 became the first manned craft to reach escape velocity. Guidance was so precise that only two of four expected course corrections were needed. The crew became spacesick— surprisingly, for Borman had seemed immune on his Gemini trip. Early on December 24, while passing behind the moon (as seen from earth), the Apollo engine fired again and put it into orbit 60 miles above the moon.

The crew found it easy to pick out and photograph potential landing sites; this was encouraging. On Christmas, after twenty hours in orbit, the Apollo engine fired once more—the one time it had to work. The astronauts were en route home, to a precise but jarring landing in the Pacific. They hit so close to the recovery carrier that some planners urged moving future recovery forces well away from the aiming point, lest a Command Module crash into a ship.

On January 6, the final schedule and crews for the flights culminating in the moon landing were decided on.

A sound version of the LM was finally ready for test in earth orbit. Apollo 9, commanded by James McDivitt, with David Scott as Command Module pilot and Russell Schweikart as Lunar Module pilot, was launched on March 3. In all operations with the LM, the commander would join its pilot while the CM pilot stayed in the Apollo. Jolted by a "pogoing" Saturn V, although not nearly as badly as Apollo 6, the crew suffered spacesickness despite dramamine. Although Schweikart was particularly sick, he tested the LM in every step needed for rendezvous around the moon. Apollo 9 landed after a completely successful mission.

The mission flown by Apollo 10 was the product of a surprising, probably unnecessary caution by NASA—surprising after the decisions about Apollo 8, at any rate. It would go into orbit around the moon; and the LM would drop to just 50,000 feet above the surface before returning to the Apollo. LM-4, named *Snoopy* (the Command Module was *Charlie Brown*), carried extra radar to survey the landing site for Apollo 11 and only half the normal fuel load for the ascent engine, so it could not actually land. Mueller and many others thought all this unnecessary and believed that Apollo 10 should have been planned as the first landing. But NASA's heads felt sure that the Soviets were nowhere near a landing and that prudence was in order.

Commanded by Thomas Stafford, with John Young as Command Module pilot and Eugene Cernan as LM pilot, Apollo 10 lifted off on May 18. They had a rough ride going into orbit, and again when the S-IVB put them on course for the moon. No one became spacesick, although they suffered from contaminated water. Some hydrogen in the fuel cells remained as bubbles in the water it produced. In orbit around the moon, the crew was disturbed to find that the LM had somehow twisted out of alignment with *Charlie Brown*. It was decided that the slippage was not so great as to be dangerous, and they pulled away from the Apollo as planned. Their new orbit took them to 47,000 feet above the surface, closely approaching the landing site for Apollo 11. They fired the descent engine again to return to the Apollo and were about to dump it and fire the half-loaded ascent stage to complete the trip when the LM whipped out of control. They had accidentally flipped a switch putting their onboard computer in control of its guidance. Shaken, they brought the LM under control and rejoined the Apollo. They landed in the Pacific on May 26.[9]

APOLLO 11: LUNAR LANDING

The crew that would land on the moon consisted entirely of veterans of Gemini. The civilian commander, Neil Armstrong, a Korean War Navy pilot, had flown the X-15 as well. LM pilot Buzz Aldrin and Command Module pilot Michael Collins were West Pointers and USAF professionals. All were capable, and Armstrong and Aldrin were commonly regarded as the smartest men in the astronaut corps. Although Aldrin had personal problems that would surface after his return (and that he would overcome), none of that was apparent on the trip. The crew had trained to the nth degree; every move they would make had been rehearsed carefully.

On July 16, 1969, they had a smooth liftoff from earth, beginning the most closely watched event in history. On their second orbit around the earth, the S-IVB fired again; after a rough ride of six minutes, they reached escape velocity. The flight out was comfortable, none were spacesick. Only one mid-course correction was needed. Going into orbit around the moon, they carefully checked their equipment and then rested for nine hours. On the morning of July 20, Armstrong and Aldrin crawled from Command Module *Columbia* to Lunar Module *Eagle*. They undocked and tested the thrusters and all vital systems. At precisely the right moment, Armstrong fired the descent engine. It took twelve minutes to reach the surface; nothing actually went wrong, but alarms caused by computer overloads were irritating. At a height of just over 2,000 feet, Armstrong saw that they were coming down next to a rocky crater in an area strewn with boulders. He made a last-minute lateral adjustment to reach a smooth surface a few hundred feet away. At 4:17 P.M. Eastern Standard Time, *Eagle* landed on a level plain that was covered with many small craters and ridges, in the east central part of the Sea of Tranquility (Mare Tranquillatis) just north of the moon's equator and just off the center of the moon's nearside. *Eagle* had twenty seconds of fuel left. Characteristically, Armstrong was not quite satisfied with his performance, but few others would quarrel with it. The first humans had reached another world.

Unknown to the men aboard *Eagle* or a watching world, those monitoring the craft on earth were very worried. Pressure sensors indicated that something was blocking a fuel line; they believed it was a bit of frozen fuel and feared that heat from the engine would make it explode. Some at

Grumman urged telling *Eagle* to take off immediately, but *Columbia* was not then in a position for the two to rendezvous. Some favored "burping" the engine, but nothing was done about the problem, and whatever it was vanished of its own accord.

Armstrong and Aldrin were supposed to take a long rest before leaving *Eagle*, but they were in no mood to wait. It took several hours to get ready to emerge. At 10:39 P.M., Armstrong clambered down to the surface, declaring that it was "one small step for [a] man, one giant leap for mankind." (Much to his irritation, he swallowed the *a* or the microphone failed to pick it up.) On the way down, he had deployed a TV camera. He examined the surface and quickly scooped up a sample in case they had to leave early. Then Aldrin emerged, pronouncing the scene one of "magnificent desolation." After examining *Eagle* for any damage, they practiced walking in low gravity. Armstrong moved the TV camera away from the LM, and Aldrin began setting up the relatively few but valuable experiments they had brought. NASA's directors had decided to make few demands on this first, relatively brief visit; the instrument package originally planned had been cut down in the face of the growing weight of the LM and to provide a greater margin of safety. Aldrin erected a solar wind sample collector. They then planted the Stars and Stripes, discovering that the ground under the surface was fairly hard. This exercise, which seems rather pointless since the United States had no intention of claiming the moon, was followed by a call from President Nixon, continuing a dubious tradition initiated by Kennedy. On the whole, however, the patriotic waste of time was kept to a minimum. The astronauts then emplaced a passive seismic experiment—four seismometers that would remain on the moon to report to earth, and a laser mirror reflector (which would enable more precise measurements of the distance between the earth and the moon, fluctuations in the earth's rotation, and the movements of the crust involved in the still controversial continental drift theory). They took many photographs and samples of rock. Fortunately, Armstrong had been the best student of geology among the nonscientists in the astronaut corps, and he made effective use of the limited time.

The controllers on earth extended the planned outing by a quarter of an hour; the crew finally returned to *Eagle* with 50 pounds of rocks and the solar wind collector. They had been outside only about two hours. After a fitful sleep, they departed at 1:54 P.M. on July 21. Four hours later, they rendezvoused with *Columbia*. The men transferred their gear and specimens, jettisoned *Eagle*, and had an easy flight home, landing in the Pacific on July 21. The sequel to the great journey was a tedious twenty-one days in quarantine, joined by a few technicians possibly contaminated by contact with lunar materials. The precautions were of dubious value, since much soil had been tracked into the LM and then the *Columbia*, and was released into the air and sea when *Columbia*'s hatch was opened. The recovery crew, at least, would have been contaminated but was not quarantined. No one had really expected life on the moon, and it was even less likely that if there were any organisms there they could harm terrestrials.

There was nothing to worry about. No evidence of life, and almost no organic materials, were found in the samples. They proved to be igneous rocks, not quite like their earth counterparts. They showed that the moon's composition was in fact different, although not grossly so, from earth's and proved that the moon had been at least partly molten and had once had a magnetic field.[10] This knocked out the old idea that the moon might have fissioned from earth; it had formed separately.

APOLLO 12: RETURN TO THE MOON

With the pressure of competition with the Soviets off, Apollo 12 was not launched until November 14. It was commanded by Charles Conrad, with Richard Gordon as pilot of Command Module *Yankee Clipper* and Alan Bean as pilot of LM *Intrepid*. Liftoff was smooth enough, but the vehicle was hit by lightning as it rose through clouds—causing worry, but no important damage. The episode again vindicated the caution of the von Braun team; against opposition, it had insisted on giving the Saturn V its own guidance system, separate from the Apollo's. The Saturn's system was unscathed, while the Apollo's was temporarily deranged.

After this, the outward trip was uneventful. On November 17, Apollo 12 went into lunar orbit. The crew took many pictures, especially of the Fra Mauro region, where Apollo 13 was to land. The next day Bean and Conrad guided *Intrepid* to a remarkably precise landing in the Oceanus Procellarum, 830 miles from where *Eagle* had landed, and right by Surveyor 3. Given the moon's lumpy gravitational field, this was a real feat by the planners, the designers of the guidance system, and the crew.

Unlike *Eagle*, *Intrepid* hauled the complete Apollo Lunar Experiment Package; the crew deployed seismometers, a magnetometer, a solar wind spectrometer (as well as the solar wind collector carried on Apollo 11 and all later flights), an ionosphere detector (to see what happened to *Intrepid*'s own exhaust gases), a dust detector, and an atmosphere gauge—the latter to pick up any volcanic emissions. The men spent nearly four hours deploying instruments and collecting samples. Unfortunately, they accidentally pointed their TV camera at the sun (or perhaps a reflection off *Intrepid*) and burned out the pickup. Returning to the LM, they recharged their oxygen cylinders and slept in hammocks (a new item). For their second trip outside, they were allowed to go much farther from base, penetrating more rugged ground (including crater bottoms). Reaching Surveyor 3, they removed parts for examination on earth. Returning with specimens and the solar wind collector, they left seven hours later, on the morning of November 20. Earth controllers slammed the LM into the moon to provide a shock for the seismometers. To the surprise of scientists, the moon "rang" like a bell. This indicated that it was a largely solid, although layered, body without much, if any, liquid core. The magnetometer found that the moon had a very weak magnetic field after all, due to eddy currents generated by the solar wind. The rocks from Oceanus Procellarum proved half a billion years younger than those taken by *Eagle*. The men who had collected the data had a good trip home but a rough landing; Bean was hurt when a camera broke loose.[11]

APOLLO 13: BRUSH WITH DISASTER

The next flight showed the dangers still involved in space flight. It was commanded by James Lovell, with John Swigert as pilot of Command Module *Odyssey* and Fred Haise as pilot of Lunar Module *Aquarius*. (The latter name came from the musical *Hair*. It is said that Lovell had not seen it when he named the LM; when he finally did so, he left in disgust!)

There were some minor problems during and after liftoff, but nothing that seemed serious. That changed fifty-five hours into the mission. The Command Module depended for oxygen, water, and electrical power on two hydrogen and two oxygen tanks, Inconel spheres at high pressure, and three fuel cells in its Service Module. Just one tank of each element was adequate for the whole trip, and just two fuel cells could generate all the power needed. One cell would suffice to bring the crew home in an emergency. Either of the two main electrical buses could carry enough power for normal functioning.

There had been some trouble in reading a quantity gauge on one oxygen tank. Accurate readings required stirring up their contents with fans; a ground controller requested a stir to check all the tanks. The astronauts felt a jolt and heard a bang.

In a test, in March 1970, one oxygen tank had been overheated. A safety switch, designed to an obsolete specification (the new one had never reached the subcontractor concerned, or the latter had not acted on it), had failed and the temperature in the tank rose to a point at which the insulation of the wiring inside overheated and cracked. (No one had watched the indicators, which would have shown that something was wrong.) The stir had been the last straw, causing a short-circuit and a fire. The tank blew open, damaging the other oxygen tank and other equipment.

The crew found a low electrical voltage on one main bus; that one oxygen tank was empty and the other was evidently leaking. The crew hastily shut off one fuel cell and all nonessential uses of power. Shortly thereafter they shut off another fuel cell and the last cell evidently had little life left. The only alternative power sources in the Apollo were storage batteries reserved for, and only sufficient for, the reentry into earth's atmosphere. As it was, the crew had to use a battery for a time just to maintain control. There remained the LM. Fortunately, Grumman engineers had foreseen the possibility of using it as a lifeboat in case something went wrong; they had provided additional "consumables" in it for such an eventuality. The crew aligned the LM's guidance system with that of the Apollo—a tricky operation that had to be done while power remained in the latter—and shut down *Odyssey*, moving into the LM. There was enough oxygen but, it turned out, not enough lithium hydroxide to remove the carbon dioxide that three men would exhale over the next few days. The canisters used in *Odyssey* would not fit in the LM, so the crew improvised a CO_2-removal system using material removed from the canisters. The LM's descent engine was fired to assure a free-return trajectory; a second firing after Apollo 13's close approach to the moon speeded its return and enabled *Odyssey* to land in the Pacific, where the recovery forces were deployed. The LM had to use a minimum of power; the men shivered in the cold. They skimped on drinking to save water to cool electronic equipment; finally the water tank in *Odyssey* froze solid. They became dehydrated, and Haise developed a kidney infection. Nor were they free of worry; there was a problem with a helium tank in the LM and worry whether *Odyssey* could be powered up again after a long spell of cold. When the crew jettisoned the Service Module before reentry, they were shocked to see how bad the explosion had been. But it had not damaged the heatshield; and they made a good landing in the Pacific.

Their survival had been a near thing. The disaster had resulted from a series of seemingly small oversights and mistakes piling up. The explosion on Apollo 13 could easily have caused worse and fatal damage. Had the blast occurred when Apollo 13 was on the launch pad, it might have destroyed the whole Saturn V. Had such an explosion taken place at any time on Apollo 8 (which did not carry a LM) or on any subsequent flight after the LM left the Apollo, the whole crew would have been lost.

Although the Service Module could not be examined, a review board reconstructed the incident by studying the telemetry record and the history of the equipment involved. The Apollo was modified to prevent any such incident in the future. Another oxygen tank was added, positioned away from the others, and wires inside "cryogenic" tanks were covered by stainless steel. A battery was installed that was capable of powering the Command Module home from any point in flight, as well as an extra water supply.[12]

Apollo 13 coincided with and intensified a general shakeup in the Apollo program. In 1969 there had been growing discontent, in and outside NASA, with the status of scientific work within the Apollo program. It had been generally accepted that at least the first two missions must be flown by men with test pilot/engineer training. But scientists had hoped that the six scientist-astronauts chosen in 1965 would start landing after that. (Russell Schweikart, recruited in 1963, had worked as a research physicist but was associated with the test pilot group. For some reason, no one deemed him a scientist-astronaut.) The announcement in August 1969 of the crews for Apollo 13 and 14 made clear that this would not be the case. At the same time, although there was no direct connection, several prominent scientists connected with the program (including Wilmot Hess, the chief scientist at the Manned Spacecraft Center, and one of the scientist-astronauts) resigned; although they did not necessarily leave because of disagreements over the program, most disliked the way things were going. Eugene Shoemaker, a geologist working for the U.S. Geological Survey who had worked at NASA, harshly criticized it and condemned Apollo's hardware for what he considered unnecessary shortcomings for scientific purposes. He pointed out, correctly, that it had been built to get men to the moon in a hurry, without much regard for what they would do when they got there. In general, scientists working on Apollo felt themselves to be second-class citizens compared to the engineers, and they grumbled at the latter's continued domination. One of Mueller's advisers, Fred Whipple, bluntly told him that there was much justification for the scientists' irritation. Mueller, who had been particularly responsible for the atmosphere described, heeded him. Mueller left the Office of Manned Space Flight in late 1969, as part of a general turnover at the top of the Apollo program. The new men were more flexible; and Gilruth, still head of the Manned Spacecraft Center, and the astronaut James McDivitt, the new head of the Apollo Spacecraft Program Office, both admitted to the scientists that they had cause for complaint. The system for exchanging information and arranging experiments was rationalized. In February 1970, a Science Working Panel was formed to adjust scientific and operational needs; a science mission manager and a mission scientist were assigned to each flight. The new system, if belated, worked well. Maximizing the gains from the remaining missions was particularly desirable, for the program was shrinking in a way dismaying even to many scientists who had not originally wanted it and had little use for manned space flight.

Underneath the general hoopla surrounding the first moon landing, there had been a good deal of grumbling at the expense involved (the real motives and nature of these complaints will be analyzed later), and it was soon clear that even many who had seemed enthusiastic had no inclination to support a big space program. When the Space Task Force appointed by President Nixon early in 1969 reported in September, it suggested three options for various levels of funding aimed at the goals of a fifty-person space station, a moon base, and an expedition to Mars, all supported by a reusable earth-to-orbit shuttle. Public reaction was bad; the very idea of a Mars trip, even at the lowest level of funding, was ridiculed. It became clear that even a shuttle and a major orbital station would be hard to get across. (In the event, only a cut-down, partly reusable shuttle was built.) Nixon had little interest in space flight (although he did not seem actively hostile to the space program) and was unwilling to do much to counter the prevailing trend of public opinion. NASA's budget was cut steadily, and retrenchments were forced even in current programs. In January 1970, the last Apollo mission, 20, was canceled. Saturn V production would be stopped after the fifteenth rocket. One Saturn V would be used to launch the small space station planned since 1963 as the Apollo Applications Program. Renamed Skylab, it was originally to have been interspersed among lunar flights; now it would follow the last moon trip. Three Apollos, launched by Saturn IBs, would be used to man Skylab for extended stays; after that, it would be deserted for an indefinite period.

In September 1970, the ax fell again. Apollo 15 and 19 were canceled; the renumbered moon missions would end with Apollo 17. NASA Administrator Thomas Paine, disgusted, resigned. The *New York Times* noted that the cuts saved one fourth of 1 percent of the money invested in Apollo; the astronomer Thomas Gold acidly likened this to a man buying a Rolls Royce and not driving because he could not afford gasoline.[13]

LAST MISSIONS

Apollo 14, commanded by Alan Shepard, finally lifted off on January 31, 1971, to carry out the mission originally planned for Apollo 13. Stuart Roosa was the pilot of Command Module *Kitty Hawk*, Edgar Mitchell the pilot of LM *Antares*. It took six tries to dock *Kitty Hawk* with *Antares* and pull it away from the S-IVB, but otherwise the flight outward was uneventful. An improved flight plan was used; Apollo 14 dropped to a lower orbit before *Antares* left to land, giving the LM crew more fuel and making the landing safer. On February 5, Shepard and Mitchell landed near Fra Mauro crater. Equipped with a rubber-wheeled cart, they roved further than ever before from the LM, but the terrain, and climbing in space suits, proved tougher than expected. They were unable to mount the rim of a big crater as hoped. They had deployed a bigger instrument package; a passive seismometer, a laser reflector (complementing the one left by Apollo 11), and ionosphere, atmosphere, and charged particle detectors. For the first time they carried out an active seismic experiment, setting off charges to generate seismic waves. On February 6, they left to meet *Kitty Hawk*, using a new technique for a quicker and simpler rendezvous. The trip home was uneventful, but the crew's time was better used than before; they performed several small experiments requiring zero gravity. Landing just over a half mile from the recovery carrier, they were the last astronauts to undergo quarantine.

Apollo 15 inaugurated a new series of missions. An improved Saturn V, with more powerful engines, and a bigger LM with a heavier payload enabled the astronauts to make more extended stays with more equipment, in more rugged areas. For these missions they would have a wheeled, battery-powered Lunar Roving Vehicle, enabling them to drive up to 6 miles from base. The Apollo spacecraft was more heavily instrumented for observations from lunar orbit.

Apollo 15 was launched on July 26 into a lower parking orbit than earlier missions; that and other minor innovations added to the payload it could carry. The flight was without incident; the astronauts were again given more scientific activities (ultraviolet photography of the earth). On July 30, LM *Falcon*, carrying mission commander James Irwin and David Scott, left Alfred Worden in Command Module *Endeavour* to land in the Palus Putredinus region, well north of the equatorial regions where earlier landings had been made. They set down near Mount Hadley and the nearby Hadley Rille, so both the mountain and the abyss could be examined.

After resting and fixing a tiny oxygen leak (a "urine dump" valve had been left open), Scott and Irwin, using improved space suits, unloaded the Lunar Rover. They were delighted to find that it worked well. Driving was one thing that proved easier than expected. They examined Hadley Rille, but ground control cautiously rejected their proposal to enter it. Returning to *Falcon*, they set up their instrument package: solar wind collector, solar wind analyzer, dust detector, magnetometer, an improved laser reflector, and seismometer package. Drilling holes proved harder than expected, so a heat-flow experiment—designed to find out how much heat was rising from the moon's interior—had to be finished the next day. On that day, they examined the lower slopes of Mount Hadley Delta and found a specimen of anorthosite, the oldest lunar rock yet seen. Completing the heat-flow job, they tested how easy it was to dig in lunar soil. On the third day, yet another excursion returned them to Hadley Rille. On August 2, they departed to rendezvous with *Endeavour*.

Worden had been given more to do than previous Command Module pilots, photomapping the moon and surveying the surface with gamma and X-ray detectors. A laser altimeter recorded surface elevations in unprecedented detail. Worden launched a subsatellite, which would stay in lunar orbit; its detectors would survey magnetic fields and particles and plasmas around the moon. A transponder would allow it to be tracked from earth, mapping the "mascons" and the moon's lumpy gravitational field. After Irwin and Scott rejoined Worden, they spent two more days in lunar orbit before leaving for earth, completing the most successful and productive mission yet.

Apollo 16, delayed for the sake of improved space suits and other gear, was launched on April 16, 1972, with John Young as commander, Thomas Mattingly II as pilot of Command Module *Casper*, and Charles Duke as pilot of LM *Orion*. Despite a mysterious but quickly fixed derangement of its guidance system, Apollo 16 reached lunar orbit. More trouble appeared when one of *Orion*'s antennas jammed and a backup control system on *Casper* went out just after the LM departed. The landing on the moon was delayed while engineers on earth found a way around the bad circuit involved. Finally, on April 21, *Orion* landed in a highland area called the Cayly Descartes formations near the crater Descartes. After eating and sleeping, Young and Duke set up their instrument package. This included an ultraviolet camera-spectrograph for the first astronomical observations from the moon, as well as a solar wind collector, cosmic ray experiment, magnetometer, seismometer, another heat-flow test (ruined by an accident), and an active seismic experiment. Navigating the Lunar Rover through the hilly, rougher than expected area proved more difficult than they had supposed. The region proved not of volcanic origin, as earth observers had expected, and it had a high local magnetic field. Late on April 23, they rejoined Mattingly, who had encountered more problems with his guidance system; yet another problem with *Casper*'s propulsion system caused a subsatellite to be launched into the wrong orbit, and it soon crashed. But the flight home was uneventful.

Everyone knew Apollo 17 was the last chance to explore the moon for a long time, although probably few imagined that even in the 1990s there would be no prospect of humans returning to the moon. The flight was slated for the rugged Taurus-Littrow area, a valley in mountains southeast of the Mare Serenitatis. It would carry the first scientist-astronaut (other than the generally ignored Schweikart), Harrison Schmitt, a geologist who served as pilot of LM *Challenger*. The trip was commanded by Eugene Cernan, with Ronald Evans as pilot of Command Module *America*. After delays, Apollo 17 lifted off on Pearl Harbor Day, 1972. Landing on the moon on December 11, Cernan and Schmitt took to the Rover. On their first excursion, they set up the instrument package; in addition to the usual instruments, this included another heat-flow experiment (this one worked) and gravimeters, as well as an active seismic experiment, a new type of meteoritic dust detector, and a scanner designed to probe for subsurface water or ice. (None was found.) A neutron probe measured the effect of cosmic rays on the soil. In three days of energetic exploration, hampered by dust, they found orange soil (indicating relatively late volcanic activity) and collected more samples than any of their predecessors. Apollo 17 was virtually untouched by the equipment problems that had come close to undoing Apollo 16. The seventh and final lunar expedition returned to earth on December 19; it had been the most effective.[14]

APOLLO AND THE MOON

The information gained by the Apollo expeditions and supplemented by the Soviet unmanned effort enabled the formation of a rough picture of the moon's structure, composition, and history. It became fairly clear that it had never had any life, and probably no free water either. But it was a differentiated body that had undergone some changes early in its history. All rocks found were igneous; none were sedimentary or metamorphic. Under a loose layer of rubble, a crust (largely of anorthosite and thicker on the far side than the near side) went down an average of 37 miles; below that there was a mantle some 625 miles deep, and, probably, a partly molten core of silicates or iron. The moon had once had a magnetic field, which had largely disappeared. The minerals in the crust contained few volatiles but a higher percentage of radioactives than the cosmic average. The moon's composition differed considerably from the earth and might well have formed in a different part of the solar system before being captured by the earth. It might never have been completely molten, but its outer layer had melted early in its history and probably had remelted in parts later. The vast basins, called seas, had been gouged out by cosmic impacts 3.9 to 4.1 billion years before; the highlands retained the oldest rocks on the moon—over four billion years old. The craters proved overwhelmingly meteoritic in origin. There had been volcanic activity, but the moon had long been dead geologically. Its crust was not rich in valuable minerals (with the vital exception, perhaps, of helium-3, deposited by the solar wind and almost unavailable on earth, which might be the best fuel for future nuclear fusion reactors). But there were ample materials for building permanent bases and, perhaps, schemes of space industrialization. Whatever its other consequences and original purpose, Apollo's true value may have been as the costliest prospecting job in history. The Soviet probes were a great achievement, but no unmanned effort could have duplicated Apollo's samples; without the larger rocks it brought back, the soil the unmanned probes retrieved would have been downright misleading.[15]

SPINOFFS AND BENEFITS

Apart from the scientific data gained and speculative long-range gains, the Apollo program had short-term side-effects and technological gains, or spinoffs, which were a significant recompense for the $25 billion expended. (The space program as a whole, including Apollo, undoubtedly paid for itself just through improved weather reporting. It was estimated that by 1971 NASA's weather and earth resources satellites alone were saving $3 billion a year, and perhaps tens of thousands of lives, by tracking storms, plant diseases, and forest fires from orbit. Of course, that sort of activity could have been carried on without Apollo, or indeed any manned flights.) Although sometimes exaggerated (for example, the useful plastic teflon, actually a product of the Manhattan Project, was sometimes hijacked by ardent advocates of Apollo), many useful techniques and products were developed. Building the Saturns involved many advances in industrial technology, especially the development of new aluminum alloys and welding techniques, new tools such as the "electromagnetic hammer," new forms of insulation, and techniques to make and store cryogenic fluids on a large scale. The project's investment in electronics, especially biomedical devices and computers, was particularly productive. It contributed to the development of CAT scanners, heart-monitoring devices and other biosensors, and portable kidney machines. And Apollo generated jobs. Charles Murray, who studied both Apollo and the social programs of the era, concluded that Apollo produced as many jobs as Johnson's whole Great Society program.[16]

AFTERMATH

While the Soviets concentrated energetically on developing space stations, with the end of lunar exploration American manned space flight gradually trailed off. (Unmanned planetary probes, despite very tight budgets, obtained some remarkable results.) NASA managed to carry out Skylab and the politically motivated linkup of an Apollo with a Soviet Soyuz (a very doubtful choice instead of another Skylab visit). The remaining Apollo capability was, almost literally, thrown away. The remaining two Saturn IBs and two Saturn Vs, still usable, although costly to maintain, never flew and were turned over to museums. (Three usable lunar modules also went to institutions; another, unbelievably, was junked.)

NASA concentrated much of its reduced budget in the Space Shuttle, which barely survived concentrated congressional attacks in the early 1970s. To cut development costs, at the price of inflating eventual operating expenses, its reusability and safety diminished steadily. Originally it was to have been a two-stage vehicle, both stages winged and piloted, with auxiliary jet engines. First the upper stage was cut down in size to depend on expendable external tanks. Then—much against the advice of the safety-conscious von Braun— the first stage was replaced by solid-fuel boosters. Finally, the jets were removed, leaving the shuttle a glider capable of just one landing pass, dependent on awkward transportation from landing to launch sites. In its duel with an unsympathetic Congress, NASA sold the Shuttle on the basis of wild overestimates of the number of flights it would make and underestimates of the overhauls and operating expenses needed—and the risks involved. It recklessly sacrificed its expendable unmanned launch vehicles, some of which had to be reintroduced after 1986. NASA, an increasingly stagnant bureaucracy, and North American/Rockwell fell from the high standards set during Apollo. The long-delayed Shuttle emerged from a plant in which drug use, drunkenness, and even sabotage were rife, much too late to save Skylab. Its flights fell behind schedule, and actual costs per pound to orbit were no better than the Saturn V's. Flaws in the solid-fuel boosters, glossed over by management, led eventually to disaster.[17]

The fatal flaw in the U.S. space program, however, lay farther back, in the derailing of the logical course of development by Apollo. Instead of committing the nation to a rational step-by-step expansion into space, with initial concentration on a space station and the solution of the central problem of space flight (economical delivery of large payloads to orbit, something chemically fueled multistage rockets like the Saturn V could never do) Kennedy opted for a one-shot leap to the moon with existing technology. The move toward a space station was stopped, then sidelined to the minor Skylab project, while radical improvements—the nuclear rocket and Orion—were supported minimally and then strangled. The promise of manned space flight was bound up with the fate of the moon project. But the latter was, almost literally, a stunt. It was started under a

President who had no real interest in space, for reasons of national prestige, and was not intended to be part of a rational program. As John and Ruth Lewis noted, the government "did not commit any funding to any goal beyond the achievement of the lunar landing. It is ironic that one of the most attractive virtues of Apollo from the political perspective had turned out to be its greatest liability; it was designed from the start as a dead end—and it was well-designed indeed. This is the reason why there is so much use of, and so little agreement about the phrase 'next logical step' in the post-Apollo world. Apollo itself was such a logical anomaly that there *is* no next logical step."[18] (It is, of course, true that the Apollo spacecraft was originally designed to support a space station, not for a moon landing. But that fact was largely forgotten after 1961; the public, and even most historians, assumed that the program produced and named the craft, rather than the other way around. There were political and commercial motives for fostering this idea. Admitting that important aspects of the Apollo program dated to Eisenhower did not suit his successors, while NASA and North American did not like admitting that it was the oldest aspect of the program that had the most delays and trouble.)

Some have blamed this state of affairs solely on the Kennedy Administration; indeed the Lewises have even described the process involved as "NASA's discovery that it could sell its soul to politicians and get rich doing it."[19] The temptation to blame Kennedy for all that went wrong must be resisted. In the first place, the danger of Soviet competition was a real one in 1961, and had to be faced. A Soviet first landing on the moon in the 1960s would undoubtedly have been interpreted throughout the world as a humiliation and a grave reverse for the West. (With a little common sense at the top, Korolev might well have gotten to the moon first, whatever the Americans did.) It may be argued that instead of indulging in an irrational race to the moon, Kennedy should have invested in a program aimed at developing basic space capabilities, and especially propulsion research, thus making certain that, even though the Soviets might (and probably would) beat the West to the moon, the United States would overtake them in real and lasting achievements. Such a strategy might have appealed to a man like Eisenhower, but not a Kennedy. But in any case that was not the sort of advice Kennedy received. It was NASA's own planners who had decided, in 1959, that the moon was the logical goal, not necessitating further steps. They, and NASA's genuine supporters like Lyndon Johnson, presumably did not mean that manned space flight should stop there, but that was the sort of conclusion others would draw. NASA did not "sell its soul," but was guilty of misjudgment.

It is conceivable, perhaps, that the Kennedy Administration should have followed a dual program, one aimed at beating the Soviets to the moon, the other at capabilities of more permanent value. It may be that some of those involved thought that that was what they were doing. But the stunt aspects of space flight drove the long-range aspects out. And, for one reason or another, the stunt side was the one that dominated the public mind—assisted by NASA's inept public relations. (The writer Robert A. Heinlein, who dealt with NASA, classed its efforts in this field as the worst of any government agency he had ever seen.) That, coupled with fierce political attacks (overwhelmingly by liberals), helps explain the otherwise perplexing fact that it was *after* the landing on the moon that public support for the space program fell dramatically. It is not the whole explanation, for there was a strong element of the totally irrational in the public's attitude and in almost all attacks on the program. (Rational, if not necessarily correct, criticisms of the sort advanced by Abelson and Weaver played a small role in the campaign against the space program.) The grandeur of space travel did not fit in with the atmosphere of mean-spirited belittling and downright misanthropy so characteristic of the late 1960s, which never really dissipated thereafter.

In retrospect, Apollo, for all the faults we have noted, may appear one of the few redeeming aspects of one of the dreariest eras of American history. But it did not seem so, to many, at the time. Even a collection of reactions by science fiction writers to Apollo 11—a group one might expect to be overwhelmingly enthusiastic—discloses much grumbling and a widespread (if incoherent) feeing of disillusionment.[20] Complaints usually revolved around the need to concentrate on ending war, poverty, and environmental problems. The space program was strangely linked, in the critics' minds, with the military and the Indochina War, both directly and as a source of vast expenditures. Indeed even defenders of the program then, and later, would sometimes link it and the war, implying that the costs of the war somehow forced cutbacks in space budgets. In fact, while the 1965 budget—coinciding with massive commitments in Indochina—began a relative decline of NASA's budget and did hurt the nuclear rocket, the steep cuts that occurred after Apollo 11 actually followed the start of U.S. withdrawal from Indochina.

By the time Congress killed the last three Apollo missions, it was quite clear that U.S. involvement in Indochina must end not long after the 1972 election. The tendency to link Apollo, or the space program in general, with the war, was bizarre as either a moral or financial comparison. To compare exploration, however extravagant the cost, with war betrayed a total collapse of moral distinctions, and the amount of money involved differed by orders of magnitude. (Presenting the military budget as *the* obstacle to the Good Society was arguably absurd enough; after the Eisenhower Administration it rarely absorbed more than 7 percent of the GNP.) Apollo took 5 percent of the annual expenditures on defense; it took less money than totally unproductive expenditures such as paying farmers not to grow crops, and it cost less than $20 per person per year. Yet it was widely presented as a fearsome drain on the treasury and an obstacle to liberal hopes. One observer sardonically noted that "organized crime devours something like $25 billion a year, but the Cosa Nostra is a hard thing to fight, and, besides, it has been around for quite a while. But, if the $5 billion a year which NASA so frivolously steals out of the mouths of the poor could but be restored to the economy, the New Eden would instantly appear."[21] Yet Senators such as J. William Fulbright professed to think that it was a choice between sewers and waterworks and rocks from the moon; former Supreme Court Justice Arthur Goldberg professed to believe that scrapping Apollo would balance the national budget.[22]

The scientists who had opposed Apollo as a poor investment found their own budgets cut, as esteem for both science and technology fell. By the 1980s, scientists would regularly be portrayed as villains on American TV screens. Science education declined even more sharply than the rest of the shambles of American public education; a growing proportion of college students in the sciences would be foreigners, as Americans flocked to law and business. Spinoffs and other benefits of the space program were, of course, ignored. Such irrationality was uncharacteristic of the liberalism of previous decades, but was a growing part of the national ethos.

Notes

PREFACE

1. *New York Times*, May 26, 1961.

CHAPTER 1

1. John D. Clark, *Ignition* (New Brunswick, N.J.: Rutgers University Press, 1972), xi; Willy Ley, *Rockets, Missiles, and Men in Space* (New York: Viking, 1968), 93–96, 297–302; David Baker, *The Rocket* (New York: Crown, 1978), 17–21.

2. *The Papers of Robert H. Goddard*, edited by Esther C. Goddard and G. Edward Pendray (New York: McGraw-Hill, 1970), Vol. 1, pp. 40, 337–406, 413–428, Vol. 2, pp. 688–698, 714–716, 800–803, 809, 810, 881–884, 1061–1062, 1076–1077, 1212–1213, Vol. 3, pp. 1332–1333, 1404, 1409; Robert H. Goddard, "A New Turbine Rocket Plane for the Upper Atmosphere," *Scientific American* (March 1932), 148–149; Milton Lehman, *Robert H. Goddard* (New York: Da Capo, 1988), 1–294; Mitchell R. Sharpe, "The Centenary of Robert Hutchins Goddard 1882–1982," *JBIS* (Journal of the British Interplanetary Society) (December 1982), 530–540; G. Edward Pendray, "Pioneer Rocket Development in the United States," pp. 19–28 in *The History of Rocket Technology*, edited by Eugene Emme (Detroit, Mich.: Wayne State University Press, 1964); Constance McLaughlin, *Ordnance Department: Planning Munitions for War* (Washington, D.C.: Department of the Army, 1955), 356. It has recently been fashionable to belittle Goddard's influence and suggest that his importance has been exaggerated. As Homer Newell puts it, "Much of what he did had to be redone" because of his "lone-wolf approach and secrecy"; *Beyond the Atmosphere* (Washington, D.C.:

NASA, 1980), 30–31. William Sims Bainbridge, author of *The Spaceflight Revolution* (New York: John Wiley, 1976), which along with Frederick Ordway and Mitchell Sharpe's *The Rocket Team* (New York: Crowell, 1979) typifies what might be called the Germanocentric approach to the history of rocketry, goes even farther, claiming that some Americans have overclaimed for Goddard for reasons of national pride. Some may have done so, but in the present writer's opinion the striking bias in historical writing has been an overemphasis on the extent of German leadership in rocketry. This is traceable to the tremendous impact of the V-2 and the fact that Willy Ley, a founder of the VfR, stressed the German role in his many excellent and ground-breaking books on rocketry.

The degree of Goddard's secrecy and in effect in reducing the influence of his work can easily be exaggerated. There is evidence that the Germans maintained a strong interest in his work up to 1939 (see Lehman, *Robert H. Goddard*, p. 220). His mere association with Lindbergh, one of the most famous men in the world, attracted attention. He did publish, albeit sparsely, and reported to well-known institutions—the Guggenheim Foundation, the Carnegie Institute, and the Smithsonian. In 1936 he described his work in detail to the American Association for the Advancement of Science, and it was covered in detail by the *New York Times*, where it occasionally reached page 1 (e.g., September 1, 1935, January 1, 1936). Above all, he secured many patents; and his heirs, aided by Lindbergh, maintained long-standing suits over their infringement, which were settled only in 1960. There were good reasons, therefore, for others in the rocket field to minimize their debt to him. Some Americans went farther than the Germans in belittling Goddard; von Braun admitted the Germans' debt to him and was responsible for erecting a monument to him. See also Erik Bergaust, *Reaching for the Stars* (New York: Doubleday, 1960), 24–28. Some of Goddard's work may have been independently duplicated, but claims of this sort should be regarded skeptically.

3. Leonard Mosley, *Lindbergh* (New York: Doubleday, 1976), 344. General Dornberger claimed that almost 90 percent of Goddard's patents were not available. See also Walter Dornberger, "The German V-2," p. 36 in *The History of Rocket Technology*, edited by Eugene Emme (Detroit, Mich.: Wayne State University Press, 1964).

4. Ley, *Rockets, Missiles, and Men in Space*, 100–149, 298–302, 419; Baker, *The Rocket*, 27–32; Frank H. Winter, *Prelude to the Space Age: The Rocket Societies 1924–1940* (Washington, D.C.: Smithsonian Institution Press, 1983), 30–53; I. Essers, *Max Valier* (Washington, D.C.: NASA, 1976), esp. pp. 67, 81, 92–97, 110–135.

5. Frank Borman, *Countdown* (New York: Morrow, 1988), 99.

6. G. Harry Stine, *ICBM* (New York: Orion, 1991), 67.

7. Walter Dornberger, *V-2* (New York: Bantam, 1979); Gregory Kennedy, *Vengeance Weapon 2* (Washington, D.C.: Smithsonian Institution Press, 1983); Baker, *The Rocket*, 33–62, 85–90; Ley, *Rockets, Missiles, and Men in Space*, 181–223, 498–499, 501; Ordway and Sharpe, *The Rocket Team*, 1–261; Bainbridge,

The Spaceflight Revolution, 92–95, 117–118; Stine, *ICBM*, 33–93; Erik Bergaust, *Wernher von Braun* (Washington, D.C.: National Space Institute, 1976), 21–84; David Irving, *The Mare's Nest* (Boston: Little, Brown, 1965), 18–43, 65, 83, 97–120, 294–295, 304–310.

8. Winter, *Prelude to the Space Age*, 73–83; Baker, *The Rocket*, 26–27, 72–76; Ley, *Rockets, Missiles, and Men in Space*, 229–232; Clark, *Ignition*, 19–21; *The Papers of Robert H. Goddard*, Vol. 3, pp. 1443–1451, 1479–1483, 1606n; Lehman, *Robert H. Goddard*, 294–384; Clayton Koppes, *JPL and the American Space Program* (New Haven, Conn.: Yale University Press, 1982), 2–39; Frank Malina, "Origins and First Decade of the Jet Propulsion Laboratory," pp. 46–66 in *The History of Rocket Technology*, edited by Eugene Emme (Detroit, Mich.: Wayne State University Press, 1964); Frank Malina, "The US Army Air Corps Jet Propulsion Research Project GALCIT Project No. 1, 1939–1946: A Memoir," pp. 153–201, Frank Malina, "America's Long-Range Missile and Space Exploration Program: The Ordcit Project of the Jet Propulsion Laboratory 1943–1946: A Memoir," pp. 339–383, George H. Osborn, Robert Gordon, Herman L. Coplen, with George S. Jones, "Liquid Hydrogen Rocket Engine Development 1944–1950," pp. 279–324 in *Essays on the History of Rocketry and Astronautics: Proceedings of the Third through the Sixth Symposia of the International Academy on Astronautics*, edited by R. Cargill Hall (Washington, D.C.: NASA, 1977); John Sloop, *Liquid Hydrogen as a Propulsion Fuel: 1945–1959* (Washington, D.C.: NASA, 1978), 4–5, 13–19, 31–33; John Sloop, "Technological Innovation for Success: Liquid Hydrogen Propulsion," pp. 225–239 in *Between Sputnik and the Shuttle*, edited by F. C. Durant (San Diego, Calif.: American Academy of Science, 1981); Frederick I. Ordway and Frank H. Winter, "Pioneering Commercial Rocketry in the United States of America: Reaction Motors 1941–1950: Part I," *JBIS* (December 1983), 542–552.

9. Baker, *The Rocket*, 76–84; Leonid Dushkin, "Experimental Research and Design Planning in the Field of Liquid-Propellant Rocket Engines Conducted Between 1934–1944 by the Followers of F. A. Tsander," pp. 79–97 in Hall, ed., *Essays on the History of Rocketry and Astronautics*; Winter, *Prelude to the Space Age*, 55–71, 80.

10. Clark, *Ignition*, passim.

11. Lehman, *Robert H. Goddard*, 131.

CHAPTER 2

1. Ley, *Rockets, Missiles, and Men in Space*, 225–236; Kennedy, *Vengeance Weapon 2*, 27, 52, 55–64; Ordway and Sharpe, *The Rocket Team*, 273–298, 310–317, 346–353, 358, 397; S. A. Curtis, "Use of the German V-2 in the U.S. for Upper Atmosphere Research," *JBIS* (December 1979), 443–448; Newell, *Beyond the Atmosphere* (Washington, D.C.: NASA, 1980), 33–36; Stine, *ICBM*, 95–98, 106, 109–120; Bergaust, *Wernher von Braun*, 189; Clarence Lasby, *Project Paperclip* (New York: Atheneum, 1971), esp. pp. 5–9, 15–19, 26,

36–42, 88, 101, 103, 113–116, 132–135, 153–154, 167–169, 185–193, 199–201, 222–223, 229–231, 252–253, 257–260; John B. Medaris, *Countdown for Decision* (New York: G. P. Putnam's, 1960), 117.

2. Baker, *The Rocket*, 126–127; Kennedy, *Vengeance Weapon 2*, 55–56; Ordway and Sharpe, *The Rocket Team*, 294–308.

3. R. Cargill Hall, "Early U.S. Satellite Proposals," pp. 67–93 in *The History of Rocket Technology*, edited by Eugene Emme (Detroit, Mich.: Wayne State University Press, 1964); R. Cargill Hall, "Earth Satellites: A First Look by the United States Navy," pp. 253–277 in *Essays on the History of Rocketry and Astronautics*; Sloop, *Liquid Hydrogen as a Propulsion Fuel*, 18–58, 63, 73–76.

4. Edmund Beard, *Developing the ICBM* (New York: Columbia University Press, 1976), 72.

5. Beard, *Developing the ICBM*, 8, 21, 33, 37–38, 44, 49, 67–75; Jacob Neufeld, *The Development of Ballistic Missiles in the United States Air Force 1945–1960* (Washington, D.C.: Office of Air Force History, 1990), 9–24; Michael Armacost, *The Politics of Weapons Innovation* (New York: Columbia University Press, 1969), 9, 155–160; Medaris, *Countdown for Decision*, 99–100.

6. Beard, *Developing the ICBM*, 49–56, 62–66, 79–96; Neufeld, *The Development of Ballistic Missiles in the United States Air Force*, 24–33, 36–38, 44–50; Stine, *ICBM*, 141–146; John L. Chapman, *Atlas: Story of a Missile* (New York: Harper, 1960), 27–35, 38–53; Baker, *The Rocket*, 97; Frederick I. Ordway and Frank H. Winter, "Pioneering Commercial Rocketry in the United States of America: Reaction Motors, Inc. 1941–1950: Part 2," *JBIS* (April 1985), 158, 161–162.

7. J. W. Powell, "Navaho: The Know-How Missile," *JBIS* (February 1987), 93–95; Russ Murray, "The Navaho Inheritance," *American Aviation Historical Society Journal* (Spring 1974), 17–21; Beard, *Developing the ICBM*, 89, 92–95; Neufeld, *The Development of Ballistic Missiles in the United States Air Force*, 57–59, 71, 76, 99, 114–128; Stine, *ICBM*, 121, 152, 191–192; Baker, *The Rocket*, 101; Roger E. Bilstein, *Stages to Saturn* (Washington, D.C.: NASA, 1980), 13–15; Martin Caidin, *Countdown for Tomorrow* (New York: E. P. Dutton, 1958), 243–249, 254; Martin Caidin, *Overture to Space* (New York: Duell, Sloane and Pearce, 1963), 68.

8. Ley, *Rockets, Missiles, and Men in Space*, 248–263; Milton Rosen, *The Viking Rocket Story* (New York: Harper, 1955); Constance McLaughlin Green and Milton Lomask, *Vanguard* (Washington, D.C.: NASA, 1971), 9–12, 58; Newell, *Beyond the Atmosphere*, 37–38, 82; Baker, *The Rocket*, 259; Milton Rosen, "The Viking Rocket: A Memoir," pp. 429–441 in *Essays on the History of Rocketry and Astronautics*.

9. Steven Zaloga, *Target America* (Novato, Calif.: Presidio Press, 1993), 111, 115–136, 140–141, 252, 259, 261; Steven Zaloga, "The First ICBM: Early Soviet Strategic Ballistic Missile Development," *Aerospace Historian* (Winter/December 1985), 268–270; Stine, *ICBM*, 131–137, 155–159; G. A. Tokaty,

"Soviet Rocket Technology," pp. 277–281 in *The History of Rocket Technology*, edited by Eugene Emme (Detroit, Mich.: Wayne State University Press, 1964); Baker, *The Rocket*, 114–118; Neufeld, *The Development of Ballistic Missiles in the United States Air Force*, 71; James Oberg, *Red Star in Orbit* (New York: Random House, 1981), 16–22; Clark, *Ignition*, 115–119.

CHAPTER 3

1. Thomas Wolfe, *Soviet Power in Europe* (Baltimore, Md.: Johns Hopkins University Press, 1970), 73–228; Lawrence Freedman, *The Evolution of Nuclear Strategy* (New York: St. Martin's Press, 1981), 145–149, 152; Christopher Bluth, "Defense and Security," pp. 194–202, Harry Hanak, "Foreign Policy," pp. 180–193 in *Khrushchev and Khrushchevism*, edited by Martin McCauley (Bloomington, Ind.: Indiana University Press, 1987). For different views of Khrushchev, see also Oleg Penkovskiy, *The Penkovskiy Papers* (New York: Avon, 1966) and Robert Slusser, *The Berlin Crisis of 1961* (Baltimore, Md.: Johns Hopkins University Press, 1973).

2. Freedman, *The Evolution of Nuclear Strategy*, 77–78, 80, 84–86; *Foreign Relations of the United States 1952–1954*, Vol. II, Part 1 (Washington, D.C.: Government Printing Office, 1984), 264–281, 323, 329–349, 360–366, 394–434, 435–440, 559–561, 576–597, 634–635, 639, 785–802, 833–834.

3. Doris Condit, *The Test of War: History of the Office of the Secretary of Defense* (Washington, D.C.: Historical Office of the Secretary of Defense, 1988), 473–475; Beard, *Developing the ICBM*, 104, 122–128; Neufeld, *The Development of Ballistic Missiles in the United States Air Force*, 66, 80, 92; Stine, *ICBM*, 149–151; Baker, *The Rocket*, 105, 116–121, 226.

4. Neufeld, *The Development of Ballistic Missiles in the United States Air Force*, 65–92; Beard, *Developing the ICBM*, 130–144; Ernest G. Schwiebart, *History of US Air Force Ballistic Missiles* (New York: Praeger, 1965), 57–59, 68; Chapman, *Atlas*, 61–71.

5. Neufeld, *The Development of Ballistic Missiles in the United States Air Force*, 93–114, 120, 255–265; Beard, *Developing the ICBM*, 144–185; Schwiebart, *History of US Air Force Ballistic Missiles*, 32, 60–61, 65, 71–89, 217–219; Herbert F. York, *Race to Oblivion* (New York: Simon & Schuster, 1970), 84–88; Trevor Gardner, "How We Fell Behind in Missiles," *Airpower Historian* (January 1958), 3–13.

6. York, *Race to Oblivion*, 87–88.

7. Neufeld, *The Development of Ballistic Missiles in the United States Air Force*, 114–128; Beard, *Developing the ICBM*, 182–185; Schwiebart, *History of US Air Force Ballistic Missiles*, 95–96; Chapman, *Atlas*, 80; Baker, *The Rocket*, 107, 231–232, 256–257; Robert Perry, "Atlas, Thor, Titan and Minuteman," pp. 143–148 in *The History of Rocket Technology*, edited by Eugene Emme (Detroit, Mich.: Wayne State University Press, 1964); Jay Miller, *The X-Planes* (New York: Aerofax/Orion, 1988), 134–137.

8. John Prados, *The Soviet Estimate* (New York: Dial, 1982), 30–36; Michael Beschloss, *Mayday* (New York: Harper & Row, 1986), 8, 15, 78, 92, 105, 120; James R. Killian, *Sputnik, Scientists and Eisenhower* (Cambridge, Mass.: MIT Press, 1977), 67–88; Thomas Powers, *The Man Who Kept the Secrets* (New York: Knopf, 1979), 97.

9. Neufeld, *The Development of Ballistic Missiles in the United States Air Force*, 120–122, 128–136; Beard, *Developing the ICBM*, 186–194; Schwiebart, *History of US Air Force Ballistic Missiles*, 172–173.

10. Neufeld, *The Development of Ballistic Missiles in the United States Air Force*, 149–167; Beard, *Developing the ICBM*, 196–207, 223; Chapman, *Atlas*, 80–165; Baker, *The Rocket*, 109–110, 233; Miller, *The X-Planes*, 94–99.

11. Neufeld, *The Development of Ballistic Missiles in the United States Air Force*, 143–147, 151–152, 163, 166–167; Armacost, *The Politics of Weapons Innovation*, 8–9, 43–172; Medaris, *Countdown for Decision*, 74, 98–112, 116–148, 161, 180; Baker, *The Rocket*, 108, 235, 255; Bergaust, *Wernher von Braun*, 244–256; Bergaust, *Reaching for the Stars*, 208–223; Julian Hartt, *The Mighty Thor* (New York: Duell, Sloane and Pearce, 1961), 5–134; York, *Race to Oblivion*, 94–100, 102–103, 105; *New York Times*, June 26, 1957, p. 1, June 30, 1957, p. 1.

12. Harvey Sapolsky, *Polaris System Development* (Cambridge, Mass.: Harvard University Press, 1972), 7–8, 11–134; Armacost, *The Politics of Weapons Innovation*, 104–110; Wyndham Miles, "Polaris," pp. 162–175 in *The History of Rocket Technology*, edited by Eugene Emme (Detroit, Mich.: Wayne State University Press, 1964); James Baar and William Howard, *Polaris* (New York: Harcourt Brace, 1960), 21–98; York, *Race to Oblivion*, 100.

13. Zaloga, *Target America*, 133–142, 156, 169, 172–180; Zaloga, "The First ICBM," 268–273; Baker, *The Rocket*, 118–122; Stine, *ICBM*, 158–161, 220–221; G. Harry Stine, "How the Soviets Did It in Space," *Analog* (August 1968), 48–71; Oberg, *Red Star in Orbit*, 26, 33–35.

CHAPTER 4

1. Philip Klass, *UFO's: Identified* (New York: Random House, 1968); Robert Sheaffer, *UFO Verdict* (Buffalo, N.Y.: Prometheus, 1986); Edward J. Ruppelt, *The Report on the Unidentified Flying Objects* (New York: Ace, 1964); David Michael Jacobs, *The UFO Controversy in America* (Bloomington, Ind.: Indiana University Press, 1975), 35–55, 78, 90.

2. Arthur C. Clarke, *The Exploration of Space* (New York: Harper, 1951); Arthur C. Clarke, *Interplanetary Flight* (New York: Harper, 1950); Ernest Stuhlinger, "Gathering Momentum," pp. 113–123 and Randy Lieberman, "The Colliers and Disney Series," pp. 135–146 in *Blueprint for Space*, edited by Frederick I. Ordway and Randy Lieberman (Washington, D.C.: Smithsonian Institution Press, 1992); Cornelius Ryan, *Across the Space Frontier* (New York: Viking, 1952); Cornelius Ryan, *Conquest of the Moon* (New York: Viking, 1953);

Werner von Braun, *The Mars Project* (Urbana, Ill.: University of Illinois Press, 1953); David Baker, *The History of Manned Space Flight* (New York: Crown, 1982), 21–23; Bergaust, *Wernher von Braun*, 155, 173–177; Bergaust, *Reaching for the Stars*, 269–274; G. Harry Stine, *Earth Satellites and the Race for Space Superiority* (New York: Ace Books, 1957), 124–150. See also John S. Lewis and Ruth A. Lewis, *Space Resources* (New York: Columbia University Press, 1987), 106–113.

3. Clarke, *Exploration of Space*, 120–130, 136–140; Poul Anderson, *Is There Life on Other Worlds?* (New York: Collier Books, 1968), 63–77; Frederick I. Ordway, "The Legacy of Schiaparelli and Lowell," *JBIS* (January 1986), 19–27; *Neighbors of the Earth*, edited by Thornton Page and Lou Williams Page (New York: Macmillan, 1965), 14, 19, 52–59, 77; V. A. Firsoff, *Life Beyond the Earth* (New York: Basic Books, 1963), esp. pp. 164–173; Alan Nourse, *Nine Planets* (New York: Harper, 1960); Robert S. Richardson, *Exploring Mars* (New York: McGraw-Hill, 1954); Willy Ley, *Mariner IV to Mars* (New York: New American Library, 1966). For modern views, see also Fred Whipple, *Orbiting the Sun* (Cambridge, Mass.: Harvard University Press, 1981) and Joseph F. Baugher, *The Space-Age Solar System* (New York: John Wiley, 1988).

4. Green and Lomask, *Vanguard*, 42–61; Newell, *Beyond the Atmosphere*, 50, 52–53; R. Cargill Hall, "Origins and Development of the Vanguard and Explorer Satellite Programs," *Airpower Historian* (October 1964), 101–112; Ley, *Rockets, Missiles, and Men in Space*, 303–304, 307; Bergaust, *Wernher von Braun*, 235–242; Bergaust, *Reaching for the Stars*, 308; Baker, *The Rocket*, 132–133, 259.

5. Green and Lomask, *Vanguard*, 61–181; Baker, *The Rocket*, 259; John Hagen, "Viking and Vanguard," pp. 122–141 in *The History of Rocket Technology*, edited by Eugene Emme (Detroit, Mich.: Wayne State University Press, 1964).

6. Medaris, *Countdown for Decision*, 68, 119–120, 134–135, 143, 147, 151; "Jupiter C/Juno I: America's First Satellite Launcher," *Spaceflight* (January 1981), 12–17; Ley, *Rockets, Missiles, and Men in Space*, 312–315; Wernher von Braun, "Redstone, Jupiter and Juno," pp. 108–113 in *The History of Rocket Technology*, edited by Eugene Emme (Detroit, Mich.: Wayne State University Press, 1964); Ordway and Sharpe, *The Rocket Team*, 376–377; Baker, *The Rocket*, 237; Caidin, *Countdown for Tomorrow*, 77–78; Martin Caidin, *War for the Moon* (New York: E. P. Dutton, 1959), 51, 60–67, 69, 74.

7. Neufeld, *The Development of Ballistic Missiles in the United States Air Force*, 144, 147, 180–181; Schwiebart, *History of US Air Force Ballistic Missiles*, 221, 224; Prados, *The Soviet Estimate*, 104–106; Philip Klass, *Secret Sentries in Space* (New York: Random House, 1971), 76–88.

CHAPTER 5

1. *New York Times*, November 5, 1957, p. 1; Albert Parry, *Russia's Rockets and Missiles* (New York: Doubleday, 1960), 192–193; Bergaust, *Wernher von Braun*, 303.

2. *Survey of International Affairs 1956–1958* (Oxford, England: Oxford University Press, 1962), 347–351, 546.

3. *New York Times*, October 8, 1957, pp. 1, 11, 13, October 9, 1957, p. 1, October 10, 1957, p. 1, October 22, 1957, p. 4; Green and Lomask, *Vanguard*, 186–190; Caidin, *Countdown to Tomorrow*, 51, 54, 57.

4. *New York Times*, October 16, 1957, p. 1, October 21, 1957, p. 13, November 3, 1957, p. 1, November 10, 1957, Part 1, pp. 1, 12, 25, 36, Part 4, p. 10; Walter MacDougall, *The Heavens and the Earth* (New York: Basic Books, 1985), 132–150; Donald Cox, *Space Power* (Philadelphia, Pa.: John C. Winston, 1958), 21–26, 107–108; *The Challenge of the Sputniks*, edited by Richard Witkin (New York: Doubleday, 1958); Caidin, *Countdown to Tomorrow*, 44–49; Edgar Bottome, *The Missile Gap* (Rutherford, N.J.: Fairleigh Dickinson University Press, 1971), 37–51; Klass, *Secret Sentries in Space*, 23–26; Eric Goldman, *The Crucial Decade and After* (New York: Vintage, 1960), 302, 309, 313–314, 341; Allen J. Matusow, *The Unraveling of America* (New York: Harper & Row, 1984), 4–5, 8–9. MacDougall, *The Heavens and the Earth*, is probably the most detailed account of the post-Sputnik debate, but it exaggerates the faults of contemporary news coverage (other than Time-Life's) in describing it as a "media riot." MacDougall understates the Administration's own worries. For examples of the most extreme and alarmist attacks on the Eisenhower Administration, see Drew Pearson, *America—Second-Class Power?* (New York: Simon & Schuster, 1958) and Alexander De Seversky, *America—Too Young to Die* (New York: McGraw-Hill, 1961).

5. Bottome, *The Missile Gap*, 41, 62–63; *Survey of International Affairs 1956–1958*, 35; Baker, *The Rocket*, 135; Armacost, *The Politics of Weapons Innovation*, 186–189.

6. *New York Times*, November 6, 1957, pp. 1, 13–14, November 8, 1957, pp. 1, 8, November 14, 1957, p. 14, November 16, 1957, pp. 1–2; Prados, *The Soviet Estimate*, 64–79; Dwight Eisenhower, *Waging Peace* (New York: Doubleday, 1965), 219–223; Bottome, *The Missile Gap*, 45–49; Killian, *Sputnik, Scientists and Eisenhower*, 6, 11, 15, 27, 96.

7. MacDougall, *The Heavens and the Earth*, 148–155; Prados, *The Soviet Estimate*, 63; Richard Aliano, *American Defense Policy from Eisenhower to Kennedy* (Athens, Ohio: Ohio University Press, 1975), 118, 133–138.

8. Green and Lomask, *Vanguard*, 196–197, 206–212, 232; Ley, *Rockets, Missiles, and Men in Space*, 318–319.

9. Medaris, *Countdown for Decision*, 165–168, 202–226; Newell, *Beyond the Atmosphere*, 82–84, 174–177; "Jupiter C/Juno I," 16–17; Green and Lomask, *Vanguard*, 198, 213–217, 237–238; Koppel, *JPL and The American Space Program*, 83, 85, 87–88.

10. See York, *Race to Oblivion*, 132, 144–146, for the opposite claim. York, for example, implies that Polaris was accelerated only by months, in flat contradiction of the facts.

11. John T. Greenwood, "The Air Force Ballistic Missile and Space Program,

1954–1974" *Aerospace Historian* (Winter/Dec. 1974): 195; Neufeld, *The Development of Ballistic Missiles in the United States Air Force*, 159, 170–174, 227; Medaris, *Countdown for Decision*, 176–184, 198; Klass, *Secret Sentries in Space*, 85–88; Armacost, *The Politics of Weapons Innovation*, 172–176, 181, 186, 221, 227–228, 234; Miles, "Polaris," 165–170; Baar and Howard, *Polaris*, 94.

12. York, *Race to Oblivion*, 117–118, 144–146; Bilstein, *Stages to Saturn*, 25–29; Baker, *The Rocket*, 136, 146–147.

13. Barbara Clowse, *Brainpower for the Cold War* (Westport, Conn.: Greenwood, 1981).

14. Cox, *Space Power*, 88–89; *New York Times*, October 17, 1957, p. 13.

CHAPTER 6

1. Zaloga, *Target America*, 78, 81–85, 148–150, 154, 164, 192–197; Wolfe, *Soviet Power in Europe*, 84–86, 105–106, 179–184; Albert Wohlstetter, "Is There a Strategic Arms Race?," *Foreign Policy* (Summer 1974), 2–20; William Baugh, *The Politics of the Nuclear Balance* (New York: Longman, 1984), 55–56; Freedman, *The Evolution of Nuclear Strategy*, 261–263; Sergo Khrushchev, *Khrushchev on Khrushchev* (Boston: Little, Brown, 1990), 21–22.

2. Zaloga, "The First ICBM," 270; Arnold Horelick and Myron Rush, *Strategic Power and Soviet Foreign Policy* (Chicago, Ill.: University of Chicago Press, 1966), 35–102, 108–112, 114–116; Wolfe, *Soviet Power in Europe*, 84–86, 177–184; Bluth, "Defense and Security," 197–202; Klass, *Secret Sentries in Space*, 36; Bottome, *The Missile Gap*, 74–75.

3. Prados, *The Soviet Estimate*, 63, 75–80, 85, 97; Francis Gary Powers, *Operation Overflight* (New York: Holt, Rinehart and Winston, 1970), 29, 59, 63, 66–69, 72; Klass, *Secret Sentries in Space*, 40, 48; Donald Cox, *The Space Race* (Philadelphia, Pa.: Chilton, 1962), 46; Killian, *Sputnik, Scientists and Eisenhower*, 144–146.

4. Cox, *Space Power*, 42–45; Parry, *Russia's Rockets and Missiles*, 132–142; Alfred Zaehringer, *Soviet Space Technology* (New York: Harper, 1961), 72–85, 98; James Dewar, *Project Rover: A Study of the Nuclear Rocket Development Program 1953–1963*, Ph.D. dissertation, Kansas State University 1974, 258n1.

5. Prados, *The Soviet Estimate*, 63, 78–84; Bottome, *The Missile Gap*, 55–56, 84–85.

6. Wolfe, *Soviet Power in Europe*, 80–81, 88–93; Jean Edward Smith, *The Defense of Berlin* (Baltimore, Md.: Johns Hopkins University Press, 1963), 155–162, 181–198, 204–206; Horelick and Rush, *Strategic Power and Soviet Foreign Policy*, 117–128; Jack Schick, *The Berlin Crisis 1958–1962* (Philadelphia, Pa.: University of Pennsylvania Press, 1971), 3–72; Eisenhower, *Waging Peace*, 329–346; Beschloss, *Mayday*, 175–184.

7. Neufeld, *The Development of Ballistic Missiles in the United States Air Force*, 161, 165, 222–226, 232–233; Medaris, *Countdown for Decision*, 180,

183–184; Armacost, *The Politics of Weapons Innovation*, 184–195, 198, 203–204; Hartt, *The Mighty Thor*, 260ff; *The Cuban Missile Crisis*, edited by Laurence Chang and Peter Kornbluh (New York: The New Press, 1992), 15, 61–62, 349.

8. Neufeld, *The Development of Ballistic Missiles in the United States Air Force*, 185–199, 201–210, 213–219, 230–238; Stine, *ICBM*, 217–230; York, *Race to Oblivion*, 94, 150; Killian, *Sputnik, Scientists and Eisenhower*, 145–147; Baker, *The Rocket*, 173–174; Schwiebart, *History of USAF Ballistic Missiles*, 25.

9. Neufeld, *The Development of Ballistic Missiles in the United States Air Force*, 182, 227–230, 237; Stine, *ICBM*, 230–232, 238; Roy Neal, *Ace in the Hole* (New York: Doubleday, 1962); Baker, *The Rocket*, 184–187.

10. Sapolsky, *Polaris System Development*, 41, 62, 65–66, 131–141, 158–159, 182; Baar and Howard, *Polaris*, 94ff; Miles, "Polaris," 164–171; Baker, *The Rocket*, 241; Stine, *ICBM*, 234–235.

11. Bottome, *The Missile Gap*, 83–104; Klass, *Secret Sentries in Space*, 36–40; Prados, *The Soviet Estimate*, 83–87; *New York Times*, January 12, 17, 1959; Thomas R. Phillips, "The Growing Missile Gap," *The Reporter* (January 8, 1959), 10–16; Thomas R. Phillips, "Mr. McElroy's Maginot Line," *The Reporter* (February 19, 1959), 25–26; Thomas R. Phillips, "We Can't Buy Time That Has Been Lost," *The New Republic* (January 19, 1959), 6; Edward Hymoff, "Some of Our Launch Pads Are Missing," *The Reporter* (June 25, 1959), 27–30; Freedman, *The Evolution of Nuclear Strategy*, 135–136; Aliano, *American Defense Policy from Eisenhower to Kennedy*, 162, 176–177.

12. Bottome, *The Missile Gap*, 111–133; Prados, *The Soviet Estimate*, 84–95; Klass, *Secret Sentries in Space*, 46–49; George B. Kistiakowsky, *Scientist at the White House* (Cambridge, Mass.: Harvard University Press, 1976), 115, 219, 250, 261; Thomas R. Phillips, "The Great Guessing Game," *The Reporter* (February 18, 1960), 26–30; Aliano, *American Defense Policy from Eisenhower to Kennedy*, 169; Cox, *The Space Race*, 49, 137–138, 141. See also York, *Race to Oblivion*, pp. 10, 57, which conveys the impression that neither he nor any other sensible person ever believed in the missile gap.

13. Beschloss, *Mayday*, passim; Klass, *Secret Sentries in Space*, 53, 91–93; Prados, *The Soviet Estimate*, 96–101, 109–110; Desmond Ball, *Politics and Force Levels* (Berkeley, Calif.: University of California Press, 1980), 15, 20–22, 34–35; Aliano, *American Defense Policy from Eisenhower to Kennedy*, 230; Bottome, *The Missile Gap*, 138, 141, 147; Michael Beschloss, *The Crisis Years* (New York: HarperCollins, 1991), 21, 26, 30.

14. Prados, *The Soviet Estimate*, 114–118; Neufeld, *The Development of Ballistic Missiles in the United States Air Force*, 215; Bottome, *The Missile Gap*, 147, 151, 155–156, 163, 165–166; Beschloss, *The Crisis Years*, 56–60; Ball, *Politics and Force Levels*, 20–22, 90–92, 98–99.

15. Ball, *Politics and Force Levels*, 44, 60–62, 68, 90–92, 96, 103, 109–111, 114, 118–121, 123, 142, 156, 166, 170–173, 175, 177, 185, 206–211, 214, 234–236, 241, 252–263, 275; Prados, *The Soviet Estimate*, 114–115; Beschloss, *The Crisis Years*, 344; Neufeld, *The Development of Ballistic Missiles in the*

United States Air Force, 213–217; Baugh, *Politics of the Nuclear Balance*, 56–63; Colin Gray, *The Soviet-American Arms Race* (Lexington, Mass.: Saxon House/Lexington Books, 1976).

16. Slusser, *The Berlin Crisis of 1961*, esp. pp. 221–222, 372–375; Klass, *Secret Sentries in Space*, 63–65; Horelick and Rush, *Strategic Power and Soviet Foreign Policy*, 122–125; Bottome, *The Missile Gap*, 163–166; Prados, *The Soviet Estimate*, 122; Beschloss, *The Crisis Years*, 150, 242–244, 256–335; Charles P. Vick, "The Soviet Super Boosters," *Spaceflight*, Vol. 15, No. 6 (December 1973), 457; Arkady Shevchenko, *Breaking with Moscow* (New York: Knopf, 1985), 117–118.

17. See also Stine, *ICBM*, p. 248, for a slightly different version of this common saying.

18. A full-scale exploration of the myth later generated about the missile gap casts light on American attitudes to the Cold War in the 1960s and after. The sport of blaming it on some sinister organization, faction, or individuals (instead of analyzing it as a mistake) began very early. Hanson Baldwin blamed it on exaggerated USAF estimates, partisan Senators, and columnists. Kennedy blamed it on the Eisenhower Administration, while Senator Symington managed to find that the real culprit was the CIA (Bottome, *The Missile Gap*, 168, 192). Theodore Sorensen's account in *Kennedy* (New York: Bantam, 1966), p. 377, is an interesting example of how to combine truthful statements with half-truths to convey a totally misleading impression. The leftist writer Fred Cook claimed that the gap had been invented by General Power in 1960 (Aliano, *American Defense Policy from Eisenhower to Kennedy*, 82, 238–239). Many sources—e.g., William Safire, *Safire's Political Dictionary* (New York: Random House, 1978), 254, 423—describe the gap as a partisan device created by Kennedy and/or the Democrats in general in 1959–1960. Herbert York, in his influential account of the arms race, implies that the "military-industrial complex" was to blame (*Race to Oblivion*, 10, 57, 123, 127). Michael Beschloss (*The Crisis Years*, 25–26, 65–66) propounds the odd thesis that Eisenhower deliberately let Khrushchev promote the myth of the gap to prevent pressure for a "real" arms race, a policy reversed by Kennedy with awful results.

19. Slusser, *The Berlin Crisis of 1961*, 386–387, 430, 467; *Penkovskiy Papers*, 56–57, 212, 215, 367–368; Jerrold Schechter and Peter Deriabin, *The Spy Who Saved the World* (New York: Scribners, 1992), 232–233, 239–240; John Baron, *KGB* (New York: Bantam, 1974), 405; Russ Braley, *Bad News* (Chicago, Ill.: Regnery/Gateway, 1984), 435–436.

20. *The Cuban Missile Crisis*, 351; Beschloss, *The Crisis Years*, 378–380, 382–389, 413, 427; Raymond Garthoff, *Reflections on the Cuban Missile Crisis* (Washington, D.C.: The Brookings Institution, 1989), 6–31, 42; James G. Blight and David Welch, *On the Brink* (New York: Hill and Wang, 1989), 30–32, 53, 140–141, 147, 157–158, 229, 235–241, 295–300.

21. *The Cuban Missile Crisis*, 63–65, 353, 354, 356; Prados, *The Soviet Estimate*, 123–135; Beschloss, *The Crisis Years*, 413, 416–429; Garthoff,

Reflections on the Cuban Missile Crisis, 43–54; Dino Brugioni, *Eyeball to Eyeball* (New York: Random House, 1991), 104, 111–112, 116, 144–151, 164–172, 182–186, 252.

22. Garthoff, *Reflections on the Cuban Missile Crisis*, 134 n241; *Back to the Brink: Proceedings of the Moscow Conference on the Cuban Missile Crisis*, edited by Bruce Allyn, James G. Blight, and David Welch (Cambridge, Mass.: Harvard University Center for Science and International Affairs, 1992), 163.

23. Gray, *The Soviet-American Arms Race*, 118; Prados, *The Soviet Estimate*, 183–200; Wolfe, *Soviet Power in Europe*, 432–437; Neufeld, *The Development of Ballistic Missiles in the United States Air Force*, 233–238; Baugh, *Politics of the Nuclear Balance*, 149–150, 158–159.

CHAPTER 7

1. Richard Lewis, *Appointment on the Moon* (New York: Ballantine, 1969), 68–99; McLaughlin and Green, *Vanguard*, 217–249, 283–289; Medaris, *Countdown for Decision*, 229–230; Koppes, *JPL and the American Space Program*, 92; Baugher, *The Space-Age Solar System*, 63; Newell, *Beyond the Atmosphere*, 174, 177; Jack D. Manno, *Arming the Heavens* (New York: Dodd, Mead, 1984), 55, 77–83; Brian Harvey, *Race into Space* (London: Ellis Harwood, 1988), 34.

2. Baker, *The Rocket*, 142, 233–236, 255–258; Klass, *Secret Sentries in Space*, 131, 138–139, 166; *NASA Historical Data Book, Vol. I, 1958–1968* (Washington, D.C.: NASA, 1983), 39, 42, 67–83; J. B. Powell, "Thor-Able and Atlas-Able," *JBIS* (May 1984), 219–224; McLaughlin and Green, *Vanguard*, 254–255.

3. MacDougall, *The Heavens and the Earth*, 164–175, 196–198; Medaris, *Countdown for Decision*, 242–243, 257–269; Loyd Swenson, Jr., James Grimwood, and Charles Alexander, *This New Ocean* (Washington, D.C.: NASA, 1966), 8, 27, 75–85, 101–102, 111; York, *Race to Oblivion*, 116–117, 142–143; Newell, *Beyond the Atmosphere*, 90, 102–103; John Logsdon, *The Decision to Go to the Moon* (Chicago, Ill.: University of Chicago Press, 1970), 19–21, 23, 28, 30–32, 47.

4. Homer Boushey, "The USAF and Astronautical Development," *Airpower Historian* (January 1958), 118–123; Koppes, *JPL and the American Space Program*, 94–95, 99–101; Medaris, *Countdown for Decision*, 186–187; Swenson, Grimwood, and Alexander, *This New Ocean*, 27; Bilstein, *Stages to Saturn*, 34; Logsdon, *The Decision to Go to the Moon*, 47.

5. Sloop, *Liquid Hydrogen as a Propulsion Fuel*, 179–180, 191, 195–196, 200–201, 205–209, 218, 220, 226–229, 232–238; Medaris, *Countdown for Decision*, 262–264; Baker, *The Rocket*, 136, 243; Bilstein, *Stages to Saturn*, 25–29, 36, 38–39, 45, 50–51, 78–79, 89–97, 105–107; *NASA Historical Data Book*, Vol. 1, p. 53.

6. Powell, "Thor-Able and Atlas-Able," 221–224; Koppes, *JPL and the*

American Space Program, 92, 100; Caidin, *War for the Moon*, 47–49, 84, 153ff; Ley, *Rockets, Missiles, and Men in Space*, 334, 345.

7. Harvey, *Race into Space*, 35–37; Arthur Smith, *Planetary Exploration* (Wellingborough, England: Patrick Stephens, 1988), 22–23; Baugher, *The Space-Age Solar System*, 109; Bevan French, *The Moon Book* (New York: Penguin, 1977), 76.

8. Swenson, Grimwood, and Alexander, *This New Ocean*, 75–81, 323, 328; Baker, *History of Manned Space Flight*, 32–62; Buzz Aldrin and Malcolm McConnell, *Men from Earth* (New York: Bantam, 1991), 40–54, 57–58; Tom Wolfe, *The Right Stuff* (New York: Bantam, 1979); Lewis, *Appointment on the Moon*, 105–112; Charles Murray and Catherine Bly Cox, *Apollo* (New York: Simon & Schuster, 1989), 62–65.

9. Koppes, *JPL and the American Space Program*, 100–101, 111–113; Baker, *History of Manned Space Flight*, 52–55; Courtney Brooks, James Grimwood, and Loyd Swenson, Jr., *Chariots for Apollo* (Washington, D.C.: NASA, 1979), 7–13, 15, 20; Bilstein, *Stages to Saturn*, 53; Logsdon, *The Decision to Go to the Moon*, 34–37, 56–57, 62; Murray and Cox, *Apollo*, 43–44.

10. Klass, *Secret Sentries in Space*, 95–105; Lewis, *Appointment on the Moon*, 81–97, 325; Ley, *Rockets, Missiles, and Men in Space*, 342–344.

11. Harvey, *Race into Space*, 38–52; Oberg, *Red Star in Orbit*, 39–43, 47–48; James Oberg, *Uncovering Soviet Disasters* (New York: Random House, 1988), 177–183; Andrei Sakharov, *Memoirs* (New York: Knopf, 1990), 195–196; Philip Clark, *The Soviet Manned Space Program* (New York: Orion, 1988), 14–18; Smith, *Planetary Exploration*, 57–58, 77–85.

CHAPTER 8

1. Harvey, *Race into Space*, 52–60; Oberg, *Red Star in Orbit*, 52–58; Martin Caidin, *Red Star in Space* (New York: Crowell-Collier Press, 1963), 28–31; Clark, *The Soviet Manned Space Program*, 18–20.

2. Baker, *History of Manned Space Flight*, 82–91; Logsdon, *The Decision to Go to the Moon*, 72–73, 83–84, 97–120; Brooks, Grimwood, and Swenson, *Chariots for Apollo*, 15, 20, 22–25; Murray and Cox, *Apollo*, 60–61, 69–81; Koppes, *JPL and the American Space Program*, 113, 116; Newell, *Beyond the Atmosphere*, 208–209, 396; Beschloss, *The Crisis Years*, 116, 165–167.

3. Swenson, Grimwood, and Alexander, *This New Ocean*, 314–331, 335–338, 342–360; Aldrin and McConnell, *Men from Earth*, 64–67; Wolfe, *The Right Stuff*, 200–224; Baker, *History of Manned Space Flight*, 72–79; Martin Caidin, *Man into Space* (New York: Pyramid, 1961).

4. Logsdon, *The Decision to Go to the Moon*, 110–111, 122–171; Murray and Cox, *Apollo*, 82–83.

5. Harvey, *Race into Space*, 63–65, 71–72, 77–79; Oberg, *Red Star in Orbit*, 63, 65–72, 84; Aldrin and McConnell, *Men from Earth*, 85–88, 110–111, 122;

Clark, *The Soviet Manned Space Program*, 19–23. See also Caidin, *Red Star in Space*, esp. pp. 222–223.

6. Baker, *History of Manned Space Flight*, 93–99; Aldrin and McConnell, *Men from Earth*, 73–85, 93–97, 106–109, 111–114; Swenson, Grimwood, and Alexander, *This New Ocean*, 365–500, 508; Martin Caidin, *Rendezvous in Space* (New York: E. P. Dutton, 1962), esp. pp. 9, 135–157, 209–211; Lewis, *Appointment on the Moon*, 129–154, 198–229; Wolfe, *The Right Stuff*, 231–242, 252–257, 263–294, 308–323, 333–343. Wolfe rightly defends Carpenter against the claims that he panicked and exaggerated stories of his incompetence, but he curiously insinuates that Grissom panicked.

7. Swenson, Grimwood, and Alexander, *This New Ocean*, 507.

8. Swenson, Grimwood, and Alexander, *This New Ocean*, 503–505; Barton C. Hacker and James Grimwood, *On the Shoulders of Titans* (Washington, D.C.: NASA, 1977), v 21–200; Lewis, *Appointment on the Moon*, 327–333; Baker, *History of Manned Space Flight*, 168–176, 182.

9. Baker, *History of Manned Space Flight*, 188–190, 196–197; Harvey, *Race into Space*, 81–82, 89–98; Oberg, *Red Star in Orbit*, 75–82; Clark, *The Soviet Manned Space Program*, 26–29; R. F. Gibbons and P. S. Clark, "The Evolution of the Vostok and Voskhod Programmes," *JBIS* (January 1985), 7–10.

10. Hacker and Grimwood, *On the Shoulders of Titans*, 184–308; Aldrin and McConnell, *Men from Earth*, 137–148, 160–165, 168–175; Lewis, *Appointment on the Moon*, 327–376; Baker, *History of Manned Space Flight*, 197, 202–203, 216.

11. Bilstein, *Stages to Saturn*, 58, 323–344; Lewis, *Appointment on the Moon*, 187, 263–267; Lewis and Lewis, *Space Resources*, 34; Ley, *Rockets, Missiles, and Men in Space*, 404–411.

12. Smith, *Planetary Exploration*, 24–29, 41–52; French, *The Moon Book*, 76–87; Koppes, *JPL and the American Space Program*, 117–165, 173–184; Lewis, *Appointment on the Moon*, 231–262; Harvey, *Race into Space*, 101, 103–107.

13. Harvey, *Race into Space*, 74–76, 88–89; Smith, *Planetary Exploration*, 57–67; Lewis and Lewis, *Space Resources*, 66–68.

14. Anderson, *Is There Life on Other Worlds?*, 69.

15. Page and Page, *Neighbors of the Earth*, 36–43; Baugher, *The Space-Age Solar System*, 135; Whipple, *Orbiting the Sun*, 182–195; Smith, *Planetary Exploration*, 68–83; Koppes, *JPL and the American Space Program*, 126–129, 194–196; Lewis, *Appointment on the Moon*, 267–282; V. A. Firsoff, *The Solar Planets* (New York: Crane, Russak, 1977), 98–116; V. A. Firsoff, *Life Among the Stars* (London: Allan Wing, 1974), 114–124.

16. Ley, *Mariner IV to Mars*, passim; Whipple, *Orbiting the Sun*, 197–214; Baugher, *The Space-Age Solar System*, 147–165; Firsoff, *The Solar Planets*, 119–147; Lewis, *Appointment on the Moon*, 282–299; Koppes, *JPL and the American Space Program*, 165–171, 200–202, 219–221; Smith, *Planetary Exploration*, 89–111; Norman Horowitz, *To Utopia and Back* (New York: W. H.

Freeman, 1986), 82–142; Benjamin Adelman, "The Question of Life on Mars," *JBIS* (June 1986), 256–262.

CHAPTER 9

1. Miller, *The X-Planes*, 194–197; Martin Caidin, *Wings into Space* (New York: Holt, Rinehart and Winston, 1964), 9–14; C. R. Turner, "Some Fundamental Aspects of the Aerospace Plane Concept," *JBIS* (September-October 1964), 454–458; P. J. Conchie, "A Horizontal Takeoff and Landing Satellite Launcher or Aerospace Plane," *JBIS* (September 1985), 387–390.

2. Caidin, *Wings into Space*, 56; Irene Sanger-Bredt, "The Silver Bird Story," *Spaceflight* (May 1973), 166–181; Ley, *Rockets, Missiles, and Men in Space*, 444–448; Baker, *The Rocket*, 90–91; Zaloga, *Target America*, 122–124, 160, 261.

3. Richard Hallion, *Supersonic Flight* (New York: Macmillan, 1972); Miller, *The X-Planes*, 15–31, 45–49; Richard Hallion, *Test Pilots* (Washington, D.C.: Smithsonian Institution Press, 1988), 214–216; William Bridgeman and Jacqueline Hazard, *The Lonely Sky* (New York: Bantam, 1983); A. Scott Crossfield with Clay Blair, *Always Another Dawn* (New York: World Publishing, 1960), 147–148, 171–178, 180–185; Frank Everest with John Guenther, *The Fastest Man Alive* (New York: Dutton, 1958), 158–160.

4. Hallion, *Supersonic Flight*, 123, 169–170, 180–182; Miller, *The X-Planes*, 20–21, 25, 27, 34–43, 210–213; Everest, *The Fastest Man Alive*, 186–238; Crossfield, *Always Another Dawn*, 150–151, 212–215, 247; Jules Bergman, *Ninety Seconds to Space* (Garden City, N.Y.: Doubleday, 1960), 67–83, 100, 162–163; Richard Hallion, "American Rocket Aircraft: Precursors to Manned Flight Beyond the Stratosphere," pp. 288–294 in *History of Rocketry and Astronautics*, edited by Kristan R. Lattu, IAA History Symposium Vol. 3 (San Diego, Calif.: American Astronautical Society, 1989).

5. Miller, *The X-Planes*, 113–119, 128; Crossfield, *Always Another Dawn*, 156, 185–186, 205–305; Bergman, *Ninety Seconds to Space*, 84–126, 160, 162–163, 212; John R. Hansen, "Transition to Space: A History of Space Plane Concepts at Langley Aeronautical Laboratory 1952–1957," *JBIS* (February 1987), 67–80; Curtis Peebles, "X-15: First Wings Into Space," *Spaceflight* (June 1977), 228–232; Hallion, "American Rocket Aircraft," 295–302; Richard Tregaskis, *X-15 Diary* (New York: E. P. Dutton, 1961), 12–16, 42, 47, 52, 130–132; Clark, *Ignition*, 104; Milton O. Thompson, *At the Edge of Space* (Washington, D.C.: Smithsonian Institution Press, 1992), 1–49, 56.

6. Miller, *The X-Planes*, 119–129; Crossfield, *Always Another Dawn*, 305ff; Tregaskis, *X-15 Diary*, 138–142, 250–290; Hallion, *Test Pilots*, 254–260; Hallion, "American Rocket Aircraft," 302–311; "Notes," *Spaceflight* (December 1968), 415; David Baker, "The X-15 in Retrospect," *Spaceflight* (June 1971), 216–219; Thompson, *At the Edge of Space*, 50ff; Wolfe, *The Right Stuff*, 167–172, 233, 251, 348–349, 365.

7. Miller, *The X-Planes*, 146–151, 162–171; Caidin, *Wings into Space*, 95–100; Curtis Peebles, "Origins of the US Space Shuttle," *Spaceflight* (November 1979), 435–442; Roy F. Houchin II, "The Diplomatic Demise of Dyna-Soar," *Aerospace Historian* (Winter/December 1988), 274–280; Borman, *Countdown*, 168–169.

CHAPTER 10

1. Robert Rhodes, *The Making of the Atomic Bomb* (New York: Simon & Schuster, 1986), 25.

2. Robert Bussard, *Fundamentals of Nuclear Flight* (New York: McGraw-Hill, 1965), 5–6; M. Vertregt, "Theory of the Step-Rocket," *JBIS* (July 1971), 420; Clark, *Ignition*, 109, 190.

3. Bussard, *Fundamentals of Nuclear Flight*, 11–18; Francis Schweik and Karlheinz Thom, *Gaseous Fuel Nuclear Reactor Research* (Washington, D.C.: NASA, 1975); Clarke, *Interplanetary Flight*, 71–72; *Review of Nuclear Reactor Program*, February 1, 1966, pp. 38–39 (Folder XII, Nuclear Propulsion: Project Rover, NASA History Office).

4. See, for example, John W. Campbell, *The Atomic Story* (New York: Henry Holt, 1947), 279; *One World or None*, edited by Dexter Masters and Katherine Way (New York: McGraw-Hill, 1946), 16–21, 30.

5. Keith Boyer, *Nuclear Rockets* (New York: American Institute of Aeronautics and Astronautics Paper 67-981, 1967), 1; Dewar, *Project Rover*, 11–25; James Dewar, "Project Rover: The United States Nuclear Rocket Program," pp. 109–110 in *History of Rockets and Astronautics*, AAS History Series, edited by John Sloop, Vol. 12 (San Diego, Calif.: American Astronautical Society, 1991); William C. House, "The Development of Nuclear Rocket Propulsion in the United States," *JBIS* (March-April 1964), 308; Stanislaw Ulam, *Adventures of a Mathematician* (Berkeley, Calif.: University of California Press, 1991), 252; Robert Bussard, "Nuclear Rockets," *Astronautics* (December 1962), 32–33.

6. Bussard, "Nuclear Rockets," 33–34; Dewar, *Project Rover*, 36–63, 96–102, 106–107, 111–113, 126; Dewar, "Project Rover," 110–111, 116; *NASA Historical Data Book*, Vol. 2, pp. 479, 482–483; Boyer, *Nuclear Rockets*, 2–3; *Project Rover: Nuclear Rocket Propulsion Program Chronology* (Washington, D.C.: NASA, no date but probably 1965); *Brief History and Chronology of the Nuclear Rocket Program*, Atomic Energy Commission, December 12, 1962, pp. 1–13; York, *Race to Oblivion*, 121. See also Richard Hewlett and Francis Duncan, *Nuclear Navy* (Chicago, Ill.: University of Chicago Press, 1974), 119–122, 153, 381–389.

7. Dewar, *Project Rover*, 105, 168; *NASA Historical Data Book*, Vol. 2, pp. 479, 486; *Project Rover: Nuclear Rocket Propulsion Program Chronology*, 9; *Study of a Manned Mars Landing Mission Using a Mars Orbit Rendezvous Profile* (Office of Systems, Office of Manned Space Flight, Nuclear Propulsion: Project Rover, NASA History Office, 1963, addendum B-17.

8. *Aviation Week* (May 4, 1959), 83; see also Lewis and Lewis, *Space Resources*, 106; Clarke, *Interplanetary Flight*, 71–72.

9. Dewar, *Project Rover*, 54, 63–75, 78–82, 102, 169–170; House, "The Development of Nuclear Rocket Propulsion in the United States," 310; *NASA Historical Data Book*, Vol. 2, pp. 479, 483–484; Boyer, "Nuclear Rockets," 3.

10. Donald Kingsbury, "Atomic Rockets," *Analog* (December 1975), 38–57; Dewar, *Project Rover*, 76–77; *NASA Historical Data Book*, Vol. 2, p. 484; Boyer, "Nuclear Rockets," 3; Bruce Knight, letter, *Science* (July 19, 1968), 219–220.

11. Dewar, *Project Rover*, 106, 131–154, 197, 206–219, 222–228; Dewar, "Project Rover," 119–121; Ulam, *Adventures of a Mathematician*, 253–255; House, "The Development of Nuclear Rocket Propulsion in the United States," 311–313; *NASA Historical Data Book*, Vol. 2, pp. 480–482.

12. Dewar, *Project Rover*, 169–189; Dewar, "Project Rover," 113–115; *NASA Historical Data Book*, Vol. 2, pp. 480, 485; Boyer, "Nuclear Rockets," 4.

13. Dewar, *Project Rover*, 190–196, 228–245; Dewar, "Project Rover," 117, 121–122; *NASA Historical Data Book*, Vol. 2, pp. 480–481; House, "The Development of Nuclear Rocket Propulsion in the United States," 309; Boyer, "Nuclear Rockets," 4; Harold B. Finger to Research Director, Office of Advanced Research and Technology, September 3, 1963 (Nuclear Propulsion Rover NASA History Office).

14. Dewar, *Project Rover*, 196, 245, 275; Boyer, "Nuclear Rockets," 4–7; *NASA Historical Data Book*, Vol. 2, pp. 481–483, 486–487; L. C. Carrington, "The Nuclear Rocket Program," *Journal of Spacecraft and Rockets* (April 1969), 465–470; Robert Schroeder, "NERVA: Entering a New Phase," *Astronautics and Aeronautics* (May 1968), 42–53; William R. Slivka, "Unique Production Problems Encountered in Development of NERVA Space Engine," *Automotive Engineering* (October 1970), 22–27.

15. *New York Times*, March 26, 1972, p. 3; Saul Adelman and Benjamin Adelman, *Bound for the Stars* (Englewood Cliffs, N.J.: Prentice-Hall, 1981), 73.

16. Ulam, *Adventures of a Mathematician*, 252–256; Eugen Mallowe and Gregory L. Matloff, *The Starflight Handbook* (New York: John Wiley, 1989), 57–58; John McPhee, *The Curve of Binding Energy* (New York: Farrar, Straus and Giroux, 1974), 167; Anthony R. Martin and Alan Bond, "Nuclear Pulse Propulsion: An Historical Review of an Advanced Propulsion Concept," *JBIS* (August 1979), 283–292.

17. Martin and Bond, "Nuclear Pulse Propulsion," 283–310; *New York Times*, September 17, 1958, p. 19, August 16, 1959, p. 1; John McPhee, *The Curve of Binding Energy*, 165, 167–178, 182–183; Freeman Dyson, *Disturbing the Universe* (New York: Harper, 1981), 110–115; Mallowe and Matloff, *The Starflight Handbook*, 61–67; York, *Race to Oblivion*, 128, 163.

18. Dyson, *Disturbing the Universe*, 114–115; Martin and Bond, "Nuclear Pulse Propulsion," 294, 297; *Study of a Manned Mars Landing Mission Using a Mars Orbit Rendezvous Profile*, B-17, B-18.

19. Mallowe and Matloff, *The Starflight Handbook*, 61; Martin and Bond,

"Nuclear Pulse Propulsion," 283–285; *Space Daily*, July 28, 1965, p. 131, July 29, 1965, p. 138, July 30, 1965, p. 145.

20. Mallowe and Matloff, *The Starflight Handbook*, 57.

CHAPTER 11

1. Bilstein, *Stages to Saturn*, 58–68, 71–72, 163, 192–194, 196; Brooks, *Chariots for Apollo*, 5–6, 23, 34, 45–52, 53–86, 100–107; Murray and Cox, *Apollo*, 113–124, 134–143; John Logsdon, "Selecting the Way to the Moon: The Choice of the Lunar Orbital Rendezvous Mode," *Aerospace Historian* (Summer/ June 1971), 63–79; Charles Pellegrino and Joshua Stoff, *Chariots for Apollo* (Blue Ridge Summit, Pa.: Tab, 1987), 20–25; Bergaust, *Wernher von Braun*, 408–409; Aldrin and McConnell, *Men from Earth*, 100–106; Arnold Levine, *Managing NASA in the Apollo Era* (Washington, D.C.: NASA, 1983), xii, 1–3.

2. Levine, *Managing NASA in the Apollo Era*, 5, 19–20, 34–42; Murray and Cox, *Apollo*, 152–154, 158–165; William David Compton, *Where No Man Has Gone Before* (Washington, D.C.: NASA, 1989), 7–10, 23–25; Brooks, *Chariots for Apollo*, 110–111, 127–131; Bilstein, *Stages to Saturn*, 348–351; Bergaust, *Wernher von Braun*, 413–414; MacDougall, *The Heavens and the Earth*, 389–397.

3. Beirne Lay, *Earthbound Astronauts* (Englewood Cliffs, N.J.: Prentice-Hall, 1971), 27–31, 39–41; Bilstein, *Stages to Saturn*, 107–127, 140–153, 162–190, 191–231, 262–264, 269, 283–291, 395–398; Murray and Cox, *Apollo*, 144–150, 179–180; Bergaust, *Wernher von Braun*, 508.

4. Brooks, *Chariots for Apollo*, 17, 26–29, 35–36, 41–44, 131–142, 165, 167–172, 194–196; Bilstein, *Stages to Saturn*, 225–226; Murray and Cox, *Apollo*, 105–107, 166–172, 183; Lewis, *Appointment on the Moon*, 180, 373–388; Baker, *History of Manned Space Flight*, 150–152, 252–253. See also Erik Bergaust, *Murder on Pad 34* (New York: G. P. Putnam's, 1968), 154–157.

5. Brooks, *Chariots for Apollo*, 208–211, 213–235; Murray and Cox, *Apollo*, 188–234; Aldrin and McConnell, *Men from Earth*, 180–188; Borman, *Countdown*, 170–183; Pellegrino and Stoff, *Chariots for Apollo*, 93–95; Compton, *Where No Man Has Gone Before*, xi, 9; Lay, *Earthbound Astronauts*, 79, 125–137. See also Bergaust, *Murder on Pad 34*, esp. pp. 126, 136–139, a bitter personal attack on Webb.

6. Pellegrino and Stoff, *Chariots for Apollo*, 33–34, 39, 46, 63, 93–95, 110–111; Brooks, *Chariots for Apollo*, 143–165, 172–178, 259; Baker, *History of Manned Space Flight*, 296; Aldrin and McConnell, *Men from Earth*, 159, 196–197.

7. Harvey, *Race into Space*, 65–68, 82–83, 85–87, 103, 108, 113, 115–122, 124–125, 127, 129, 132, 138; Aldrin and McConnell, *Men from Earth*, 97–98, 149–150, 178–179, 189–190, 200–204, 213, 219–220, 228–232, 246–247, 283–284; Vasili Mishin, "The Moon Programme that Failed," *Spaceflight* (January 1991), 2–3; Clark, *The Soviet Manned Space Program*, 23–25, 32, 36, 41–42;

Oberg, *Red Star in Orbit*, 86–95, 98, 112–125; Smith, *Planetary Exploration*, 31–38.

8. Brooks, *Chariots for Apollo*, 232–235, 241–253, 256–260, 265–272; Bilstein, *Stages to Saturn*, 341–345, 347, 352–366; Aldrin and McConnell, *Men from Earth*, 194, 197–198, 205–206, 212–218; Lewis, *Appointment on the Moon*, 408–447; Murray and Cox, *Apollo*, 238–250, 308–324; Compton, *Where No Man Has Gone Before*, 132–133; Borman, *Countdown*, 189–191; Lay, *Earthbound Astronauts*, 140–147.

9. Borman, *Countdown*, 20–219; Compton, *Where No Man Has Gone Before*, 133–134, 137–139; Brooks, *Chariots for Apollo*, 274–312; Bilstein, *Stages to Saturn*, 367–369; Aldrin and McConnell, *Men from Earth*, 212–214, 217–218, 220–231; Murray and Cox, *Apollo*, 336–339; Lewis, *Appointment on the Moon*, 465–499.

10. Brooks, *Chariots for Apollo*, 313–357, 363; Murray and Cox, *Apollo*, 347–370; Aldrin and McConnell, *Men from Earth*, 243–274; Michael Collins, *Carrying the Fire* (New York: Bantam, 1983), 359–461; Pellegrino and Stoff, *Chariots for Apollo*, 152–179; Richard Lewis, *The Voyages of Apollo* (New York: Quadrangle, 1974), 65–88; Lewis, *Appointment on the Moon*, 499–539; Compton, *Where No Man Has Gone Before*, 134, 142–155, 267.

11. Murray and Cox, *Apollo*, 371–386; Compton, *Where No Man Has Gone Before*, 177–189; Lewis, *The Voyages of Apollo*, 90–132.

12. Henry S. F. Cooper, *Thirteen: The Flight That Failed* (New York: Dial Press, 1973); Murray and Cox, *Apollo*, 387–446; Compton, *Where No Man Has Gone Before*, 386–393; Lewis, *The Voyages of Apollo*, 149–168, 175; Pellegrino and Stoff, *Chariots for Apollo*, 184–205.

13. Compton, *Where No Man Has Gone Before*, 167–171, 193–197, 201–203; Lewis, *The Voyages of Apollo*, 149–151, 170–172; Newell, *Beyond the Atmosphere*, 101, 292–293; Brooks, *Chariots for Apollo*, 362; Brian O'Leary, *The Making of an Ex-Astronaut* (Boston: Houghton Mifflin, 1970), esp. pp. 169, 176–178, 207–216; William David Compton and Charles Benson, *Living and Working in Space* (Washington, D.C.: NASA, 1983), xi, 68, 85–86, 102, 116.

14. Compton, *Where No Man Has Gone Before*, 206–253; Lewis, *The Voyages of Apollo*, 182–290; French, *The Moon Book*, 97–115; Bilstein, *Stages to Saturn*, 376–378.

15. Compton, *Where No Man Has Gone Before*, 257–262; Lewis, *The Voyages of Apollo*, 290–300; Whipple, *Orbiting the Sun*, 133–169; French, *The Moon Book*, 23–25, 114–115, 117, 267; Lewis and Lewis, *Space Resources*, 184–185, 266.

16. Frederick Ordway and Mitchell Sharpe, *Dividends From Space* (New York: Crowell, 1971), esp. pp. 7–11, 15–16, 18–28, 34, 42, 50–53, 101–103, 118–119, 138–139, 165–167, 187, 189, 220–231; Bilstein, *Stages to Saturn*, 395–400; Charles Murray, *Losing Ground* (New York: Basic Books, 1984), 274n2.

17. Lewis and Lewis, *Space Resources*, 77–85, 98–106, 379–380; Compton

and Benson, *Living and Working in Space*, passim; Malcolm McConnell, *A Major Malfunction* (Garden City, N.Y.: Doubleday, 1987); Joseph Trento, *Prescription for Disaster* (New York: Crown, 1987); Richard Lewis, *Challenger: The Final Voyage* (New York: Columbia University Press, 1987).

18. Lewis and Lewis, *Space Resources*, 112–113.

19. Ibid., 97, 112, 378; see also Baker, *History of Manned Space Flight*, 287.

20. Donald Wollheim, ed., *Men on the Moon* (New York: Ace Books, 1969), 148–191; Robert A. Heinlein, *The Expanded Universe* (New York: Grosset and Dunlap, 1980), 513.

21. Wollheim, *Men on the Moon*, 174.

22. Lewis, *The Voyages of Apollo*, 149–151, 169–171; Jerry Grey, *Enterprise* (New York: William Morrow, 1979), 65, 76, 100–101.

Select Bibliography

Adelman, Saul, and Adelman, Benjamin. *Bound for the Stars*. Englewood Cliffs, N.J.: Prentice-Hall, 1981.

Aldrin, Buzz, and McConnell, Malcolm. *Men from Earth*. New York: Bantam, 1991.

Aliano, Richard. *American Defense Policy from Eisenhower to Kennedy*. Athens, Ohio: Ohio University Press, 1975.

Allyn, Bruce; Blight, James G.; and Welch, David, eds. *Back to the Brink: Proceedings of the Moscow Conference on the Cuban Missile Crisis*. Cambridge, Mass.: Harvard University Center for Science and International Affairs, 1992.

Anderson, Poul. *Is There Life on Other Worlds?* New York: Collier Books, 1968.

Armacost, Michael. *The Politics of Weapons Innovation*. New York: Columbia University Press, 1969.

Baar, James, and Howard, William. *Polaris*. New York: Harcourt Brace, 1960.

Bainbridge, William Sims. *The Spaceflight Revolution*. New York: John Wiley, 1976.

Baker, David. *The History of Manned Space Flight*. New York: Crown, 1982.

Baker, David. *The Rocket*. New York: Crown, 1978.

Ball, Desmond. *Politics and Force Levels*. Berkeley, Calif.: University of California Press, 1980.

Baugh, William. *The Politics of the Nuclear Balance*. New York: Longman, 1984.

Baugher, Joseph F. *The Space-Age Solar System*. New York: John Wiley, 1988.

Beard, Edmund. *Developing the ICBM*. New York: Columbia University Press, 1976.

Bergaust, Erik. *Murder on Pad 34*. New York: G. P. Putnam's, 1968.

Bergaust, Erik. *Reaching for the Stars*. New York: Doubleday, 1960.

Bergaust, Erik. *Wernher von Braun*. Washington, D.C.: National Space Institute, 1976.

Bergman, Jules. *Ninety Seconds to Space*. Garden City, N.Y.: Doubleday, 1960.

Beschloss, Michael. *The Crisis Years*. New York: HarperCollins, 1991.

Beschloss, Michael. *Mayday*. New York: Harper & Row, 1986.

Bilstein, Roger E. *Stages to Saturn*. Washington, D.C.: NASA, 1980.

Blight, James G., and Welch, David. *On the Brink*. New York: Hill and Wang, 1989.

Borman, Frank. *Countdown*. New York: Morrow, 1988.

Bottome, Edgar. *The Missile Gap*. Rutherford, N.J.: Fairleigh Dickinson University Press, 1971.

Bridgeman, William, with Hazard, Jacqueline. *The Lonely Sky*. New York: Bantam, 1983.

Brooks, Courtney; Grimwood, James; and Swenson, Loyd Jr. *Chariots for Apollo*. Washington, D.C.: NASA, 1979.

Brugioni, Dino. *Eyeball to Eyeball*. New York: Random House, 1991.

Bussard, Robert. *Fundamentals of Nuclear Flight*. New York: McGraw-Hill, 1965.

Caidin, Martin. *Countdown for Tomorrow*. New York: E. P. Dutton, 1958.

Caidin, Martin. *War for the Moon*. New York: E. P. Dutton, 1959.

Caidin, Martin. *Man into Space*. New York: Pyramid, 1961.

Caidin, Martin. *Overture to Space*. New York: Duell, Sloane and Pearce, 1963.

Caidin, Martin. *Red Star in Space*. New York: Crowell-Collier Press, 1963.

Caidin, Martin. *Wings into Space*. New York: Holt, Rinehart and Winston, 1964.

Chang, Laurence, and Kornbluh, Peter, eds. *The Cuban Missile Crisis*. New York: The New Press, 1992.

Chapman, John L. *Atlas: Story of a Missile*. New York: Harper, 1960.

Clark, John D. *Ignition*. New Brunswick, N.J.: Rutgers University Press, 1972.

Clark, Philip. *The Soviet Manned Space Program*. New York: Orion, 1988.

Clarke, Arthur C. *The Exploration of Space*. New York: Harper, 1951.

Clarke, Arthur C. *Interplanetary Flight*. New York: Harper, 1950.

Collins, Michael. *Carrying the Fire*. New York: Bantam, 1983.

Compton, William David. *Where No Man Has Gone Before*. Washington, D.C.: NASA, 1989.

Compton, William David, and Benson, Charles. *Living and Working in Space*. Washington, D.C.: NASA, 1983.

Condit, Doris. *The Test of War: History of the Office of the Secretary of Defense*. Washington, D.C.: Historical Office of the Secretary of Defense, 1988.

Cooper, Henry S. F. *Thirteen: The Flight That Failed*. New York: Dial Press, 1973.

Cox, Donald. *Space Power*. Philadelphia, Pa.: John C. Winston, 1958.

Cox, Donald. *The Space Race*. Philadelphia, Pa.: Chilton, 1962.

Crossfield, A. Scott, and Blair, Clay. *Always Another Dawn*. New York: World
    Publishing, 1960.
De Seversky, Alexander. *America—Too Young to Die*. New York: McGraw-Hill,
    1961.
Dewar, James. *Project Rover: A Study of the Nuclear Rocket Development
    Program 1953–1963*, Ph.D. dissertation, Kansas State University, 1974.
Dornberger, Walter. *V-2*. New York: Bantam, 1979.
Eisenhower, Dwight. *Waging Peace*. New York: Doubleday, 1965.
Essers, I. *Max Valier*. Washington, D.C.: NASA, 1976.
Everest, Frank, with Guenther, John. *The Fastest Man Alive*. New York: E. P.
    Dutton, 1958.
Firsoff, V. A. *Life Among the Stars*. London: Allan Wing, 1974.
Firsoff, V. A. *Life Beyond the Earth*. New York: Basic Books, 1963.
Firsoff, V. A. *The Solar Planets*. New York: Crane, Russak, 1977.
Foreign Relations of the United States 1952–1954, Vol. II, Part 1. Washington,
    D.C.: Government Printing Office, 1984.
Freedman, Lawrence. *The Evolution of Nuclear Strategy*. New York: St. Martin's
    Press, 1981.
French, Bevan. *The Moon Book*. New York: Penguin, 1977.
Garthoff, Raymond. *Reflections on the Cuban Missile Crisis*. Washington, D.C.:
    The Brookings Institution, 1989.
Goddard, Esther C., and Pendray, G. Edward, eds. *The Papers of Robert H.
    Goddard*. New York: McGraw-Hill, 1970.
Gray, Colin. *The Soviet-American Arms Race*. Lexington, Mass.: Saxon House/
    Lexington Books, 1976.
Green, Constance McLaughlin, and Lomask, Milton. *Vanguard*. Washington,
    D.C.: NASA, 1971.
Grey, Jerry. *Enterprise*. New York: William Morrow, 1979.
Hacker, Barton C., and Grimwood, James. *On the Shoulders of Titans*. Washington,
    D.C.: NASA, 1977.
Hallion, Richard. *Supersonic Flight*. New York: Macmillan, 1972.
Hallion, Richard. *Test Pilots*. Washington, D.C.: Smithsonian Institution Press,
    1988.
Hartt, Julian. *The Mighty Thor*. New York: Duell, Sloane and Pearce, 1961.
Harvey, Brian. *Race into Space*. London: Ellis Harwood, 1988.
Heinlein, Robert A. *The Expanded Universe*. New York: Grosset and Dunlap,
    1980.
Hewlett, Richard, and Duncan, Francis. *Nuclear Navy*. Chicago, Ill.: University
    of Chicago Press, 1974.
Horelick, Arnold, and Rush, Myron. *Strategic Power and Soviet Foreign Policy*.
    Chicago, Ill.: University of Chicago Press, 1966.
Horowitz, Norman. *To Utopia and Back*. New York: W. H. Freeman, 1986.
Irving, David. *The Mare's Nest*. Boston: Little, Brown, 1965.

Kennedy, Gregory. *Vengeance Weapon 2*. Washington, D.C.: Smithsonian Institution Press, 1983.

Khrushchev, Sergo. *Khrushchev on Khrushchev*. Boston: Little, Brown, 1990.

Killian, James R. *Sputnik, Scientists and Eisenhower*. Cambridge, Mass.: MIT Press, 1977.

Kistiakowsky, George B. *Scientist at the White House*. Cambridge, Mass.: Harvard University Press, 1976.

Klass, Philip. *Secret Sentries in Space*. New York: Random House, 1971.

Koppes, Clayton. *JPL and the American Space Program*. New Haven, Conn.: Yale University Press, 1982.

Lasby, Clarence. *Project Paperclip*. New York: Atheneum, 1971.

Lay, Beirne. *Earthbound Astronauts*. Englewood Cliffs, N.J.: Prentice-Hall, 1971.

Lehman, Milton. *Robert H. Goddard*. New York: Da Capo, 1988.

Levine, Arnold. *Managing NASA in the Apollo Era*. Washington, D.C.: NASA, 1983.

Lewis, John S., and Lewis, Ruth A. *Space Resources*. New York: Columbia University Press, 1987.

Lewis, Richard. *Appointment on the Moon*. New York: Ballantine, 1969.

Lewis, Richard. *Challenger: The Final Voyage*. New York: Columbia University Press, 1987.

Lewis, Richard. *The Voyages of Apollo*. New York: Quadrangle, 1974.

Ley, Willy. *Mariner IV to Mars*. New York: New American Library, 1966.

Ley, Willy. *Rockets, Missiles, and Men in Space*. New York: Viking, 1968.

Logsdon, John. *The Decision to Go to the Moon*. Chicago, Ill.: University of Chicago Press, 1970.

MacDougall, Walter. *The Heavens and the Earth*. New York: Basic Books, 1985.

MacKintosh, J. M. *Strategy and Tactics of Soviet Foreign Policy*. Oxford, England: Oxford University Press, 1963.

Manno, Jack D. *Arming the Heavens*. New York: Dodd, Mead, 1984.

McConnell, Malcolm. *A Major Malfunction*. Garden City, N.Y.: Doubleday, 1987.

Medaris, John B. *Countdown for Decision*. New York: G. P. Putnam's, 1960.

Medvedev, Zhores. *Soviet Science*. New York: W. W. Norton, 1979.

Miller, Jay. *The X-Planes*. New York: Aerofax/Orion, 1988.

Murray, Charles, and Cox, Catherine Bly. *Apollo*. New York: Simon & Schuster, 1989.

NASA Historical Data Book 1958–1968. Washington, D.C.: NASA, 1983.

Neal, Roy. *Ace in the Hole*. New York: Doubleday, 1962.

Neufeld, Jacob. *The Development of Ballistic Missiles in the United States Air Force 1945–1960*. Washington, D.C.: Office of Air Force History, 1990.

Newell, Homer. *Beyond the Atmosphere*. Washington, D.C.: NASA, 1980.

Nourse, Alan. *Nine Planets*. New York: Harper, 1960.

Oberg, James. *Red Star in Orbit*. New York: Random House, 1981.

Oberg, James. *Uncovering Soviet Disasters*. New York: Random House, 1988.

O'Leary, Brian. *The Making of an Ex-Astronaut*. Boston: Houghton Mifflin, 1970.

Ordway, Frederick, and Sharpe, Mitchell. *Dividends From Space*. New York: Crowell, 1971.

Ordway, Frederick, and Sharpe, Mitchell. *The Rocket Team*. New York: Crowell, 1979.

Page, Thornton, and Page, Lou Williams, eds. *Neighbors of the Earth*. New York: Macmillan, 1965.

Parry, Albert. *Russia's Rockets and Missiles*. New York: Doubleday, 1960.

Pearson, Drew. *America—Second-Class Power?* New York: Simon & Schuster, 1958.

Pellegrino, Charles, and Stoff, Joshua. *Chariots for Apollo*. Blue Ridge Summit, Pa.: Tab, 1987.

Penkovskiy, Oleg. *The Penkovskiy Papers*. New York: Avon, 1966.

Powers, Francis Gary. *Operation Overflight*. New York: Holt, Rinehart and Winston, 1970.

Powers, Thomas. *The Man Who Kept the Secrets*. New York: Knopf, 1979.

Prados, John. *The Soviet Estimate*. New York: Dial, 1982.

Richardson, Robert S. *Exploring Mars*. New York: McGraw-Hill, 1954.

Rosen, Milton, *The Viking Rocket Story*. New York: Harper, 1955.

Ryan, Cornelius. *Across the Space Frontier*. New York: Viking, 1952.

Ryan, Cornelius. *Conquest of the Moon*. New York: Viking, 1953.

Sakharov, Andrei. *Memoirs*. New York: Knopf, 1990.

Sapolsky, Harvey. *Polaris System Development*. Cambridge, Mass.: Harvard University Press, 1972.

Schechter, Jerrold, and Deriabin, Peter. *The Spy Who Saved the World*. New York: Scribners, 1992.

Schick, Jack. *The Berlin Crisis 1958–1962*. Philadelphia, Pa.: University of Pennsylvania Press, 1971.

Schwiebart, Ernest G. *History of US Air Force Ballistic Missiles*. New York: Praeger, 1965.

Shevchenko, Arkady. *Breaking with Moscow*. New York: Knopf, 1985.

Sloop, John. *Liquid Hydrogen as a Propulsion Fuel 1945–1959*. Washington, D.C.: NASA, 1978.

Slusser, Robert. *The Berlin Crisis of 1961*. Baltimore, Md.: Johns Hopkins University Press, 1973.

Smith, Arthur. *Planetary Exploration*. Wellingborough, England: Patrick Stephens, 1988.

Smith, Jean Edward. *The Defense of Berlin*. Baltimore, Md.: Johns Hopkins University Press, 1963.

Sorensen, Theodore. *Kennedy*. New York: Bantam, 1966.

Stine, G. Harry. *Earth Satellites and the Race for Space Superiority*. New York: Ace Books, 1957.

Stine, G. Harry. *ICBM*. New York: Orion, 1991.

Survey of International Affairs 1956–1958. Oxford, England: Oxford University Press, 1962.

Swenson, Loyd Jr.; Grimwood, James; and Alexander, Charles. *This New Ocean*. Washington, D.C.: NASA, 1966.

Thompson, Milton O. *At the Edge of Space*. Washington, D.C.: Smithsonian Institution Press, 1992.

Tregaskis, Richard. *X-15 Diary*. New York: E. P. Dutton, 1961.

Trento, Joseph. *Prescription for Disaster*. New York: Crown, 1987.

Ulam, Stanislaw. *Adventures of a Mathematician*. Berkeley, Calif.: University of California Press, 1991.

Von Braun, Wernher. *The Mars Project*. Urbana, Ill.: University of Illinois Press, 1953.

Whipple, Fred. *Orbiting the Sun*. Cambridge, Mass.: Harvard University Press, 1981.

Winter, Frank H. *Prelude to the Space Age: The Rocket Societies 1924–1940*. Washington, D.C.: Smithsonian Institution Press, 1983.

Witkin, Richard, ed. *The Challenge of the Sputniks*. New York: Doubleday, 1958.

Wolfe, Thomas. *Soviet Power in Europe*. Baltimore, Md.: Johns Hopkins University Press, 1970.

Wolfe, Tom. *The Right Stuff*. New York: Bantam, 1979.

Wollheim, Donald, ed. *Men on the Moon*. New York: Ace Books, 1969.

York, Herbert F. *Race to Oblivion*. New York: Simon & Schuster, 1970.

Zaehringer, Alfred. *Soviet Space Technology*. New York: Harper, 1961.

Zaloga, Steven. *Target America*. Novato, Calif.: Presidio Press, 1993.

Index

About the Author

ALAN J. LEVINE is a historian specializing in Russian history, international relations, and World War II. He has published numerous articles about World War II and the Cold War and is author of *The Soviet Union, the Communist Movement and the World: Prelude to the Cold War* (Praeger, 1990) and *The Strategic Bombing of Germany, 1940–1945* (Praeger, 1992).